PAGANISM—CHRISTIANITY—JUDAISM

TO

the memory of the composer Adolf Schreiber,
that brilliant, humble, truthful man—
my unfortunate friend

PAGANISM—CHRISTIANITY—JUDAISM

A Confession of Faith

MAX BROD

*translated from the German
by William Wolf*

THE UNIVERSITY OF ALABAMA PRESS

University, Alabama

Translated into English from
Heidentum Christentum Judentum: Ein Bekenntnisbuch

Copyright © 1921 by Kurt Wolff Verlag, Munich

English translation Copyright © 1970
by The University of Alabama Press

Standard Book Number: 8173-6700-4

Library of Congress Catalog Card Number: 78-104937

Manufactured in the United States of America

CONTENTS

FOREWORD TO

THE ENGLISH TRANSLATION

I AM WRITING THESE INTRODUCTORY LINES IN THE SPRING OF 1968 IN Tel Aviv, where I have been living for almost thirty years. The book itself was written in Prague and Marienbad in the last years of World War I—1917 and 1918. As may be deduced from the mention of Gustav Landauer's death, the last part of the book was written in the days of the Raete Rebellion in Munich. The epilogue to the second edition (1921), "Concerning the Talmud," must have been written in 1920.

Thus some fifty years separate the original composition of this book and the present English language edition, the first in this language, published under the good auspices of the University of Alabama Press.

It is hardly surprising that during this long interval the author's experiences—mostly painful ones—have multiplied and his insights have somewhat matured. A Greek sage said long ago: "Only beatings lead to education"—an observation that Goethe would later make the motto of his autobiography. My own generation has received too many beatings in the school of life. Many hundreds of millions did not, to use the expression of Heinrich Mann's Professor Unrat, "reach the goal of their class." Hitler and World War II offered quite a mad course of studies, into which mankind was forced to enroll by several rabid tyrants.

Fire, storm, and stress—fanaticism—are the prerogative of youth. This book of my own youth contains many thoughts that I chose to express more sharply than I would express them today. But this does not touch on the merits of the basic ideas. All I had to do when revising this book was to smooth out certain especially sharp and harsh points. For the rest, unless truth was at stake, I preferred not to obscure the passionate language of the young man through the circumspection of the later years.

By way of corrective supplement, I must emphasize, first, that classical antiquity has not been done justice enough. At the time of writing I saw only Homer's world, and it was not until a long time after this book was first published that I saw the religious significance of Plato—and also of Goethe. Even so, the present book does include certain instances of a proper evaluation of that factor.

Second, the book lacks a detailed discussion of the great Christian authors—except for Dante and Kierkegaard. Additional reference to the ideas of Thomas Aquinas, Novalis, Hölderlin, Flaubert, Tolstoi, and others would have given a truer and fairer picture, I think now, in consideration of what was initiated in the second Vatican Council.

Third, it is no longer quite true "today" that the forces of the "Caucasian" nations determine world history. The "today" of yesterday has changed into "at that time." Currently, the Afro-Asian peoples are increasingly expressing their independence from Europe and America. One of the new creations is the State of Israel, established twenty years ago, and this is opening up significant avenues, for the first time in two thousand years. Many of the new nation's spiritual aspects have yet to be clarified, and many things that were and are hopes are far from being fulfilled. It is regrettable that many expansionist states prevent the settlement of the Arab-Jewish conflict, which could be solved through a realistic approach. In their efforts in that direction these states use means of propaganda that have nothing to do with truth.

Our world is involved in a stormy process of change, and the very danger that this change could well lead to total destruction adds actuality to the present book, which was written during a wild and merciless war. For the main theme of the book is the distinction between "noble" and "ignoble" misfortune. War *is* an avoidable and thus, according to my terminology, an ignoble misfortune. It depends solely upon man's will whether he wishes to utilize all possibilities for the ultimate abolition of war, without rising luciferically above all things irrational, without giving up the humility he owes those metaphysical powers on which our spiritual nature depends.

"To venerate *and* to help"—this is the proper double watchword, as against the one-sided materialistic motto of the East, the totalitarian states.

To venerate—to recognize noble misfortune as an essential part of being human, which means to have religion; and at the same time *to help*—to abolish, exercising all one's power, ignoble misfortune, exploitation, and war.

It sounds very simple, and yet putting it into practice is a complicated and confused undertaking. This may be clarified by a practical example, beyond all conceptual theories, but in the genuine language of the poet Shin Shalom, one of the most important Hebrew lyricists. In *Davar*, one of Israel's leading daily newspapers, he published the poem reproduced below. It caused a sensation. May the poet's words of peace be listened to, when politicians fail. It is true that the poem refers specifically only to a tiny place on earth, the Middle East. Unhappily, a mere change of the proper names used would make the poem applicable to large parts of the globe.

Ishmael, Ishmael
by Shin Shalom

Ishmael, my brother,
How long shall we fight each other?

My brother from times bygone,
My brother—Hagar's son,
My brother the wandering one.

One angel was sent to us both,
One angel watched over our growth—
Thee in the wilderness, death threatening through thirst,
I a sacrifice on the altar, Sarah's first.

Ishmael, my brother, hear my plea:
It was the angel who tied thee to me.

The caravan progresses, out of breath,
Crossing the desert, a march to death.
But we have seen a mission divine,
Eternal secrets are thine and mine.
Why should we blind each other's eyes?
Let us be brothers; brother, arise!

The heat of the desert has narrowed our mind,
Our common grazing ground we cannot find.

Let us remember our father's kind heart,
Let brothers never again from each other part.

Remember "the well of the Living God Who sees me,"
Let bonds of friendship bring me to thee.

Time is running out, put hatred to sleep.
Shoulder to shoulder, let's water our sheep.

Tel Aviv   MAX BROD
Spring, 1968

PAGANISM—CHRISTIANITY—JUDAISM

1

THE THREE POWERS

IT IS NOW CUSTOMARY FOR AUTHORS WHO PROPOSE TO WRITE OF RATH-
er general matters to include a few introductory remarks on the
shortcomings of man's conceptual language.

I am of the opinion that such ceremonies are of no value. We
simply have to remember that concepts are all we really have to
work with. Even when we wish to attack formulations of concepts,
we can only do so by using formulated concepts.

The shortcomings of such a procedure are well-known. The visible and tangible world cannot be caught. It escapes through the holes
of the net. The author is hence reminded not to over-estimate himself and particularly his first formulas, but rather to refine them
more and more so as to come close to reality, keeping in mind all
the time that he can never expect to grasp reality itself.

The same warning must be addressed to the reader. He too must
beware of seeing final conclusions in his first formulations. Nor
should he make the mistake of believing he has finished the book if,
while holding his place in the second chapter, he browses through
the last. A book such as this one, the sum total of many years' thinking, can be properly appreciated only if the reader feels himself to
have reached its focal point, from which he may view the whole
with one glance, seeing simultaneously all the modifications of one
basic thought as if they were so many transparent plates.

The earth is dominated by three spiritual powers—paganism,
Christianity, Judaism. These represent three ways of interpreting
ultimate things, three attempts to relate the visible world with a
divine superworld, three ways in which the human soul reacts to the
religious experience. How they stand in relation to each other, how
their spheres of influence rise and drop—these are basically the elements which determine all events.

Even the universal destruction of human civilization (world wars etc.) is but the last consequence of the dispersion of power among paganism, Christianity, and Judaism. In saying this, I am not referring to any official power but to the secret vibrations which these three modes of life have woven around all senses of mankind. When these three religious possibilities shift places in relation to each other, the future of the earth looks different. I am thinking particularly of Europe and America and some bordering areas, not of the central regions of Asia and Africa, although there too some active powers seem to be on the move. Yet for the time being the body of the Caucasian peoples is shaped by their will to assume a form, and this restricts them in such a manner that it cannot oscillate nor send forth independent waves. The Caucasians do rule. But who rules the rulers?

Everything depends on whether paganism, Christianity, or Judaism will become the guiding spiritual ideal of the future. In anticipation let us state that paganism has the best chances, or rather that an amalgamation of paganism and Christianity is today on the rise and threatens to dominate the world. Somewhere on the sidelines and in darkness is a misunderstood Judaism.

This is how things stand. This is the situation that calls forth my critical essay.

But how can we speak of three paths, since there is only one absolute value, and one heaven?

In one of his articles on the history of religion and sociology, Max Weber replied to this objection as follows:

> Like all other inner experiences, the religious one is, of course, irrational. In its highest mystical form it is even *the* experience par excellence; and, as has been beautifully demonstrated by William James, it is characterized by its absolute incommunicability. It does have a *specific* character and appears as *perception*, yet it cannot be adequately reproduced with the instruments of our speech and concepts. . . . But in spite of that irrationality it is of the highest practical importance to know what the *thought system* is like which the religious experience occupies and maps out. For here is the source of the important ethical differences among the various religions of the earth.

I am selecting three such thought systems, three typical spiritual attitudes. They are extreme and primary possibilities of the human soul—the simplest elements—to which all other attitudes can be reduced and which occur everywhere under various guises. In defining them in their extreme forms, I am not concerned with the fact that historical experience recognizes additional variations and borderline cases. For the time being, my concept of the three systems must be accepted, the entire book being devoted to their investigation.

Paganism is dedicated to the idea of the *continuation of this world*. The divine sphere is seen as a continuation of this world.

Christianity is dedicated to the idea of the *denial of this world*. It sees divinity in the image of a denial of this world, and it strives after the dissolution of the visible world and hopes for the invisible one.

Judaism . . . Here I cannot even try to present an approximation. For the time being, however, I am offering this description: Judaism neither affirms nor negates this world. This third possibility will be discussed in the course of this book.

It is true that "denial of this world" does not apply to Christianity as a whole but only to the basic trend of its European development. In the original Christianity of the synoptic Gospels and in the work of outstanding individual Christians such as Dante, Kierkegaard, etc., there are germs of a quite different development. This will be discussed further on in greater detail.

Tentative Definition

Here we shall give a rough sketch for a tentative understanding of pagan, Christian, and, Jewish attitudes.

Paganism approves of the material world without any restriction. It is true that today's pagans call themselves Christians, but they like to walk about in the wraps of pagan animal hides. A harmless name for this is "archaization." All Aryans, Germanics, swastika people—also Gauls, Romans, Hellenes—eagerly revert to the unbaptized state of their respective nations. But the same holds true of the estheticizing Hellenism of the entire world, the great wave of the Renaissance, the "anti-Christ" Nietzsche, and, with qualifications, the "Olympian" Goethe, the "egoist" Stendhal, and Stirner (*The Only One*)—every philosophy that acknowledges this world without an attempt at modification; physiocracy and the Manchester doctrine; the liberal motto of *laissez faire*; the ancient polis and the "old Prussian spirit"; monism; biological attitudes, Treitschke's idea of the State and the adoration of "what has evolved historically"— all these are evolutionary forms of the same pagan idea which seeks its divine world in a straight continuation of this one. All those drives which prevail here and now are considered holy. If at one time the power of the individual is preferred, at another time that of the state, this makes no difference in principle. One and the same matter produced the heavens and the earth. Heroes and half-gods are the bridge that leads from man to the gods. Divine things are patterned according to earthly ones. The virtues of paganism are heroism, aristocracy, health, strength, daring, survival of the fittest, the morals of the masters. Paganistic society is based on service and obedience, on heroism and allegiance, ducal leadership and 'loyalty' of the subjects.

Christianity means a complete turning away from all natural drives, and thus the utter negation of paganism. The drives are "sinful," they are "the old Adam," which must be driven out, the "original sin," which, according to the clerical authority of Bellarmin, consists of the loss of our supernatural, which means spiritually free, nature *(ex sola doni supernaturalis ob Adae peccatum amissione)*. According to Luther "the clay from which we have been formed is damnable," and Calvin put it most severely: *"ex corrupta hominis natura nihil nisi damnabile prodire"* (only damnation can come from man's corrupt nature). Therefore even man's "good works" are entirely worthless; and, in Augustine's words, they are only "racing along very fast next to true life" *(cursus celerrimus praeter vitam)*. The century-long struggle between Protestants and the mildest Catholic attitude (as formulated by Moehler, for instance) concerns itself only with the problem whether good works and love *(fides formata)* have a secondary value next to saving grace, or not even that. Out of the entire life in this world, which becomes increasingly dim, the Christian chooses one complex, which gathers all light, and only that complex is to him important and worth experiencing—the Savior's sacrificial death. This achieved a vicarious satisfaction *(satisfactio vicaria)* for all sins, and created grace, the bridge to a purer world, the *only* bridge. This *uniqueness*, the historical fact of the transcending event, is characteristic of all of Christianity, although individual Christian sects differ as to the conditions under which grace invades the personal life of the individual (the Catholics believing in faith and sacraments, the Protestants in faith alone). This uniqueness of the spiritually decisive event is only a symbol of the devaluation by Christianity of all other life in this world. It is, so to say, the other side of that devaluation and draining. If any deed or experience could bring consolation or salvation of a metaphysical importance, "Christ would have died in vain," as Paul expressed it. But the earth must be viewed as a vale of tears, for "My kingdom is not of this world." If, therefore, the individual becomes the sole bearer of inner experiences, it is not because Christianity considers the individual important (it is simply nonsense to credit Christianity with the discovery of the "I" or the "individual," as has become the fashion) but rather because any social intercourse and any outward movement of the soul is a concern of this world; for carnal existence is basically uninteresting and incomprehensible. The "I," however, represents the minimum of existence and besides is indispensable, and thus it can only be tolerated by the Christian. The isolated individual—the monk and the ascetic—is the type of that morality.

At this point we can only mention in passing that *Judaism* does not deny this world all its importance, and yet it does not take part in the pagan idea of "only this world." It has not always been understood that Judaism ascribes importance to a certain order in this world, although the role of the "Law" in Judaism has been widely misinterpreted. What is true in such and similar descriptions is that Judaism never took its eyes off this world, off nature, good deeds, social work, or the joy of the spirit. In that respect Judaism has always been quite "worldly." But that "worldliness" is of a different kind. It is a worldliness not for its own sake but for God's sake, whose throne is the world, and for the sake of the *miracle*, which can bring man so close to his God, who is aglow with love, that he may exclaim: "Let Him kiss me with the kisses of His mouth, for Thy love is sweeter than wine" (Song of Songs I:2). This miracle which happens to man does not take him out of life, as is demanded by Christian teaching, but it is just that miracle which enables him to work, in the midst of life, through deeds blessed by grace. Thus I have called that miracle "this-worldly miracle." "A miracle has occurred to me, therefore I shall do something useful," said Rabbi Simon bar Yochai. This is a statement which may offend the ears of a degenerate Europe. But to me it is the central statement of Judaism. Later

I shall have more to say on this. But one thing must be anticipated at this point. To the Jew the visible world is not the scene of a miracle which has happened once—a saving deed performed two millennia ago once and for all—but in this miracle the world opens itself up, and in unpredictable ways, to the miracle, to the encounter with God, although such encounters are rare occurrences. (Every generation is said to have thirty-six righteous men!) We must never follow the pantheistic self-illusion of considering these encounters as a matter of course. But since the possibility of a miracle can never be excluded, and since it is not tied to any definite "marching route" (the experience of Christ), but rather claims for itself the entire expanse of earthly diversity—at least potentially—Jewish thinking considers the entire visible world as eminently important. Everywhere there slumber "sparks of divinity," not only in so-called sacramental deeds but also in our entirely rational or purely physical functions: in study, in the washing of one's hands, in partaking of food, etc., and—again potentially—even in sin, according to the profound teaching by Rabbi Akiba. We must never disregard material situations and shades of meaning in the world of phenomena. Judaism is the least abstract of all religions, and so its great and original codification, the Talmud, contains life in its entirety, with its most minute details, the day and the hour of the individual as well as that of the group, medical experience, science, legality, history and its interpretation, literature, agriculture, the culinary arts, etc.—in short, existence in all its fullness. And yet all this is not pagan, it is not simply an affirmation, but it stands under the aspect of the miracle, of sanctification, of eternity. Now those two worlds—that of temporality and that of the miracle—are not placed side by side or against each other in a rational manner; but out of the innermost heart, out of the structure of the work, there emerges that which gives Judaism its incomparable character and a significance which has not yet been properly utilized by mankind. It is a charmingly impenetrable integration of otherworldly wisdom *(Aggadah)* with the wisest worldliness *(Halachah)*, of poetry and deed, of myth and practice—an integration incomprehensibly concise to those who have not studied the Talmud thoroughly. This integration sometimes occurs in one single sentence or even one single syllable. Since I have made mention of the great and symbolic word "Talmud," I take this opportunity to declare emphatically that I am not thinking of today's infirm

Judaism in connection with this enthusiastic description of the creative power of the Jewish genius. I am thinking only very little of today's attempts at a new Jewish life, something that tries to rid itself of weakness and shadowy existence, in contrast to the immeasurable treasure of tradition, which has been so badly administered, so little utilized, so greatly abused and yet is so rich in what is important to this time of need.

The Amalgamation

It is just because of the exaggeration of their contrasts that paganism and Christianity show a strong affinity for each other. We come now to the strange fact of *amalgamation of Christianity and paganism*, and one of the main tasks of this book is to prove the existence of and the need for that amalgamation. Judaism, which moves outside of that strict contrast of pagan Yes and Christian No in a sphere which has as yet been hardly understood, is less prone to such an amalgamation. On the other hand, the form which today's Christianity has adopted, and which I shall call neo-Christianity, is particularly fit to melt with paganism into a seductive illusion of faith. It is thus quite understandable that a literary leader of neo-Chrisianity points out that Christianity has left its Jewish origin and has become a European concern of Aryan nations. That popular "de-Judaizing" of Christianity is nothing but another expression of the Christian-pagan amalgamation.

At the beginning of World War I another of those neo-Christians, the brilliant and subtle philosopher Max Scheler, wrote a book *(Der Genius des Krieges)*, in which, out of the principles of Catholicism, a "heroic," "German"—which means utterly pagan—*Weltanschauung* is justified and war is sanctified.

It is true that other tendencies in Christianity are opposed to these trends of amalgamation, and it is there that the Jewish spirit finds affinity with Christianity. Dante, the great lover and the great universal politician of a realm of peace on earth, and Kierkegaard, who takes hold of this world "by virtue of the paradox," are the exalted figures of that strict Christianity which is furthest removed from the temptations of paganism. Along with Dante and Kierkegaard, we should remember those Christian geniuses referred to on page 54.

I am writing this book not as a leisurely bystander; rather, in these last years, I have penetrated more deeply into the machinery of the world and of the hearts of men than ever before. Many things of which I had been convinced have become unclear to me. Answer came from other quarters and led in different directions from those expected. Paganism, Christianity, and Judaism were important to me only so far as they gave me an answer to what happens to us today and to the world as a whole.

The fact that all nations today commit murder and robbery and that all "official" politics is as ungodly as it is inhuman must not be identified with the principally antipolitical attitude of Christianity, although it is true that the present situation easily lends itself to such an identification. It is clear that politics, the way it is being handled these days, must lead to the agony of mankind. At the same time we hear it said that this world, with all its forms of societies and organizations, is not only irrelevant but a menace to the salvation of the human soul. It is very tempting to accept our experience with politics today in light of this theory, regardless of the fact that perhaps not every possible kind of political intervention must be condemned by the judgment of the eternal spirit and regardless of the fact that the Christian denial of politics could open the door to mischief committed by ungodly elements—not only could but actually does. Does not anyone recognize the terrible guilt of Christianity for World War I? And I do not mean only the guilt of official Christianity which, in millions of prayers and ritual ceremonies, asked God's blessing on this war (ably assisted therein by official Judaism)—no, worse still, I am speaking of the unofficial and honest Christianity which, through its unconcern with the order of the world, recognized to a certain extent all evil powers as legal rulers over this world. Even a man as sensitive as Novalis said in *Heinrich von Ofterdingen*: "War is at home in this world, there must be war on earth." And although Theodor Haecker in his epilogue to Kierkegaard's *The Concept of the Chosen*, openly fights against the cruelties of the state and of the church, he also quotes with approval Tertullian's statement that "nothing is more alien to us Christians than politics." He does not even see that through such a resignation he helps promote the very evil that he abhors.

Max Scheler has best expressed this antipolitical tendency by differentiating between *tension* and *relaxation* as the two basic possibilities of mankind (*Abhandlungen und Aufsätze* I:19). The hero of tension, mistrusting the meaning and the course of the world, trusts only himself and his will. His ideal is to have a good hold on himself and the world. He who goes the way of relaxation, on the other hand, trusts the world; he yields to that trust, he renounces his own power and his own value, and finally he abandons all care, all responsibility, all personal merit, etc. Scheler's love belongs to this second, "humble" type. In praising relaxation he restated, albeit with more delicate means, what was taught during the war in the elementary classes of literary clubs; namely, that to the radical, uncompromising spirit, politics is a defilement. Politics and social work are spiritually degrading.

We must not be misled by the fact that this anti-political attitude appears in conjunction with a very sympathetic "brotherliness" and "humanity," with a cosmopolitan view of man that finds a solution in theatrical effects. This universal abstraction is part and parcel of the essence of neo-Christianity. Soon after the war a strange thing occurred. A great number of writers who had been against politics became Communists. This would be inexplicable if the attentive observer did not detect in extreme communism the very same unconcern with this world that had been characteristic of the "relaxed" man. This obscurity of the projects, in which only destruction becomes clear, this gesture which cannot grasp wide enough and thus grasps nothing, this elimination of all differences, the emptiness and abstraction—all this is again neo-Christianity, somewhat louder and more expressionistic than before, and yet without a direct and loving relation to the real world in time and space. Whatever has been gathered on the opposite side as "active spirit" and "activism" overestimates, even in its best representatives, the sphere of influence of politics, of ratio, and of the human share in the work of nature. This is true of Kurt Hiller, for instance, who demands of his "non-dominating master type" that he should free mankind, free it of all physical and metaphysical needs.

My place is neither among the neo-Christians nor among the "activists" of this world. It is hard enough to make myself understood in a world that adopts one of these two contrasting attitudes, and neither of them recognizes or even knows of a third attitude—not a synthesis of the other two but something entirely different, situated on another plane. That third attitude is the Jewish feeling for the

world. Many years ago it entered my consciousness as the distinction
between noble and ignoble misfortune. Many things that I have experienced in the meantime have been lost in those many years as
untrue or uncertain. But this one fundamental insight has stood its
ground, and in the midst of great despair I have been enabled by that
insight to maintain a firm judgment in the face of certain facts. Since
it has thus shown itself to be reliable, I shall now try to convey it to
the reader.

2

NOBLE AND IGNOBLE MISFORTUNE

The Principle

MAN, ENDOWED WITH A BODY, IS ENTIRELY FINITE. ENDOWED WITH a soul, he is still mostly finite. Only in exceptional moments of *ecstasis* does this infinite being confront the Infinite. This is his deepest sorrow and an unavoidable misfortune. Always to feel one's limitations, the changeability of the heart, the decay of the body, the dependence of the highest functions on the lowest ones, weakening during enthusiasm, the deception in the midst of the most sincere attempt at honesty—this is the organ point of all human melodies.

Clearly distinguishable from that unavoidable misfortune there is a demonic horde of obscure abominations which seem to attach to man in an equally inescapable manner, and yet, as seen again and again from the examples of individuals and of historical development in general, they are rejected and burst like bubbles. In this cruel existence of ours it is hence important to remember that beside the *unavoidable misfortune* there is also *avoidable* misfortune, there is a misery which has been delivered to man's hands and will, and it is man's destiny to change it. Yet this is not his entire destiny, for unavoidable misfortune must also be somehow considered.

An immeasurable decline of human existence has been caused by the fact that these two kinds of human misfortune have been thrown together and placed as one bundle on the back of unhappy Adam. The Christian concept of original sin has done indescribably dreadful harm.

It would be a pointless effort to distinguish those two forms of misfortune logically and by means of definition. What general axioms can decide whether a misfortune is avoidable, surmountable, or whether it is insolubly tied up with man's own shortcomings? But fortunately there is no need for such a theoretical distinction. For when the Creator forced us out into this confusion, He gave us the wonderful gift to differentiate between avoidable and essential misfortune *by means of our feeling*. Although this feeling has too often been suppressed, it seems to me that it is one of the clearest and strongest.

It is a strange and inexplicable fact that unavoidable misfortune appears to human feelings as something *noble*, and the greater the arbitrary and unnecessary human share is in the bungling of a situation, the more *ignoble* does the pain connected with that situation appear to uncorrupted feeling.

Here are two extreme examples. A bookkeeper permanently attached to his armchair, devoted for years and centuries to the entirely irrelevant fact that five plus seven is twelve—he, the sum of the most costly cells, of the most complicated capillary vessels, which, filled with magic liquid, perform magic motions—and that work of art, capable of infinite joy, that most exalted form of creation writes a thousand times every day, in beautiful script, the same empty business letter concerning three dozen cotton socks. Who would dare to tell this miserable creature with conviction that this is the way it must be? This will not change in all eternity, as long as there are human beings! This is a noble and tragic outbreak of our chronic sickness of being human.

And now a different view. Søren Kierkegaard awoke in the middle of the night in order to write down the story of his suffering *Guilty—Innocent*, torn asunder by an unending love, which finds in itself the obstacle that prevents its fulfilment. Kierkegaard feels that only through suffering that is shut up in itself, through *Fear and Trembling*, can he come close to the godhead. Of the two cabbalistic appearances of the highest Being, *Din* and *Hessed* (strict judgment and grace), he knows only the first one, and thus as a true Knight of the Faith, must not compromise by foregoing any terror that offers itself to him . . . Here the observer prostrates himself, touched by ultimate mystery. Here we are on sacred soil, for the misfortune which is displayed is a fundamental one. It is the cry which finite man sends out to the unveiled image of infinity. It is the gaze of a blinded eye, unable to behold the countenance of God. This is noble misfortune . . .

The experience of ignoble misfortune generates in every sane man, be he the object or a mere spectator, the feeling of objection and rebellion. Noble misfortune leads us to humility. Ignoble misfortune carries with it the clear incidental noise of "being wrong." Noble misfortune, the confrontation of finite man with the absoluteness of his idea, lies wrapped up in itself in a higher sphere. It is "right" and does not incite to anything. The highest moments of that misfortune can hardly be distinguished from highest exaltation, for they are the immediate passing of infinity into consciousness. The boundaries between misfortune and exalted joy fade in the highest regions; or rather, fortune and misfortune have lost their material meaning.

"Whereas man, being chastised, easily hardens, he loses himself when God's judgment falls, and in the love which wants to educate he forgets the pain" (Kierkegaard). Thus there arises an ambivalent state which represents, so to say, man's last word before entering heaven—the word on the threshold, a sigh which, in the realm of this earth, may signify pain as well as bliss, contrition as well as exaltation; and yet proclaimed in the direction of God, it means an entire integration into his purity.

Noble misfortune is misfortune in purity. It is the objectionable quality of ignoble misfortune that it disturbs that purity. Ignoble misfortune must be fought not because it cancels our fortune (only ignoble misfortune can be canceled in that manner), but rather because it prevents us from experiencing our noble misfortune in all its purity and in its ultimate concentration, and because it takes our mind away from the only essential experience—the confrontation with infinity. The human and inferior evil of this world, quite different from sadness willed by God, is the fact that all his life the bank teller complains of the additions he has to take care of, which rob him of all ideas, and that because of that grief, which I can feel well without being able to feel it in its entirety, he is cheated out of experiencing the awe of the finiteness of his boldest thoughts.

That everything is limited leads, besides to the eternally yearning misfortune of finiteness, also to the happiness of the form, the miracle of beauty. Ignoble misfortune does not reconcile through any equivalent. It is not only torturous but also small and ugly.

The moving force of ignoble misfortune is passion, and therefore sexuality is at its center. Of all God's messengers, Eros speaks most

forcefully. It drags man most speedily before the glory of God, it
contrasts him in his smallness with infinity, causes a penetrating ray
of purity to fall on him, and points out to him the ugly blemishes of
his deceptive mantle of virtue.

In the field of noble misfortune we cannot expect any help from
reforms and from deliberate human efforts. Salvation can come here
only through a supernatural act of grace, by means of the grant of
a "new heart" (Ezekiel), through *ecstasis*, and through abandoning
the maze of material and causal means. It is important to grasp this
clearly if one is to approach any kind of reform. We cannot get away
far enough from the idea of a general attempt to make the world
happy.

In his book *Das Junge Geschlecht* Heinrich Mann writes: "You
people twenty years old: your fundamental feeling in life will be the
certainty of happiness. You will not refrain from considering it re-
alizable. Nobody will dare to tell you that it would be against an
inner law to extract happiness from you without duties." Even if
happiness is absolutized by the ambivalent term of "spirit," I suspect
that the "realizableness" of happiness does not mean that greatest
happiness which is identical with the highest noble misfortune. For
that happiness has no duration: it cannot be enforced by the political
activism of Heinrich Mann and Kurt Hiller. One cannot even strive
after it.

This does not mean, however, that we reject activism in general.
On the contrary, it is very much in place in case of ignoble misfortune. For the moving power in ignoble misfortune is not an excess
of passion but a lack of foresight and cleverness. One cannot fight human finiteness with the tools of organization. This would at best lead
to a regrouping of that finiteness, as if one were to try to restore to
its original spherical form a toy balloon which has lost some air: the
indentation on one side would immediately reappear on the other.
The deep conviction of the uselessness and even sinfulness of eliminating finiteness by a pressure of the finger has led to the belief that
all human suffering comes from God and is unavoidable. This indulgence in the face of ignoble misfortune is as evil as the insolence
concerning noble misfortune. One should learn to be selective as far
as one's sufferings are concerned. Nonessential suffering, which bars
the way to absolute suffering, must be fought with the same energy

as nonessential happiness. In this case then, activism has a place.

In all this we have to swallow the bitter pill that the boundary line between noble and ignoble misfortune has not been set once and for all; it is not clearly defined, but admits of shifting and even certain mixtures. Thus, classical antiquity considered slavery to be indispensable, and Plato and Cicero—we are not passing judgment by placing one next to the other—thought that it was "noble misfortune." But we have learned that it can be avoided, and so it was ignoble. Similarly, many people who think highly of themselves see war as a scourge inseparable from man. "There will and must always be war." Really? We shall see in about two or three hundred years. Even today my feeling of indignation suffices to diagnose war as ignoble misfortune.

Let us further mention a secondary criterion that enables us, in some cases, to distinguish between noble and ignoble misfortune. In the case of ignoble misfortune, imagination weakens and compassion cannot remain in step. I can imagine the agony of someone injured and hanging on barbed wire. I can spend sleepless nights thinking of a certain battle in the world war, but whether in that battle two soldiers were killed or seventy thousand makes no difference any longer. It is as if imagination refused to penetrate into something that, although it has happened, is immanently unnecessary. Imagination does not find a firm soil under its feet or a divine justification. But it is strange that, in the case of noble misfortune, where infinite numbers are at stake, imagination and with it feeling is quite willing although not always able. This willingness cannot be described. He who has experienced it understands me.

An Allusion to the Talmud

The distinction of noble and ignoble misfortune presses itself upon me again and again, and I am surprised to notice that so far—except for a confirmation during a dialogue with Dr. Thieberger, who conveyed to me his similar distinction between suffering of existence and suffering of coexistence—I have found only in the Talmud a related thought. There (Babylonian Talmud, Tractate Berachoth 5a) a detailed controversy distinguishes between "chastisement of love" (which corresponds somehow to noble misfortune in a theological guise) and other sufferings. Here is an excerpt from that debate:

> Rabba, or, according to others, Rab Hisda, said: "When man sees that he is afflicted by suffering, he should investigate his deeds. For it is said (Lamentations 3:30), 'Let us search our ways and investigate them, and return to the Lord.' If, after having searched his deeds, one has not come upon a sin, not even neglect of study, it is certain that they are chastisements of love. For it is said: (Proverbs 3:12): 'The Lord correcteth him whom he loveth.' "

In other words, first the Talmud looked for a causal nexus between misfortune and human failing (ignoble misfortune). Only after that attempt proved unsuccessful is misfortune considered noble and a part of the divine plan for the world. In the subsequent paragraph the "chastisements of love," noble chastisements, are defined as those which do not prevent prayer and study. This is an admirable insight. Rabbi Simeon declares that God's best gifts have been attained only by means of such chastisement—the Torah, the land of Israel, and the world to come.

The opinion that *all* suffering must be considered chastisement of love, is rejected violently yet with a clumsy casuistry. Rabbi Yochanan said, "Leprosy and barrenness are not chastisement of love. It is true that leprosy is an altar of atonement but it is not chastisement of love." This paragraph concludes with a profoundly Jewish story, which is, however, worlds apart from the rigid orthodoxy and unrealistic attitude of today's Judaism:

> Rabbi Yochanan went to visit Rabbi Eliezer, who was ill and was lying in a dark room. When the latter bared his arm, a ray of light broke forth out of the darkness. This is how handsome Rabbi Eliezer was. Then Rabbi Yochanan saw that Rabbi Eliezer was crying. He addressed him thus: "Why are you crying? Is it perhaps because you did not devote more time to study? But we have a tradition that we do not consider the amount being brought to God, as long as one's direction is towards the heaven. Or are you crying because of lack of food? Not every one is worthy to have dessert. Or perhaps because you have no children? I had ten sons. Here is the tooth of the youngest. They are all dead." Rabbi Eliezer replied, "*I am crying because of the beauty of my body, which will rot in the ground.*" Rabbi Yochanan said, "*This is indeed a good reason for crying.*"

And both of them cried. After a little while Rabbi Yochanan asked, "Do you love these chastisements?" Rabbi Eliezer answered, *"Neither them nor their reward."* Rabbi Yochanan said, "Give me your hand." He did, and when Rabbi Yochanan helped him to sit up, he was cured.

One might say that this beautiful story contains all the elements of the teaching concerning human misfortune, though not systematically separated but confused. We find the noble and the ignoble misfortune, the changeability of their boundary, human rebellion, and divine grace.

Is politics possible?

There are a great number of objections to our distinction of noble and ignoble misfortune, and their rebuttal will be the subject of the subsequent chapters of this book.

I will first point out one objection which reappears frequently. It has to do with the image of the office slave, tied to his chair. It is said that this "ignoble misfortune" is just one of the many consequences of the capitalistic system, which in turn is supposedly based on the innate and unavoidable, fundamentally boundless greed of the human heart. Therefore it should be considered an immanent and "noble misfortune." It is then added that, just as in this case, every "ignoble" misfortune is only apparently so and can be traced back basically to the evil and guilty essence of creatureness. What sense then would it make to eliminate some peripheral symptoms of worldly misery, say, to shorten the working time of the office slave by a few hours? We would still be faced with the fact that during his new leisure time the same evil hearts would do their mischief, and this can in no way be solved by some kind of an organization. In short, we remember what it says in the Bible (Genesis 8:21): "The imagination of man's heart is evil from his youth." In connection with this verse and with the misunderstood second chapter (the fall of man), the Christian theory of the *culpa originalis*, original sin, was developed, and in extreme cases (Luther, Saint Augustine) it went so far as to say that mankind as a whole is like a *massa perditionis,* a pillar of salt, a log, or a rock.

It is true that Jewish wisdom and experience have taken up that

statement from the story of Noah and accepted the "evil imagination of man's heart," called "evil inclination"; but mankind does not
exhaust itself in that one inclination: it has been endowed by nature
with an additional one, "good inclination." The duality of those inclinations, of course, means an unavoidable imperfection and therefore shortcoming, eternal longing; or, in other words, "noble misfortune" is characteristic to man. But in that basic shortcoming those
two inclinations are opposed to each other. The "good inclination"
wants the shortcoming to become conscious, it wants to contrast
finiteness with infinity, duality with absolute unity, in order to be
profoundly shaken in this confrontation with God. Indeed, this
alone, the ability to experience the purity of noble misfortune, is
worthy of being called human existence, according to good inclination. "Evil inclination" wishes to escape noble misfortune and create
instead an imaginary happiness on this earth. In doing so, it creates
an entirely new, purely human and ignoble, superfluous misfortune,
a hellish addition to the divinely ordained and substantial sufferings
connected with being human (the latter are threads, through which
God has chained us to Himself and which he plucks so as to remind
us again and again of our origin). So far as the "evil inclination" creates that hell only for its own sake, it cannot be destroyed by any
interference from the outside, since it is identical with its own archi-
tect, and is basically self-punishment. By itself, the evil inclination
is entirely ignoble misfortune. The *homo capitalisticus* who burns to
death in the fire of his own work can not be extinguished. But as
long as there is a "good inclination," we do not have to tolerate this
fire devouring other souls in addition—souls which are not greedy
and whose moral wound is somewhere else. We do not have to permit this fire, because of its organization and its system, to become
victorious and fight the "good inclination" of other people or, so far
as it still exists in the *homo capitalisticus*, to prevent him from fulfilling his task and from maintaining noble misfortune.

It is hence not true that unavoidable misfortune corresponds to the
good inclination, and avoidable misfortune to the evil one. Rather,
there is also unavoidable and noble misfortune in correspondence
with evil inclination, since that evil inclination is part of mankind as
a whole and of human essence. This must simply be accepted; *all
struggle would be useless, if it were not for the fact that misfortune
which has its origin in the evil inclination tends to spread beyond its*

necessary boundaries by taking hold of innocent sections of mankind and also by ruining, through the evil inclination of one's fellow man, innocent domains of individual souls, and thus alienating them from their proper destination, which is noble misfortune. It is only at this point that *true politics* becomes possible. It is not the purpose of all true politics to fight the evil inclination. Such a fight would be a fight against windmills. Still less is it the purpose of politics to eliminate noble misfortune. This would be sinful since it would mean eliminating the good inclination. Politics can only prevent excesses which arise out of evil inclination. Its task is mainly restricted to coercion, to defense, to negativism. It presupposes the existence of a good inclination, original innocence side by side with original sin. It can neither create goodness nor abolish the evil inclination. It has reached its ultimate goal as soon as every human being has the ability to live up to his good inclination, to the passion of noble misfortune, provided that he is not prevented from doing so by his own evil inclination. *No one should be forced to indulge another man's evil inclination.* The power of evil cannot be eradicated, only the power of evil men over good men. If this is achieved, ignoble misfortune fades from the general picture of mankind. Nevertheless the same office slave may still sit tight in his chair. But then he does this out of his own evil heart, not out of that of his boss. For such a sin repentance and redemption are possible. Only ignoble misfortune carries its own shame, its own pitiful and boring shame, where no seed can grow.

Gorki

Here we come to the crossroads. Is all misfortune noble? Or is all misfortune ignoble? Or is there the one as well as the other?

In the entire literature of the world we shall hardly ever (perhaps never) find the right answer. Our thinkers and poets are either humble (even at the wrong place—in the field of avoidable misfortune, which is the Christian type), or else they rely on their own strength, on humanity, progress; but then they attack even at the wrong place, and do not stop in the face of unavoidable misfortune. And here I am talking of our good authors! Besides these, there are others who are humble or self-confident, as the case may be, only in the wrong places (quietists, degenerated mystics).

In most cases an author who has the right attitude towards noble misfortune has the wrong one towards ignoble misfortune, just as if this had to be so, and vice versa. This is however not surprising. For here appears the problem of all problems, the "incompatibility of correlated things." (See part five of this book.)

In his book *The Bourgeois and the Revolution*, Gorki *rightly* carries on a controversy against Dostoevski's "Suffer" and Tolstoi's "Do not resist force." He is here concerned with those doctrines which concern the social and political domain, but it goes almost without saying that in doing so he is equally *wrong* in mocking the deep yearning of the anti-Westerners for religion and purity. Just like other European authors, Gorki fails to distinguish between the two areas and to demand a different approach to each of them—an active one for social misery and a humble one for the affairs of the heart and heaven.

Is it possible that neither of them has eyes, and I do see? I would feel entirely forsaken, a strange curiosity, caught up in a monstrous error, were it not for a lucid passage in the Talmud, to which I refer often, and which does agree with my view. There we read (Tractate Kiddushin 40): "Rab Iddi explained to me: 'It says (Isaiah 3:10): Tell the righteous that he is good, for he shall eat the fruit of his deeds.' " Is there then a righteous man who is good, and a righteous man who is not good? This is indeed so. He who is good concerning heaven and his fellow men is a good and righteous man. But he who is good concerning heaven yet evil concerning his fellow men, is a righteous man who is not good. But on the other hand, the following verse reads, "Woe to the wicked man who is evil." Is there a wicked man who is evil, and a wicked man who is not evil? This is indeed so. He who is evil concerning heaven and towards his fellow men is an evil wicked man, but he who is only evil concerning heaven but not so concerning his fellow men is "a wicked man who is not evil." Thus the Talmud would call Gorki "a wicked man who is not evil," and Dostoievski "a righteous man who is not good."

At the "waters of strife" (Numbers, Chapter 20) Moses disrespected God in his zeal—Moses, who was careless because he wanted to be particularly certain and speedy in bringing water to his thirsty people (instead of merely talking, he hit the rock twice with his staff). Moses is the great, moving figure, the deepest symbol of that deepest of all human conflicts. If that incident were not understood symbolically, the cruel punishment for a small offense (God tells him that he would not be allowed to enter the Holy Land), that deeply symbolic punishment, would be incomprehensible. We shall come back to this later on.

Jouve

All through the first world war, the noble Frenchman P. J. Jouve was a male nurse. I read his poem "The Song of the Hospital." What heroism from the chaste nurse and the other attendants, fine boys who do superhuman work. At the end Jouve exclaims: "I see no other truth than to bring relief to the sick, and to live patiently, so that they may live!"

Something in my deepest soul does not say "Yes" to this statement. I see men sick with typhus and their indefatigable nurses, the disfigured victims of the war and their mothers who see them for the last time—all of them comforted by our poet. Suddenly all this appears to me as the terrible statistics of a hellish abyss. We do not have two parties opposite each other, those who suffer and those who bring comfort; no, there is only one party of poor inhabitants of hell—the machinery of disaster, of dung, which revolves in rage, without exit, without success.

If I want to understand that feeling afterwards, I may come to the following conclusion, without, however, being sure that it is identical with the original feeling: it might sound like an apology offered for those sufferings if one states that the hearts of other people (those of the nurses and assistants) are purified by taking care of the sufferers. If the *only truth* tells us to help the shattered targets of the grenades, if there are men who do that service in joy and happiness and see here the full meaning of their existence, the prime form of their divine souls, then the most cruel devastations of the war have found a meaning behind which an angelic glow appears, and from there it is not far to the "Christian insight" that suffering is the highest purpose of life.

Such an approach means the raising of the "ignoble misfortune" of the military hospital to the level of a "noble misfortune." And this is something we should be very careful of. There is nothing to be said against serving in such a hospital, as long as one feels, in deep rebellion and unrest, that all the misery spread out there is the consequence of the entirely *unnecessary* lunacy of war, committed by some rulers whose lunacy may appear to be immanent, but whom mankind obeys only because of a misled organization. To be calm and noble under the flag of the Red Cross—red with blood—this seems to me to be already going astray. It is more important to sabotage war than to serve it, even if this is done with a philanthropic intention. If war has already broken out and part of the disaster can only be alleviated through service in a military hospital, this is done only out of an inner rebellion against that superfluous species of a universal misfortune. Let me quote from the book of another poet who took part in the war as a medic (Armin T. Wegner: *Der Weg ohne Heimkehr*). Out of this book there speaks a beautiful defiance, real rebellion, and insight: "This was not the will of necessity." Rather, it is resignation, peace of mind, the loving intoxication of compassion, patience—which almost create companions in guilt.

Concerning all sicknesses, not only those criminally produced by the human industry of bullets but also "natural" ones, we have the strange feeling of rebellion against injustice. This may prove that our way of living or our methods of healing—or both—are wrong, although this consideration does not necessarily lead to vegetarianism, nature cure, etc. The feeling which distinguishes between arbitrary and necessary misfortune says, like Socrates' Daimonion, only No, never Yes.

Colonial Wars

Once I had a similar mood when going through some old yearbooks of *L'Illustration*.

Those gay colonial wars with the elegant Parisian ladies visiting in the tent of the "heroic general," those lightweight tropical helmets, the pleasant white color, and how easily the modern—I almost said "fashionable"—small guns fire into the thatched roofs of the enemy capital. One virtually feels how useless is the resistance of some Siamese or Moroccans against the perfected and precise technique of the latest inventions, how smoothly and clearly such an illusory battle must be fought . . . But just wait! Those "savages" will revenge themselves a thousand times for all that has been done to them in their defenselessness, and in carrying out this revenge they will not be using their own hands. In his own mysterious way God sees to it that other foreign powers, technologically equal to the colonial victor, carry out this revenge. Does not anyone feel that it is just this "defenselessness" of the colonial peoples, their ability to become an object of exploitation, which must become a snare to Europe? Whenever a new object is seized, whenever cruel deeds are committed during colonial expeditions—apparently without great sacrifices on the part of the victor—new cruelties appear again and again on *European* battle fields. The more Asia and Africa yield, the greater becomes the greed of the "civilized" nations. Every Negro who has been shot to death has been succeeded by thousands of Britons, Frenchmen, Germans, and Italians who have killed each other. As long as Europeans do not unanimously give up the capitalistic "penetration" of the weaker nations, the Europeans will be forced as a punishment to "penetrate" each other with their bloody swords.

The above considerations will sharpen our feeling for the difference between noble and ignoble misfortune. But I do not know whether theory and the religious system will ever make use of that feeling.

Is all misfortune noble? Or is all misfortune ignoble? Or do the two exist side by side? Here differences of opinion arise.

At this point I see the main difference between Judaism and Christianity.

3

THE REALM OF FREEDOM

IN JUDAISM

The Basic Difference between Judaism and Christianity

IT IS CHARACTERISTIC OF *Judaism* THAT IT ASSIGNS TO *ignoble as well as to noble misfortune* a place in the plan of the world, and considers the effect of the two on man's attitude. *Christianity*, on the other hand, *neglects ignoble misfortune for noble misfortune*. Christianity regards almost *all* suffering as *necessary* and *noble*.

I shall prove later that *this deviation* of Christianity from the Jewish attitude is *not a coincidence*. It is not a secondary distinction but rather an immediate consequence of the *basic structure of Christianity* with its belief in Christ or, more exactly, in the vicarious sacrificial death of the Son of God, for the sins of all mankind and mankind's justification. The basic difference between Judaism and Christianity can therefore apparently be formulated very simply and in a very elementary manner: Judaism is the religion of noble *and* ignoble misfortune; Christianity is the religion of noble misfortune alone.

Unfortunately this simple distinction is hidden by a whole cloud of misinterpretations and misunderstandings. The reason for this is that, at first glance, there is a more elementary and primitive distinction, a misleading error in observation, which bars proper insight. That wrong distinction sees in Christianity the teaching that there is only noble misfortune, but all too simply it assumes that Judaism is just the opposite of Christianity. Judaism thus occupies the role which really is that of Pelagianism, whereas in reality Judaism is much more complicated. In many respects it agrees with Christianity; in others, equally important ones, it differs from Christianity. By no means can we simply say that Judaism is only the opposite of the main principle of Christianity.

This wrong view that Judaism is the opposite of Christianity ascribes to Judaism the axiom that all misfortune is ignoble and thus avoidable. Even though these words might not be used, and only minor factors and mere consequences seem to be the issue, it is this position which is tacitly attributed to Judaism, and this is done by Jews as well as by non-Jews. The consequences of this cardinal error are incalculable.

Judaism as the Religion of Freedom Alone (my error)—"Tycho Brahe's Way to God"

The theory of the absolute and complete avoidability of human suffering and of evil in the world must correspond to a *one-sided* emphasis on *moral freedom*, which is considered Jewish, as against the Christian teaching of grace. According to the "Jewish" view, man's freedom is unlimited. The fate of the development of the world is placed in his hands, so that he may virtually consider himself to be God's assistant in the creation of the world. The world has not been finished once and for all, but creation is an on-going process; therefore the most indefatigable activity is demanded of man. There is no doubt that every man, out of his own good will, can do decidedly good things and can help all his fellow men out of all their distress. Thus God is really dispossessed, and man is responsible for the government of the world. Moral man works at the reshaping and completion of the world. Only he can do this, and he is not assisted by anyone. Since only he can do it, he has the full responsibility for the future of the world. In other words, God stops being transcendent. He becomes immanent—a mere function of man. He represents the individual soul that redeems itself and mankind, which rises to greater and greater moral heights. Thus there is no god who is completed once and for all, but only a becoming god, an immense center that we help construct.

I know this error particularly well, for I have gone far astray here. I myself have misunderstood Judaism, and for many years I thought of it as a pure religion of freedom with no room for grace. Today I know that all those quotations which I used in support of my opinion refer only to the *domain of ignoble misfortune*. Shattering experiences were necessary in order to teach me my catastrophic error and to lead me away from the wrong path on which I had gone. Judaism as I see it now has nothing in common with that power which is rational and human and strictly limited to man. Nevertheless it is as far removed from Christianity, which leaves everything to itself and to grace, as it is removed from my earlier illusory image of Judaism. My view now, which comprises noble as well as ignoble misfortune, is, in spite of its clarity, something so unusual, with boundaries so delicate, that I sometimes doubt whether I shall be able to present it properly. But since just that labor has been entrusted to my weak hands, I shall try it.

The idea of human autonomy in the face of God is so often expressed in Jewish literature that it cannot be by-passed in silence. But even before I became acquainted with that literature, I reached the concept that if God was all-loving he could not be omnipotent. I called this idea "God in need of help." This may well have been the natural reaction of a sensitive heart which, in early youth, catches for the first time the immeasurable suffering of all human beings. My soul felt hurt as if struck by a thousand swords. This mood had already developed into my first sketch of *Tycho Brahe's Way to God*, when I received encouragement through Hugo Bergmann's essay *Die Heiligung des Namens*. This led me in the same direction and caused me to identify that concept with the basic attitude of Judaism.

Later I wrote *Das grosse Wagnis* and *Eine Königin Esther*, books of recantation. In great catastrophes—and this is the only way for the soul to learn—it had become clear to me that the idea of the "God in need" expressed only *one* side of the Jewish belief, whereas the equally important domain of noble misfortune leads us to impotent man in need of superhuman assistance. Only out of the fiery clash of these two images does the ultimate impulse of religiosity break forth. An unconscious allusion to this can be found even in the final vision of *Tycho Brahe*: "God below me, who has helped me, and God above me, whom I help."

The Proper Boundaries: Freedom as the Province of Judaism

Once this limitation is properly understood, we notice that it is typical of Judaism that it impresses on man, with the greatest emphasis imaginable, his mission among men; namely, the struggle with ignoble misfortune. This province God has left to man. One might say that God has given up his claim to that area and appointed man to act as His representative, in full freedom and in accordance with man's insights. Man is therefore responsible for all those sufferings that, although they can be eliminated and in spite of human freedom, have not yet been abolished.

But Judaism does not exhaust itself in this idea of divine resignation and the sovereignty of human freedom which stems from it and which again leads necessarily to a certain lessening of God's own sovereignty. We must go one step further.

This idea is also mentioned with typical clarity in the essay by Hugo Bergmann:

> Without a doubt it would be a misinterpretation of the Jewish idea of God to believe that that idea must entirely be changed into a goal of mere thinking, into a Telos which has to be realized. To the Jew it is beyond any doubt that God exists, independently of whether I realize Him within myself or not. . . . Divinity has that strange duality that it exists and is also a task for him who stands outside that unification.

But in the course of the essay, Bergmann does not concern himself any more with God's transcendent "being" but he deals—and the whole structure of his work requires this—exclusively with the God who is a "task" for a future goal. The accomplishment of that task depends unilaterally on man's will (not also on God's), and if man only wishes to do so, he can become united with God. So, for all practical purposes, God is excluded, and his intervention has become superfluous. "Since man can make decisions freely, since he can escape the nets of conditionality, he is God's chariot."

Bergmann proves this point by quoting many instances from Jewish literature. Here is one excerpt from his essay:

> In the account of the creation of the world, as presented in the first chapter of Genesis, it is known that in connection with the second day we do not read the otherwise so frequent statement: "And God saw that it was good." But at the end of the sixth day it says: "And behold it was *very* good."
>
> This strange fact has been of the greatest interest for the Jewish imagination. Out of the many interpretations I choose one which is

important to our point of view. On the second day God creates the "expanse," which is meant to distinguish between water and water. For the first time we have here duality in the world. It is for this reason that God does not find His work to be good. But when, on the sixth day, man was created, man who was supposed to achieve unification, duality was basically overcome. Therefore God could not only bless the work of that day but, looking back also to the work of the second day, He could include the latter in the blessing: "And God saw that it was *very* good." The Midrash explains: "*Very* good—this alludes to the evil inclination." Since man can also be evil, because, in freedom, he can resist temptation, therefore he is the center of creation.

Thus, in the Jewish view, man is creature and Creator at the same time. He is a mere creature as long as, pushed around from the outside, he depends on conditions in order to act. But he is a creator if, freeing himself from the fetters of outside forces, he freely rises to the level of the moral deed. The Talmud (Sanhedrin 99b) teaches specifically that as a moral being man creates himself.

If man then is morally entirely free, he is not only in his very core independent of God but, bringing that thought to its logical conclusion, it is only man who works at the construction of the world. It is only through man that God can influence the development of the world, and God depends on man. For this more or less decided sharpening of the idea, too, Bergmann finds confirmation in Jewish literature. It is already alluded to in the famous verse Leviticus 3:22: (God says) "Do not profane the name of My sanctity, so that *I may be sanctified* in the midst of the children of Israel." Similarly in Leviticus Rabba: "If ye do thus, saith God, if ye become one community, in that hour *do I rise and become exalted.*" Or again: "The righteous *add strength* to the Power on high." In Genesis Rabba: "Evil men exist through their God. But as to the righteous, *God exists through them*, for it says (Gen. 28:13): Behold, the Lord stood on him." Or: "He who judges fairly becomes a co-worker with the Holy One in the work of creation."

There are a great many additional proof texts in support of Hugo Bergmann's view concerning human autonomy. Rashi, usually a very conservative commentator, remarks (in Gen. 24:7) that Abraham, when referring to the God who had led him out of his father's home and his country, called him "the God of the heavens," whereas usually (and immediately before that) it says: "The God of the heavens and of the earth." Rashi comments that only through Abraham's fulfilling God's commandments (leaving his father's house etc.) did God become the God of the earth. Before that he had only been the God of the heavens ... This beautiful thought may be said to hold the middle line between the view that human deeds are meaningless to God and the almost heretical statement by Angelus Silesius: "I know that without me God cannot live for one moment." Incidentally, that remark proves that the feeling of human omnipotence is not restricted to Judaism but is shared by all mystics. In Judaism, on the other hand, it is not limited to the writings of the Cabbala and later mystics—as is maintained by too rationalistic criticism and those frivolous fault-finders who like to trace all great things in Judaism back to foreign influences—but, as evident from the proof text, it goes through the entire Jewish literature, from the oldest times.

Here is another appropriate quotation: "When is 'the time of grace'? When the congregation is at prayer. The Lord said, 'All those who study the Torah and do deeds of loving kindness and pray with the congregation are considered as if they had redeemed me and my children from exile.' " Man redeems God! What a bold conception! The following formula is found frequently in the Talmud: "He who does this or that brings redemption to the world." Thus we read: "He who quotes a statement in its author's name brings redemption to the world"—a very touching remark, which reveals a feeling for absolute literary honesty. We also find the contrasting formula, which states that by committing a certain evil deed one "causes the divine presence to go into exile." Rabbi Meir warns that whenever faced with a decision one ought to imagine that in the whole world as well as in one's own soul the good and the evil are equally balanced so that the deed to be performed just then would make all the difference in the world. The same teacher says, "*Great is repentance; for because of one person who repents the whole world may be forgiven.*" Although this is but a metaphor, it is born of the same spirit as the great "I will not let thee go except thou bless me." (Gen. 32:27) or the statement in Isaiah: "I have put my words in thy mouth, and I have covered thee in the shadow of my hand, to spread the heavens anew and to establish the earth anew." (51:16)

It appears (I repeat: it appears) that such and similar statements prove the basic view of Judaism that man is an absolutely free, creative, and god-like being.

But according to the truly Jewish opinion man is only relatively free. He is free in the domain of avoidable misfortune. It is true that God's resignation in that domain is real and not a mere illusion. World history is not a puppet theater in which, when everything goes wrong, God waits like a life guard. Yet that resignation, being voluntary and limited, is acceptable *even to the faithful.* Even to the faithful! In this respect the idea of the "freedom of the human will as a limitation of God's power" is, I think, religiously unique, a particularity of Jewish religion. This has also been stressed by Oskar Wolfsberg in his essay *Die Zeitkultur und die traditionelle Anschauung* (*Jeschurun*, vol. VII, p. 336f.). But the problem which has not been solved by hardly any modern commentator on Judaism is how to reconcile that basic Jewish thought with the undoubtedly equally Jewish one of God's omnipotence and transcendence. All those interpreters consider this an important point, but not one of them succeeds in solving the problem. Simon Bernfeld's chapter on the freedom of the will in his *Die Lehren des Judentums nach den Quellen* is unimportant and open to objections. But in one of the most mysterious of the Psalms (82), I did find the integration of the problem. "How long will ye judge unjustly and join hands with the wicked?" (v. 2). This is how God scolds those who so badly administer the sphere of "ignoble misfortune" which has been entrusted to them, and which is symbolized by the office of the judge. The succeeding verses emphasize that we are here dealing with ignoble, social, avoidable misfortune. "Rescue the poor and the needy; deliver them out of the hand of the wicked" (v. 4). God thrusts into the face of the sinners the fact that what is expected of them is not beyond human power: "They are without insight and understanding; they walk in darkness; all the foundations of the earth shake" (v. 5). Then follows the grandiose statement of resignation which says everything there is to be said, provided we restrict it to ignoble misfortune, to material situations, "the foundations of the earth," with which alone that chapter deals: "I have said that ye are God, and sons of God altogether" (v. 6). Incidentally this verse shows that the famous "sonship of God" is to be found in the Old Testament! Concerning the area of ignoble misfortune, man is indeed God. He has received a mandate from God, for that particular field. That this is indeed a mandate, something derived and secondary, is seen from the expression "sons of the Most High," but that it is also a real and essential omnipotence of man is seen from the use of God's holy name in the phrase "Ye are God" (not "gods"). But that mandate can be revoked, and the resignation can be cancelled. Thus the Psalm concludes like this: "But ye shall die *like men*, ye shall fall like one of the princes. Arise, oh God, and judge the earth, for thou art the Lord of all nations."

I have nothing to add to that Psalm. It is self-explanatory. It defines clearly the proper restriction of freedom and of avoidable misfortune.

Among the many passages in Jewish literature that deal with a certain problem, there is always at least one that clearly gives the entire solution. A correct collection and arrangement of those passages will show that, side by side with that main passage, others point out one side of the problem, thus complementing the solution or, by exaggerating one aspect, contribute to the clarification. Unfortunately we do not have such a systematic collection, which, guided by interests of religious philosophy and not by historical or philological ones, could become a "Guide for the Perplexed." Dr. Simon Bernfeld's book mentioned above (*Die Lehren des Judentums nach den Quellen*) tries to lead in this direction. It is true that this book is an interesting attempt. But the collection of source material has been done from a very shallow viewpoint, namely from the theory of the absolute freedom of the will. In the index we look in vain for the word "grace" (*Hessed*). This is typical of a liberal and rationalistic concept of Judaism, and it is about time to correct that. What a low level of present-day Jewish apologetics! People think that they have achieved a great thing by proving that what is essential in Judaism is not the deed but the proper intention. But such an intention is demanded by many a "Thou shalt." (Concerning this, see the next part of this book.) This is supposed to counteract the reproach of an "over-emphasis on the deed" in Judaism, whereas the effect is just the opposite. Such a primitive underestimate of the Christian objections to Judaism allows Christianity to triumph easily. We then have on our own side common sense and moral Philistinism, on the Christian side ethical depth and deeply experienced conflicts. We should, however, remember that this is not the fault of Judaism but of its defenders.

Naïvete in Judaism

Where there is freedom, there is also naïvete. It may therefore be taken for granted that the Jewish soul with its great realm of freedom, which it defends even in the face of God, is the proper field for the sane naïvete of the heart. Nevertheless, as is well known, the Jew is not considered a naïve type, but a man of rationality and deliberate artificiality, the very opposite to all immediacy and vigorous strength.

Whenever a Jewish artist dares to enter the non-Jewish world outside, this is just what he is told. But this would still not be so wrong. The worst is that we Jews ourselves have lost the facility for understanding our own peculiarities—we do not understand our soul any longer. More and more we look at ourselves with alien and dull eyes, and we believe in what others have concocted about us. We push the misunderstandings of others between us and our soul, which longs for life. We become stereotyped. Overly concerned with foreign evaluations, and too conscientious, we misvalue and undervalue ourselves. And if once—and this is even more painful—we do overestimate ourselves, we do so by adopting strange models. For instance, our "chosenness" and our "religiosity" are supposedly identical with these concepts as applied by other nations. And just because our naïvete differs from that of a German or a Frenchman, does this mean that we have no naïvete whatever? A group of blond people has reached an agreement that he who has black hair is considered bald. The black-haired one obediently submits to that verdict, and eventually he does not believe any longer that black hair, too, may be called hair. Thus a group of German-Jewish critics expect a Jewish poet to have the naïvete of, say, Germans; and, without investigating whether our naïvete may differ, they simply state that Jews have no naïvete . . .

Back to our sacred sources! What a naïvete reveals itself in those books, and just where one would least look for it—in the volumes of the Talmud. There the human-divine relationship in Judaism has

been treated in this spirit with a great soulfulness, with a sweet simplicity and depth. Out of this tradition there speaks to us a familiarity
and guileless intimacy and a naïvete about the concepts for which
we long with tears. Moses speaks to God on Mount Sinai, and, as the
Tractate Sabbath tells us, he finds God busy making crowns for the
adornment of the letters of the Torah. God asks Moses, "Do people
in your city not have the custom of greeting each other?" Moses
replies, "Certainly, but a servant must not greet his master." God
answers, "But you should have wished me success in my work."
Whereupon Moses blesses God with these words: "May God's
strength be great, as thou hast spoken." What a paradise, in which
God Himself binds Eve's hair before He takes her to Adam. (In his
infamous book on the Talmud, Professor Rohling quotes this passage from the Tractate Berachoth under the heading "The corrupt
religious teaching of the Talmudic Jew," as a proof then for Talmudic blasphemy.) I am using this opportunity to suggest to those
who persevere in seeing in Jewish religiosity something rigid, sophis-
ticated, unpoetical, and unmythical—and among these are also Renan
and all those who think that the epithet "Pharisaism" implies a
judgment—to read the Aggadic passages in the Talmud. A good
collection of such passages would cast out the spell of "Jewish rationalism." Out of our world of fairy tales—though it is not a blond
one—here is one of the innumerable stories which are part of the
subject of "man in the image of God" and which breathe the style
of intimacy with the Absolute, a naïve and defiant style, a little
scurrilous and yet grandiose. It is found in the Tractate Baba Metzia
(59b) and goes somewhat like this:

One day Rabbi Eliezer disagreed with all other rabbis (members of
the council). When his arguments were of no avail, he said, "If I am
right, this tree shall testify on my behalf." Whereupon the tree left
its place and was thrust a hundred miles away or, according to
others, four hundred miles. (How beautiful is that strange tendency
to be exact!) But the sages replied coolly, "Trees cannot testify."
Then Rabbi Eliezer said, "If I am right, this creek shall prove it."
The creek began flowing upwards. Again the Sages answered, "No
argument can be deduced from water." Rabbi Eliezer exclaimed, "If
I am right, the walls of this house of study shall confirm it." Immediately the walls bent down. But Rabbi Joshua, the President, called
out to them, "Ye walls, what business is it of yours when scholars

discuss the law." Whereupon, in respect to Rabbi Joshua, the walls
did not bend any further, yet, in respect to Rabbi Eliezer, they did
not straighten up either. And thus they stand slanted to this day.
Rabbi Eliezer did not give in but finally exclaimed, "If I am right, let
God himself say so." Then a heavenly voice was heard, "Why do ye
fight with Rabbi Eliezer, since in all points of the law his decision is
the acceptable one." But even then Rabbi Joshua arose and said,
"The Torah is no longer in heaven. It has been proclaimed publicly
on Mount Sinai, and ever since then we do not listen any longer to
heavenly voices. It says in the Torah that the majority decides!"
The meeting was adjourned. Some time later Rabbi Nathan, who
had taken part in the discussion, met the prophet Elijah—even today
he walks among us in human shape—and asked him: "What did God
say at that time to our argument?" Elijah answered, "God smiled
and said, 'My children have defeated me.' "

"My children have defeated me." I believe that in the entire literature of the world there is no instance of such sweet trust, burying
one's head in God's infinite breast. But we allow it to be said that
only Christianity created the idea of man as God's child. And yet it
was the authors of the Mishna, the Tannaim, who, in the simplicity
of their hearts, proved to be poets and God's real children, sometimes even, as we have seen, his naughty children. What did those
pure and straight-thinking—which means naive—masters believe concerning God's daily work? The Tractate Avodah Zara gives us some
information:

> The day consists of twelve hours. During the first three hours God
> studies the Torah, during the next three He judges the world. See-
> ing, however, that all men deserve to be found guilty, he gets up
> from His throne of justice and sits down on the throne of mercy.
> In the third period of three hours He prepares food for all those
> alive. In the last three hours He plays with the Leviathan, as it says:
> "Thou hast created Leviathan in order to play with him" (Psalm
> 104:26).

This is a legend of the most naive joy in artistic creation. At the end
of the day, and every day, after having completed His work, God
plays with the monster, that big fish, which He has created out of an
excessive fullness of power. When discovering in Jewish literature
the "purposefulness" of the Jewish soul, Werner Sombart wisely
overlooked that artistic atmosphere in the heaven, and that purpose-

lessness. But Professor Rohling, eager to find anthropomorphisms in Judaism, discovered it! This proves what we have to be aware of when our psychology is described by our enemies. But we, the critical people, have sunk so far as to believe them, so that in this one point we are naïvete personified.

Concerning Martin Buber's Basic Concept

It is with great energy that Martin Buber has tried to place decision, choice, and the deed—which means man's autonomy—into the center of Judaism.

According to him the European is the man of feeling, and Jews, as well as Orientals in general, are men of action. Thus we read in his book *Der Geist des Judentums*:

> The basic psychic act of the man of motion is a centrifugal one. A stimulus starts in his soul, and it becomes a motion. . . . The world is not given to man, but it is his task, which consists in making the true world the real one. Here the motoric character of the Oriental is revealed in its highest sublimation—it is the pathos of demand. . . . He has more substance in acting than in perceiving, and what he does in his life is more important than what occurs to him. . . . In all spiritual attitudes of mankind, Judaism is the only one in which man's decision becomes thus the center and the meaning of all that happens. . . . God's face rests invisibly in the rock of the world; it must be brought forth and chiseled out, etc. . . .

We notice that here the "essence of Judaism" consists of elements which are strictly part of Scheler's concept of "tension." Ricarda Huch (in *Luthers Glaube*) would even call them Luciferic; for whatever man undertakes in the belief that everything depends merely on him and his good intention to do what is right—all this is Lucifer's work, and conceit is *the* sin. He who wants to be good, and fight his inclinations, he who deliberately does not want to sin, commits *the* sin, according to Ricarda Huch.

It is true that in demanding "unconditionality" Buber removes the meaning of the "deed" out of the realm of exteriority, relativity, and moralizing. Nor is Buber's "deed" done as an artificial tension against man's inclinations, but it emerges from a "unity." I am sure that, to Buber, "unity" means the right and experienced things. Yet he does not clearly state that "unity," "unconditionality," "realization" are no longer man's work or the free choice of a morally disturbed soul, but something new, *divine grace*, which goes out towards man's efforts in a mysterious way, and without which salvation cannot be hoped for. As the Talmud says, "He who wants to defile himself through sins may do so, but he who wants to remain pure is given help." Thus does the Talmud draw the Jewish line of demarcation. "Relaxation," human humility, and impotence are recognized, side by side with Buber's tension and omnipotence, which are unduly stressed. Nevertheless, this is not Luther's and Ricarda Huch's wrong way to sin. To repeat, it is proper and essential to point out that in Judaism there is the requirement of "active intervention," in contrast to Christianity, where no independent active will is left to man. Yet it is as wrong and dangerous to stress again and again Jewish "activity," and to overlook "reception," "dependence on God" for our existence, and to see in the lack of that element of stillness the real difference between ourselves and the Christian attitude. And yet the deepest essence of Judaism is to be found in the fact that it combines both elements within itself, with the whole fullness and fatefulness of such a tremendous possession.

Is Judaism without grace?

The erroneous view that Judaism makes everything dependent on man's own will and nothing on God's mystery, which is removed from that will, is spread by Christian theologians in every possible manner. They like to state that Judaism is no religion at all but merely a moral teaching, that it is not concerned with the relation of God and man but only with social ethics (man to man).

Since our young people hardly know Judaism from Jewish *sources*, but rather from misleading descriptions written by novelists and theologians of another faith, the most tender souls, the best ones, and those who are open to God are driven away from Judaism by such propagandists. I have in my possession letters written by a young poet who turned away because, under the influence of the book by Ricarda Huch mentioned above, he considered "hoping for grace" something un-Jewish, and he could not live without it. According to these false ideas, to be Jewish is to insist on one's own strength and goodness, on the freedom of the human will, on being awake—the arrogant denial of the core disaster in the image of the world, "ignoble misfortune." If one thus surgically removes one of Judaism's main themes, it is easy, and this is done generally, to see in it a mere "entrance hall," a less valuable and preliminary stage of Christianity. Mere historical succession is clothed with a logical meaning, as if one were to see in Islam a "fulfilment" of Christianity, just because it came later. A number of alleged advantages of Christianity as against Judaism, superficially presented and kept in very general terms, serves the same argumentation, which is supported by a *reckless and often outright grotesque ignorance of Jewish literature, an ignorance which has never prevented anyone from senselessly repeating unproven opinions in that field.* Considering this state of affairs, it seems to me often that only a lunatic would start a fight with such time-honored prejudices.

Rabbi Hannina's Guiding Principle

We must admit that, since our sages were not concerned with rational formulations and since they trusted in the freshness of Jewish life and its instincts, they did not create an easy access to Judaism.

Thus for many years I had been misled by a Talmudic statement from the mouth of Rabbi Hannina: "Everything is in the hands of God, except the fear of God." Today I know that this declaration must not be interpreted too broadly, and that "fear of God" does not mean "general moral freedom." Neither does it mean "love of God" or "union with God," which then, according to that saying, would depend on man and not on the heavenly powers. But we must stick closely to the plain words, "fear of God." Only this, in the words of Rabbi Hannina, does not lie in God's hands but has been entrusted to human powers. But this is not a small matter, it is something tremendous, a brilliant insight, which has not been recorded anywhere else. Think of it clearly and steadfastly! You know that your feelings are decidedly beyond your control. You may wish to have this or that feeling, but you cannot raise even the strongest wish to the level of the weakest shadow of a living sentiment. You may wish to love your sweetheart, but once she starts to become irrelevant to you, your wish does not do any good. Perhaps you would like to love her again, but you cannot do so. Or you may wish that a certain man should be irrelevant to you, or that you would like to hate him. But we love, hate, or are noncommittal regardless of the feeling we would like to harbor within ourselves. But is there supposed to be a feeling that falls quite outside of this axiom? Is the "fear of God" supposed to depend exclusively on your wish to fear Him? What a shattering thought! A psychological discovery of incalculable consequences! It is exactly the way Rabbi Hannina has put it. Detailed into sober words, it means that the fear of God—the feeling of anxiety and uncertainty caused by the fact that we, as finite beings, have been placed in an infinite context which will always remain unknown to us—that feeling is something so elementary, so original and innate in human nature that nobody can evade it. One may deliberately cover it up, silence it, and forget it; but it returns at will. The "confrontation with the Infinite" waits for us and is always ready. Even man can, if he only wills it, become conscious of the "noble misfortune." But this is all that he "can do, if he only wills it," in the terms of religion—no more and no less. To *love* God—not only to recognize the infinite domain through which we love but also to be inflamed with it—this is a requirement which cannot be fulfilled just by good intentions. But all who will it (or better, who do not work against it) can do this—not be blind to God, not feel chained in a sober cycle of purely human calculation, in the narrow circle of today and tomorrow, but rather be aware of the superhuman not only as a menacing danger and an absolute terror. In this sense the opposite of the faithful person is not the sceptic or the atheist but the Philistine. To fear God without loving Him—this comes close to atheism, if the atheist acknowledges the existence of a superhuman power. He may call it chaos or blind accident instead of calling it God, but this is only another word for his fear. That fear may be combined with mistrust (this is properly called atheism), but there is also a fear that waits in humility, and that is the fear of God of Rabbi Hannina and the *timor castus* of Saint Augustine. But the Philistine lives without any fear, without any thought of the powers above, without even probing himself concerning trust or mistrust, and only interested in himself and his earthly needs. It is then the meaning of Rabbi Hannina's statement that we do not have to be Philistines, that it depends only on us whether we wish to be that small or not. We stand immediately in this grace. With this minimum of feeling for the Infinite we are attached to transcendental truth, by that small step we are ahead on the way to salvation, and with this advantage we were born. Thus does Judaism state its case for original innocence side by side with original sin (which is also recognized in Judaism), whereas Christianity knows only original sin. Therefore, in Jewish teaching, side by side with "man's heart is evil from his youth" (Genesis 8:21), we read in the Daily Prayerbook, "O Lord, the soul that Thou hast given unto me is pure." This statement can only be understood in connection with what Rabbi Hannina said. In strict opposition to that attitude, the Protestant Church states: *Omnes homines secundum naturam propagati nascuntur cum peccato, i.e. sine metu dei*, etc.

Against Asymptotism

If we were to interpret that statement too broadly we would be in danger of making man's entire moral value depend on his "good intention." "Everything goes" is a favorite saying of my character Tycho Brahe. But this is not true. Not only are we not always successful, but even inwardly it does not work, and the "moral deed," to which one forces himself, looks desperately thin and asthmatic. We are then misled into supporting the first false supposition with an additional false hypothesis. We do not have a certain feeling just because we wish to have it, and this in spite of Kant, to whom man's moral sovereignty appeared like the starry heaven above. (Kant was a demi-discoverer of Jewish thought, and therefore Jewish thinkers from Maimon to Hermann Cohen were attracted by him, just as the ghetto was attracted by Kant's disciple Friedrich Schiller.) Neo-Kantianism tries to pacify a rebelling empiricism by saying that man is not sovereign but progresses steadily towards the absolute. The typical symbol for that theory is the asymptote—the straight line that comes closer and closer to the circle but remains separate from it. I do not deny that this is a striking image. A curve is not reached, the distance becomes smaller and smaller, and thus we have both elements of life—noble misfortune, which cannot be changed, and ignoble misfortune, which is defeated by and by. This is an understandable labor, although we remain at the same time eternally stuck. Nevertheless, I do not like it, since there is the danger of forgetting that a small distance always remains. We do not lament the fact that God and man cannot join in all eternity, but we are happy exclaiming "Nearer my God to Thee." Even the fact that we can never reach our goal leads to some comfort. There is continuous progress. We can never finish our job, and thus life cannot become boring. The main fault in the picture is that the approximation is considered a divine affair. In spite of all reservations of "not being able to reach out," it does not divide the process sharply enough into two dimensions, an arithmetic and a geometric progression. It is true that, according to strict arithmetic, the sum of the series $1/2$ plus $1/4$ plus $1/8$ plus $1/16$ is closer to 1 than the series $1/2$ plus $1/4$ plus $1/8$. But once we understand that the series is progressing, and that "one" is a deliberately chosen quantity which can be submitted to a microscope and be extended at will, we see that it makes no difference whether we are separated by $1/16$ or by $1/32$ from the destination, since every next step means only one half of the preceding one. This means that the distance always remains infinite in the sense that it can only be bridged by an infinite number of steps.

In his essay *Hermann Cohens Philosophie des Judentums* Klatzkin writes: "Historical development as such must never be regarded as the development of morality. There is always a distance between the being as morality and the being of reality. But it is continually reduced." This is true, but Klatzkin ought to have added that the continually lessening distance will always remain infinite. Then things will look differently. Then it becomes clear that the approximation is meaningless and only apparent, for a goal in infinity is no goal at all. God cannot be brought down to earth and, in the strict sense of the word, there cannot be a "kingdom of God on earth." This means the end of the "interpenetration" of earthly things with divine ones and the "reshaping" of this world, as opposed to the Christian negation of this world, and the pagan continuation. The reshaping which does exist refers only to "ignoble" misfortune and thus only to one part of Judaism; it does not yield an overall characterization.

"Asymptotism"—as we may call that wrong application of the mathematical formula—dangerously confounds acts with activities, as has been described by Oskar Baum in his beautiful novel *Die Tür ins Unmögliche*. Neither must we identify organization with the idea. (See Albrecht Hellmann in *Der Jude* 1917, no. 3.) We call asymptotists those people who are very kind and generous, so as not to have to be without compromises. To be kind is often the most subtle deception and frequently merely another word for cowardice. I would like once to meet a man who is bold and kind at the same time. But bold people are mostly disrespectful and irresponsible, and kind ones are without the ultimate blessing of a temperament.

We have to realize that the "union with God" cannot be accomplished on the level of everyday life. Religious values lie in a "jumping forth" (ecstasis), a miracle. Here no slow approximation is possible but rather the seizure of the entire moment.

> Too feeble for such flights were my own wings;
> But by a lightning flash my mind was struck—
> And thus came the fulfilment of my wish.

(Dante, Paradiso 33)

The Messianic Time

But does not what we have said contradict Messianism, which, undoubtedly a main element in Judaism, teaches that a time of fulfilment, of the kingdom of God on earth, will come?

It has not always been taken into consideration that Judaism knows of two Messianic times. The division corresponds to that between noble and ignoble misfortune, as presented here. It is quite possible that the two persons of the Messiah also have something to do with that. The Talmud speaks of the Messiah, the son of Joseph, who falls in battle, and the perfected Messiah, the son of David.

For when the Messiah is mentioned as the one who redeems man from all evil, even from that of finiteness and the evil inclination, his advent is promised for "the end of the days," which means that metaphysical time in which all time has been cancelled. On the other hand, when the Messianic time is described as a possible earthly experience, it has a much more modest effect. It will cancel ignoble misfortune or only part of it, and it is contrasted with a characteristically different time—"the future life." Thus we read in the Tractate Sabbath:

Samuel said: There is no difference between present time and Messianic time except that the political oppression from which Israel will suffer up to that period will end, for it says (Deuteronomy 15:11),

"The poor will never cease in the land." This is in agreement with a statement by Rabbi Hiya the son of Abba: "All prophets have only foretold events in the Messianic times, but the essence of the future life has not been seen by any human eye, it is known only to God."

The complex of ignoble misfortune is also an infinite quantity. The fight against ignoble misfortune can never come to an end, since the later stages are proportionally more difficult, which means that the closeness of noble misfortune is felt more and more. But at least we are here on a visible road, and at a certain point we may say that the troubles which we have overcome were tougher and crueler than those which are still ahead of us. The latter, although less urgent, are more complicated. For instance, once the proper socialized manner of production has been found for mankind and put into practice, another problem will appear in front of all. The struggle with this new problem—although of smaller importance—will take no fewer centuries for its accomplishment than the fight for socialism. Yet we must not despair, since that fight will be less important. And this is progress! At least to the historian who looks back objectively, such progress exists, although to the new generation with its more refined needs the new problem will appear to be no less urgent than socialization had been before. But we are here in the human domain—human evaluation, human speech, human yardsticks. It is different when God, noble misfortune, and religion appear on the scene. Then disorder enters the junk yard of our knowledge. Concepts are turned upside down, and all human things become nonsense, inessential, paradox, impure, evil.

I shall try to discuss the Jewish point of view concerning that basic fact.

4

THE REALM OF HUMILITY

IN JUDAISM

Serving in Joy

THAT MAN IS BASICALLY AND ESSENTIALLY A MERE TOOL IN THE HAND
of God, without power, direction, or dignity, without the ability to
will the good out of himself—this "progress of Christianity," as it is
commonly called—goes back to Jewish sources.

The problem is how to reconcile this with the equally Jewish trust
in man's sovereignty and free will, as has just been described.

For the time being we are not concerned with the freedom of the
will. The question is not whether man's will is predetermined but
rather how far the influence of the will reaches, be it determined or
not. Here we conclude that our decision can create the deed, the
proper conduct, but not the desired feeling, like kindness, love of
man, Eros. It is in my power to give alms to a beggar, but to do so
joyfully is not in my power. Our consciousness can generate motives
for a deed but not a feeling. Our consciousness can lead to the fulfilment of a commandment, but not to the "Simchah shel Mitzvah," the
joy in serving, which, according to the Talmud, is as essential as the
commandment itself.

The spontaneity of the deed is perhaps possible, but not so the
spontaneity of the feeling. When I once asked a pious Jew about this,
he replied (and his answer is typical for part of today's orthodox
Judaism, not for their ideas), "To be able to fulfill a commandment
of the Torah is enough to give me satisfaction and joy." Such a joy
has nothing to do with the joy of having done something and which,
virtually *ex post facto*, coincides with the fact that a duty has been
performed. I can very well imagine that praying is a profound joy

of being one with God, and that it arises out of an instinctive urge. That urge, which goes the right way, is also a duty. The urge and the duty have been combined, and this is the real Simchah shel Mitzvah, goodness coming out of man's nature. The greatest grace occurs when goodness has become natural to man. It is not the joy in prescribed prayer but joy in prayer itself and the satisfaction of knowing that God wants what I want. We cannot compare this with the purely bureaucratic joy of servile and religious spirits in mechanical prayer and welfare! It is of course possible that, through long training and regular habits, substitute feelings can be generated. People can be trained in identifying the joy in a deed, which happens to be in the direction of duty, with the schoolboy-like joy in the mere fact of having done one's duty. This seems to be the meaning of Foerster's training in virtue and also of all military drill. But such a greenhouse product must never be confounded with an honest and natural feeling, which cannot be enforced by a decision of the will.

The Three Levels of the Good Deed

There is a primitive and hardly contestable experience, which stands right behind the door leading into the world of ethics. And yet not everybody has had this experience which teaches that the good deed is done on three levels.

First there is the level of outward reward or other advantages. Here goodness itself is not intended.

Second, doing good is the purpose of the deed. Here we do have the intention, according to Kant's categorical imperative. One feels a sense of duty. Religion would call this "the fear of God." Fear of God is of course not the same as a superstitious fear of punishment or a hope in reward (we would then still be on the first level) but rather to be awake, to listen to the inner voice of infinity, a confrontation with the Infinite. (Remember Rabbi Hannina's statement!)

For a long time I believed that such a pure and undiluted intention to do good would suffice. I thought that such a victory of moral man over himself, as it is taught in all textbooks of ethics, is the apex of existence, and that only he who did good works with an impure intention could be accused of being sanctimonious. I had to undergo many sufferings before I became aware of the much more tragic fact that every victory over myself is also a defeat. In such a fight the I is both victor and loser. One can come to know this only by experiencing it. Whatever has been recognized as good can become morally valid only if it breaks forth out of man's deepest night, over which he has no power. A good deed is done only where nature itself becomes love.

Here is a little story, an experience from life. It is not my own story, nor is it the main experience which led me to the third level but only a small and incidental enrichment of my insight. I owe it to an acquaintance of mine, who, and this is important in this case, is a very kind person and justly enjoys a good reputation. He once told me,

A good and loyal friend of mine came to visit me one day. He came from out of town, and I had not seen him for many years, but I had maintained a connection with him by means of cordial and honestly warm letters. He had come to take care of important business matters. Since I knew that he was poor, I invited him to be my guest, which I would not have done for anyone else. I would do anything for other people except that favor, for my apartment is quite small. During the day I work hard in my business, and once I am at home I urgently want to be left alone and to arrange the few leisure hours of my life for myself alone, without having to consider others. I want to relax physically and mentally. But this time I could not think of myself only. It is true that there were plenty of hotel rooms available, but my friend would never accept a gift of money from me. But he could not, on the other hand, reject an invitation to my apartment—just as I could not avoid offering it—for this is a service of friendship which cannot be expressed in money. My duty was therefore quite clear, especially so since the matter which brought my friend was of common interest in addition to its private side. Thus he appeared at my apartment. Then followed some days which were torture to both of us. It is true that no damage was done to our friendship, for the matter was too small, and I mention it only as a symbol for greater things. But life itself became almost impossible. We did not speak of it at first because we had the best intentions, and then because we were ashamed. My friend, to whom this matter was as painful as to me, did not wish to disturb me. He made himself almost invisible. He did not demand the slightest service, he even in exaggeration tried to be of service to me. He refused to dine with me. This again led to endless discussions, which threatened to end in serious arguments. I had to force him to take a simple meal in my room, I had to tell him not to ruin himself by bringing home costly desserts and thus reverse the entire meaning of my hospitality. Finally he tried to polish my shoes. I had to keep them out of his hands, and in order to do so, I had to get up an hour earlier in the morning. The less he wanted to trouble me, the more he did so. His affairs dragged along and were supposed to take a few more days, perhaps a few more weeks. I made heroic efforts to overcome my grief and always tried to show a kind and friendly face, and I did succeed. The porcelain surface of my conduct did not show any break. But my soul was unhappy, and a small matter led to a big problem. How is it possible that something which had clearly been recognized as a duty, is done with so little joy? Why does God allow that resistance to remain, not permit it to melt away in recognition of a good decision and our perseverance to bring it to fruition? But God did not help, not even at the end, which was a small occurrence, full of that "devil ishness of everyday life," which seems to make its appearance whenever we deserve to be scolded. I had offered my friend the use of my bathroom. Afraid of disturbing my comfort and that of the maid, he took his bath at a time when everybody else was still asleep. Now the furnace which heats the water in the bathroom has a complicated mechanism, which one has to be acquainted with if one is not to do great mischief. My friend, without asking anybody, innocently opened the cold water tap and the water from the shower came down without letup. More and more water poured out of the wall, and the unfortunate man tried in vain to stop it by turning the faucet again. Finally he had to wake me up, a real flood was in progress, and the janitor, summoned in a hurry, could only stop it by shutting off the main pipe which served the whole house. It was hard for me to calm my friend's mind concerning the damage he had caused. This incident did not make it easier for me to put into practice what I had recognized as right. My rage was indescribable, particularly because I was in a rage.

At last his affairs were concluded, and my friend departed. The strangest thing was that, while returning from the railroad station, I knew that I could not have acted differently and that, if the occasion were to arise again, I would do the same thing over, yet I felt that all through those days I had lived in great sin, because the good things I had performed had not become a joy unto me but had definitely remained contrary to my nature. I despised myself, an innocently guilty man, more than ever.

Without taking the conclusion of that anecdote into consideration, we state, for the purpose of this examination, that the third level of the good deed is only attained by him who integrates that which has been recognized as a duty with that which he strives after. He must not carry virtue like a burden, not even like a burden that he has become fond of, but rather like an airy wreath, or a mighty aureola of his essence.

That integration of duty and nature lies outside human intention, and the strongest wish cannot accomplish it. It appears like a gift from God, like "grace." It is true that the place in which that gift is received is the I, and therefore it may make sense to say that the road to God leads through the I. Yet it is a road which one cannot walk on. One can only stand on it and wait. At this point man becomes aware of the emptiness of his "moral freedom of the will." For the effort of the human will can only reach a Thou Shalt, a dry and loveless fulfilment of duty, which, cut off from the soil of life, fails to reach its goal even after many tortures. The good deeds, urged on by the will and arrived at after fighting opposite inclinations, are rewarded by the ruins of the entire structure built on good deeds.

What an irony of fate that the central section of Kant's city of Königsberg is called "Löbenicht"—*live not*. This seems to be God's answer to the categorical imperative.

Does Judaism overemphasize the deed?

He who is satisfied with the second level of the good deed is "sanctimonious," which means he puts too much stress on the deed. He lacks the experience of the higher level, the third one, which comprises two ideas forming one unit as far as feeling is concerned. The first idea is that a deed which does not flow out of joy, out of the love of God, is of a lower degree. The other insight is that such a love cannot be commanded, that no Thou Shalt is applicable here, that everything depends on God's free gift of grace, which, placed into man's heart, overwhelms him.

I would not think of lowering myself to prove at first that the preference for the love of God, as compared with the respect for God, is part of the very essence of Judaism, although it may seem that in this field nothing is taken for granted or superfluous. Christianity is like a younger sister, who by her noble manner attracts the common attention to such a degree that the fine qualities of the older sister are only recognized through the younger one. Some time ago, in the constitutional national assembly of Czechoslovakia, a "well educated man," an attorney and even anticlerical, could maintain without being contradicted that the advantage of Christianity over Judaism could be found in the verse "Thou shalt love thy neighbor like thyself," although that verse can be found in Leviticus 19:18. It is not surprising then to find people stupid enough to say that in Judaism there is no "love of God," in spite of the prophetic word "I desire mercy and not sacrifice" (Hosea 6:6) and other statements like this, in spite of Hassidism, whose enthusiastic wave welled up from the deep feeling that "God can only be worshipped through joy," and in spite of the Song of Songs, whose admission into the canon is a testimony for all times of the most grandiose genius of love. That love of a shepherd for his sweetheart, a love which was a "flame of God," but which also revealed a true expression of the physical, was considered a sanctuary, a "miracle of this world." In a great moment of inspiration and of revealed grace, this love was taken to be the symbol of the loving relationship of God and the soul, of God and Israel. That interpretation became an identification, and the identification became faith, and the faith became tradition—all this was a work of *Jewish* intuition (similar to Mahler's world of music), and yet it was misinterpreted, and its relation to Judaism was denied. In any other case such an heroic deed of love would have been found worthy of the highest praise. It would have been absurd to suspect its originators of a lack of love or of a knowledge of divine love.

But I refuse to write an apology to the invisible clan of ignoramuses and hypocrites who surround us on our road of suffering; however, I want to quote a passage from the Talmud which, with an intimate and delicate feeling, sets up a hierarchy of goodness:

> There are seven kinds of pious people: 1) those who do God's will out of material motives: 2) those who say, 'Wait a bit for me, I have a good deed to perform'; 3) those who smash their heads against a wall in order to avoid looking at a woman; 4) sanctimonious people; 5) those who demand that their friends mention some duties for them to perform; 6) those who are pious because they fear God; and 7) those who are pious because they love God.

Now what of the thought that love cannot be commanded? The

third level not only praises the love of God as the incomparably highest value, it also states that it cannot be enforced through good will and that it is unattainable on the earthly road. Is that opinion too Jewish? Is it not true that generally the opposite is maintained? Do not most people see in Judaism a rigid "religion of the law," as against Christian love and forgiveness? (Incidentally, the word Torah does not mean Law but Teaching; many errors concerning Judaism can thus be traced back to a mistranslation). Does not Judaism, with its many Thou Shalt's of the Pentateuch, demand a strict observance of the commandments, is it not presumptuous with its requirement of "loving God with one's whole heart"? *(thou shalt love, as if there were wooden iron!)* Is not Christianity warmer and closer to life by pointing out man's weakness and sinfulness, his incompleteness and need for grace? Is not Judaism a cold and lifeless schoolmaster, and Christianity the pulse beat of the feeling heart of a redeemer? Is not Paul's penetrating dialectic correct, when he states that the sole reason for Jewish law is to terrify the souls by proving to them that the law cannot be fulfilled, so that we must doubly burn for an exit towards the supernatural and towards faith? ("For what comes through the law, is recognition of the sin." Romans 3:20; 5:20; 7:7.) We read often enough that it is the sin of Judaism that it obstinately rejects the Savior, and that its Pharisaic conceit is convinced that man's intention not to sin suffices to protect him from sin.

But Judaism, which has been reduced by its attackers, and, alas, sometimes also by its defenders, to the level of a shallow self-sufficiency, has also, together with Christianity, given an insight into natural sinfulness. Judaism has not only that depth of insight but also the idea, quite alien to Christianity, that, side by side with all noble misfortune, man has been tragically given the task of fighting ignoble misfortune.

Those who are better acquainted with Jewish sources can quote hundreds of passages to prove that man is sinful. (Long after the writing of this chapter, I came across the excellent essay by J. Wohlgemuth, *Das Sündenbewusstsein,* in *Jeschurun* VI, 430ff.) But it would be enough to quote from Psalms (130:3): "If thou shouldest remember iniquities, who could stand? But with thee there is forgiveness." Remember also the promise of a "new covenant" (Jeremiah chapter 31) or Psalm 103 or God's "division of daily labor," quoted above from the Talmud, where we read that God changes

from the Throne of Justice to that of Mercy. Let us also quote from
the daily prayerbook: "When we pray to thee, it is not because we
rely on our merits, but because we trust in thy great mercy. What
are we? What is our life? What are our good deeds?" Furthermore,
there are many prayers on the Day of Atonement, in which God is
referred to again and again as the God of forgiveness. Some of those
paragraphs are of a shattering force: "What shall we say before
thee, O Lord our God and God of our fathers? Are not all the
mighty men as naught before thee, the men of renown as though
they have not been, the wise as if without knowledge, and the men
of understanding as if without discernment." The need for divine
grace is clearly expressed in these words: "May it be thy will, O
Lord my God and God of my fathers, that I may sin no more."

A beautiful and clear instance is Psalm 51, in which we find the
thought that God must take the first step, that He must lay the foundation so that man's goodness may come "from the truth inside," out
of one's nature, and not against nature, for in that case man would
remain a wicked man who only does good deeds! We read in that
chapter:

> Thou desirest truth in the inward parts; let me know wisdom in my
> inmost heart. Cleanse me with hyssop so that I may become clean;
> wash me so that I may become whiter than snow . . . *Give me, O*
> *Lord, a pure heart and implant in me a new and strong spirit.* . . .
> Cast me not away from thy presence, and do not take thy holy spirit
> away from me. Make me again glad with thy salvation, and support
> me with a spirit of willingness . . . O Lord, open my lips, and my
> mouth will tell of thy praise . . .

It is in the same spirit that the Talmud (tractate Kiddushin) teaches:

> Rabbi Simon the son of Levi said, "The evil inclination takes hold of
> man all his days and wishes to slay him, as it says (Psalm 37:12),
> 'The wicked one lies in ambush for the righteous man and wants to
> kill him,' and if the Holy One, blessed be He, were not to help man,
> he would not be able to prevail over the evil inclination, as it says
> (verse 33), 'The Lord will not leave him in his hands.' "

Here are more proof texts: Rabbi Eliezer wept when he came to
the following verse (Genesis 45:4): "His brothers could not answer
him, for they were afraid of him." The brothers could not answer

the rebuke of a mortal man, how then will we be able to reply to God's rebuke? Rabbi Ami started crying when he came to the following verse (Zephaniah 2:3): "Seek ye the Lord, all ye humble of the earth, who have obeyed His laws. Seek righteousness and humility. Perhaps you may hide in the day of the Lord's anger." He remarked, "All these things they had to do, and yet it says only 'perhaps.'" Rabbi Yochanan started weeping when he came to the following verse (Job 15:15): "God does not trust His holy ones; the heavens are not clean in His sight." If he does not trust His holy ones, whom will He trust?" Rab Hisda said: "God says of the arrogant man, 'We cannot live together in the world.' God raises those who humiliate themselves, and He humiliates those who raise themselves. He who chases after power is forsaken by it. He who tries to evade it, is reached by it without having to look for it." The above texts show what we must think of the accusation that the Talmud emphasizes the deed, as is maintained by Christian professors of theology.

I have now reached one of the most important points of my investigation. We must destroy a prejudice which has been perpetuated by many generations of scholars and has been easily spread. That prejudice states that Judaism is basically unmetaphysical and rationalistic, mainly concerned with organization and social improvement, some transfigured social hygiene, decorated with some old-fashioned meaningless ceremonies, the disciplinary order of a cosmic reform institution. Even Solovyev, although on the whole friendly to Judaism, onesidedly sees here only "activism and practical materialism." Similarly a Jewish theoretician of the Jewish conviction, Benzion Kellermann, wrote, as if this were the most self-evident matter: "Social suffering is true suffering." Thus we are accused by others and by our own people, and our soul and those of our youth fall by the wayside, yearning, exhausted, looking for refreshment of spirit. At the end we become a prey to Christian propaganda, as it is presented in the theater of Strindberg, in Tolstoi's diaries, in Parsifal rites, in art, poetry, and legend.

Is this surprising and incomprehensible? The false teaching that in Judaism the soul can find an outlet *only* in social reforms must mislead every young heart concerning Judaism, as soon as it gets involved in its first serious and lonely conflict. That heart wills what it ought to, but it is not capable of it. It feels the insufficiency of its good intentions, the profound worthlessness of a good deed tremblingly accomplished against the dictate of nature. And should religion have nothing to do with all that? Has it nothing to teach as to this most important concern? In those moments offering a terrifying view into the abyss, the miserable one loses forever the illusory image of a Judaism taught in school or gathered from Kantians, and another Judaism does not exist for him. Smooth sermons, the mediocre humanism of Lazarus, the organ music of reform Judaism will not do. But the same holds true of that type of orthodoxy where the top hat has become almost as symbolic as the Sabbath candles. I am always surprised at the guilelessness of our teachers and leaders who cannot believe that the best of our youth, our intellectuals, tend towards Christianity out of conviction because they are not impressed by the way today's Judaism and Jewish religiosity are presented to them. The "teachers" do not believe it. They still believe that the only reason for converting to Christianity is the prospect of a better job. Our "teachers" do not know that Christianity, as developed by such honest and profound minds as Pascal, Novalis, Kierkegaard, Amiel, Dostoevski, and Claudel, exercises a very powerful attraction upon the most truthful among us; that it has been revived by the brilliant systems of Eucken, Troeltsch, and Scheler; that it tries to give an answer to all moral and burning questions of the present time. We cannot compete with neo-Christian art and philosophy, as far as actuality is concerned. Our sages of old would have been up to the challenge. We must allow them to use the style, the terminology, and the formulations of modern man. If we addressed our questions to them in the words of today, I am sure we would receive a satisfactory reply. But even Zionism has done this only in fragmentary allusions. This is the present situation. Unbelievable ignorance, coupled with the inaccessability and neglect of the garden of Jewish dogmas, drives our desperate youth into the coffee houses of neo-Christianity. There they hear of a love which does not obligate to anything, a wishy-washy humanitarianism which can never be put to a test, an empty radicalism which may be part of a personal selfishness. The Christian "negation of this world" can easily be recognized in the "negation of all existence" in which revolutionaries, without any responsibility, try to shorten the hours. Much can be made of the false theory that in Judaism there is no grace and of the equally false assumption that grace can be attained only through Christ. There is room enough for respectable self-torturing efforts, but also for false poses and untruthfulness.

The vast literature of the Jewish religion naturally does not reveal everywhere the basic views at which we have just arrived. Just as in all other literatures, many hands have been at work. In addition, it was written with little concern for dogmatic formulation, far away from the filing system of the Aristotelian logic. It comprises many contrasts, and the constant reconciliation of those contrasts is its very life, felt by all those, but only by those, who live in it.

In Jewish literature, it is mainly a few apocryphal works, the so-called Chochma literature, which, in a sober and moralizing tone, stress human autonomy and seem hardly to know of the human need for grace. Thus we read in Ecclesiasticus (15:11ff and 22:11): "He who obeys the law, is master of himself." This is a bloodless Judaism, already half Stoic and Hellenized. Anticipating Kant, the fourth book of Maccabees states: "Our Torah says: Thou shalt not covet thy neighbor's wife nor anything that belongs to thy neighbor. This proves that the will can dominate one's inclination and all those which stand in the way of justice." Here nothing is left of the metaphysical depth of the Bathsheba Psalm. According to Graetz, the fourth book of the Maccabees was written "in a Hellenistic community, among Jews with a Greek upbringing and a Greek taste." It is a clear symptom of that assimilation to paganism which eliminates from Judaism whatever is infinite and ungraspable. Such a religious assimilation always goes together with a cultural one. The half-assimilated German Jew Graetz applauds the Greek Jew, with whom he finds affinity. But the religious instinct of Jewish development apparently thought differently. For it seems that such imitators had no influence on Jewish tradition. The Talmud was not concerned at all with such mediocrities. It is true that there are ugly and petty statements in the Talmud, and some passages are intolerable to me. But even there it is greater, more powerful and more colorful or, at least, more paradoxical, than that colorless Philistinism, which seems to have been written with our terrible elementary school books in mind.

Rabbi Elijahu Gutmacher

An actual Jewish life will teach us more in this respect than all debates. It shows how deeply rooted in Judaism is the insight that to do good is man's concern, but to act out of love is God's affair. Here then is a sketch of the life of Rabbi Elijahu Gutmacher, as reported by S. L. Zitron in *Der Jude*, II, 5.

Gutmacher (1796–1874) studied at the Yeshiva (Talmudical college) of the famous Rabbi Akiba Eger in Poznan and quickly became his favorite disciple.

> In his early youth he was a veritable monk, always by himself. From childhood on, he went from one Yeshiva to the other in Silesia, everywhere studying the Torah, serving God. In his wanderings he studied people, became acquainted with life, and tried to understand it. That study had a double effect on young Gutmacher: on the one hand, it softened him and made him accessible to human suffering; on the other, it alienated him from mankind, since he realized that man himself was man's greatest foe and oppressor. Consequently he did not attempt to win friends. He tried to avoid meeting acquaintances, learned to cherish lonesomeness, and held conversation only with his soul.

Influenced by his study of the Zohar, he developed a strange philosophy of Judaism, as described by Zitron: According to the original blueprint of creation, man was supposed to be the image of the Infinite. Then the serpent caused the fall. Through the revelation on Mount Sinai order was reestablished in the chaos, and an integrated and inseparable triple substance was formed, consisting of the Jew, the Torah, and the Divine Presence. Making use of the terminology applied so far in this book, and in view of that great man's life, which will be described on the following pages, we may characterize the individual particles of that "triple substance" as follows: 1) the I; 2) the "fear of God" as commanded from the outside (categorical imperative, moral insight); and 3) the love of God (the joyful impulse to do good, in accordance with one's own character and having its source in one's nature). In the perfect man, all these elements must be together. It is not enough to fulfil the commandments of the Torah (to do good). The Divine Presence must do its share, if the right deed is to be done with the right strength and intensity and with proper satisfaction. According to Gutmacher, this was the case in the Holy Land. "Israel and the Divine Presence joined hands under the heaven of the Promised Land. There arose that spirit which gave the world the great prophets, those first creators and carriers of general human morals and ethics." Because of their sins—they had not kept alive the sacred triple substance—the Jews were driven out of Palestine. The Torah then accompanied them step by step into the Exile, but the Divine Presence vanished. It abandoned the other two elements.

Here we have a shocking symbol and a clear recognition of the fact that in certain situations—and we must remember that the Jewish soul in exile stands for all states of human cleavage—truly good and pure deeds cannot be done and that, in His mysterious ways, God Himself does not allow perfection, no matter how hard man tries. To fight means here already to be defeated. The Torah and the Divine Presence have parted ways. The "Thou Shalt" has remained, but the "I want it, and I like to do it" does not work. How closely this teaching is tied up with Rabbi Gutmacher's deepest feeling and how clearly it was the expression of deepest suffering and truthfulness, can be seen in this excerpt from his biography, quoted here from Zitron's essay:

> Rabbi Elijahu Gutmacher became a rabbi at a very early age. Rabbi Akiba Eger told him to get married at once and to accept the rabbinate at Pleschen. At that place then, the process of purification began which he had dreamed of and which he had chosen as the exact purpose of his life. He suppressed all passion and permitted himself the enjoyment of this world only to the extent necessary for the upkeep of his body. Whenever he found an individual or a group in distress, he was the first to come to assistance, and he did so beyond his powers. He distributed his entire salary among the needy. He sat at the bedside of poor patients and of women in labor, he gave them comfort during their times of hardship. He was the spokesman and the protector of all poor orphans and widows. He helped those whose hearts had been embittered and took their sufferings upon himself. In order to help his fellow men, he had no regard for his own health; and neither inclement weather nor great distances could prevent him from giving assistance. Nor did he discriminate among different people. All people, he used to say, are in need, and all people must be helped. He always thought that whatever he did was not enough, that here and there he had to show greater effort and bring greater sacrifices. He was thus never satisfied with himself. Every night before retiring he used to write down the reasons for his dissatisfaction. In that diary he recorded what good deeds he had performed during the day, and almost always he concluded that list

with a self-accusation and self-flagellation. After a day filled with
good deeds he fell asleep late at night sighing, "Today I have not
fulfilled my duty towards my soul."

While Gutmacher was dissatisfied with himself and found many
faults, all those around him admired him. In Pleschen and its surroundings he was known as a saint. Gutmacher had established a
Yeshiva in Pleschen, where 400 students gathered from near and
from far, and he trained them in his own spirit. He hoped that his
disciples would become the core for that host of purified souls which
should bring about redemption. For over 34 years he was the head
of his Yeshiva in Pleschen. In those years, hundreds of young men
were instructed there, but his dream about them was not to be realized, and this was a great disappointment to him. As he mentioned
in his diary, he took the blame for this upon himself alone. He
thought he had not perfected himself sufficiently to be a model for
the young generation.

Then Gutmacher left Pleschen and became the rabbi of Graetz
in the province of Poznan, near the Russian-Polish frontier. There he
made more efforts towards self-purification. He spent many hours
in solitude, served God under the open sky, stood in the midst of the
trees of the forest, and cried loud and bitterly. At that time he had
already passed the sixtieth year of his life. His age clothed him with
a very dignified appearance. Tall and slender, with large black eyes
and a long white beard, he had a majestic and patriarchal air. All
this, combined with his ascetic way of life, made many people see in
him a godly man, and various legends and miraculous stories about
him spread among the population. Those legends were not restricted
to his country; they exercised a great influence on the Jewish masses
in Poland. After some time, from many Polish frontier towns there
came sick people and barren women and people in need. These made
their journey to Gutmacher in order to ask him for advice. But
Gutmacher felt embarrassed and did not want to be considered a
miracle-working rabbi. On the other hand, his merciful heart did
not allow him to send those miserable people away without giving
each of them an appropriate word of consolation. Thus eventually
hundreds of people came to him from long distances. For their sake
he had to neglect his studies and give up his passionate prayers and
his isolation. He objected to this, and in the Hebrew journal *Ham-
maggid* he published an open letter, calling on the people to cease
their pilgrimages, since he was a simple mortal man, unable to help
himself. "If my prayers are really as pleasing to God as you believe,

I assure you that I do not pray for myself alone but for all Jews."
But this did not help, for the people believed that such a humble man
had to write that way, and they did not stop visiting him.

The conflict of that life was wonderfully serious and truthful, and
so was the resolution of that conflict. Gutmacher did not die without
having been granted "grace"—his own grace. For, as I shall explain
later, every man has his own possibility of grace. (It is the error of
Christianity to see in the belief in Christ the only grace possible.) In
every man there is a potential coming-together of what he does with
his whole heart and what he believes to be right and good. This, however, is only a *potential* coming together, which does not necessarily
become actual. The actuality of grace is God's secret. For Gutmacher that grace consisted in the rise of the pre-Herzlian idea of
Zion, which filled him for the first time with *hope*, with the belief
that his efforts would not remain in vain and fruitless, and that it
would again become possible to work at the renewal of mankind in
a grand style, and not in senseless waste. Zitron reported as follows:

One day an old good friend of his, the famous Rabbi Zvi Hirsch
Kalischer, invited Gutmacher to come to see him in Thorn, in order
to discuss with him a highly important matter of common concern.
That was the first assembly of Jewish dignitaries and rabbis in Germany, called together by Rabbi Hirsch Kalischer at the end of the
year 1860. It was to debate the question of settling Palestine, and
then the foundation stone was laid for the Hibbath Zion movement,
which comprised a large section of German-Jewish orthodoxy and
spread from there to other countries.

In Thorn, Gutmacher saw suddenly the solution for the entire
problem of Jewish redemption, which had occupied him for so
many years. His eyes lit up with a youthful fire, and his beautiful and
patriarchal face shone with great enthusiasm, when he saw that his
dream was alive in the best Jewish minds and had seized the noblest
Jewish hearts. From that moment on, the idea of Palestine became
the very center of his life. Gutmacher was one of the first to lead the
movement and to devote himself to it with his body and his soul.
With energy and courage he fought against its adversaries.

He was extremely happy when in 1861 the first Palestine Society
was established in Frankfurt on the Oder. With tears of joy he extended his hands to its founders.

When Moses Hess published his book *Rome and Jerusalem*, Gutmacher was one of the first to receive him cordially and warmly. The great Jewish scholar and Cabbalist greeted in the Jewish social- ist and philosopher a brother in arms.

Gutmacher was close to eighty years when he wrote the last lines in his diary, the summing-up of his soul:

"I am dying in peace; the Divine Presence is longing for its old friend. I feel that the triple substance, which had fallen apart, is being reunited."

Thou shalt . . .

Many a time it has been said that the main difference between Christianity and Judaism is "grace." But this is an element of the Jewish religion. Paul, Augustine, Luther, and others have stressed a hundred times that the fulfilment of moral commandments is not enough to make one perfect, and that divine assistance is needed in order to perform the commandments wholeheartedly. But this state- ment is not a Christian creation, it has already a central place in Ju- daism. The difference between Judaism and Christianity thus does not lie here but in a consequence derived from it, as will be explained presently.

But how can we reconcile the many "Thou Shalt's" of the Penta- teuch with this basic thought, particularly the requirement to "love the Lord thy God with all thy heart, with all thy soul and with all thy might?" It seems that here an a priori impossible thing is de- manded of man. He is told to harbor a certain feeling—love—whereas we have pointed out that such a feeling can only come as a gift from God, as grace!

I had been bothered for a long time by that problem. And yet it may merely be a problem of a necessarily inexact translation. It does not really say "Thou shalt love." The form of the Hebrew verb can be explained as future tense as well as in the form of an imperative. In other languages we have no parallel for such an ambiguity. We should translate, "You *will* love . . ." Then the entire passage, taken together with the preceding verse, our declaration of faith, gains an- other meaning and becomes one of the most exalted testimonies of hope and faith. Making use of Hugo Bergmann's translation, the passage then reads thus (Moses' words): "Hear O Israel, the Eternal is our God, the Eternal is One and the only God. You will love the

Eternal your God with your whole heart. . . ." Then nothing is demanded that, according to Rabbi Hannina's statement, not everybody can do—the vision of "noble misfortune," of ephemeral man,
man in doubt, facing the eternal and One God. A promise is made
that if man is deeply concerned with that vision, and if he does not
withdraw from the innate "fear of God", the "love of God" will
mature in his heart. The love of God is thus not commanded—this
would be absurd—but that love, this identity of duty and inclination,
is foretold as a consolation. If this interpretation is questioned, I find
support in a statement by Rabbi Akiba, one of the most profound
Talmudical statements. Rabbi Akiba explains "with all your heart"
by pointing to the identity of duty with nature. With all your heart—
you will love Him with your good as well as with your evil inclination. It is significant that Rabbi Akiba died with the word for "one"
on his lips. When he was being tortured to death by the Romans, he
reminded his disciples of the importance of that statement: You will
love. As a statement of consolation, this verse may thus be compared
with Deuteronomy 4:29: "You will seek there the Lord your God
and you will find Him, if you long for Him with all your heart and
all your soul." We must also remember the prophetic word, "If you
seek Me with all your heart, I will let Myself be found, says the
Lord." (Isaiah 29:14)

But how are we to explain all the other "Thou Shalt's" in the
Pentateuch? We certainly cannot say that these are also in the future
tense and not imperative. Although they do not all refer to feelings,
many of them refer to acts. They are commandments and laws of
state. This is expressed very distinctly in the Book of Deuteronomy,
where we have first a repetition of the Decalogue, which had been
proclaimed on Mount Sinai with fire, thunder, and the sound of the
Shofar (chapter five). Now the Decalogue is concerned with behavior, not with love or inclination or "doing the good with all one's
heart," but it says strictly: "Thou shalt have no other gods before
Me." This may be commanded. It is controllable, and what is expected is not a hatred of idols. Or else it says, "Thou shalt not
murder." The only exception seems to be the tenth commandment
with its prohibition of "coveting." But perhaps, after the nine commandments had been promulgated with their insistence on duty, the
last one was meant to remind man of humility and make him be wary
of sanctimoniousness. The Decalogue is followed by a revelation

given to Moses personally. It is that intimate, person-to-person teaching which starts with the confession of faith and the consolation analyzed above, "Thou wilt love." Then comes a sharp incision, and the state law begins with a clear conditional clause that even a blind man can see: "When God will take you into the Promised Land . . ." (6:10) But here "love with all one's heart" is not mentioned. It says quite logically (verse 13): "Thou shalt fear the Lord thy God, respect Him, and swear by His name." We have thus reached the lower level of the material world, in which there are territorial and juridical conditions, fear, coercion, laws, and the freedom to follow the laws.

Duty vs Nature: the Jewish Solution

But here Moses proclaims an unconditional requirement: the moral law, which is also the law of the state, must be observed. In case of a conflict between the law and personal inclinations, the law must prevail.

Here the basic difference between Judaism and Christianity, which I have mentioned above, takes on a new shape. Other forms of that difference will become clear later on. But they all can be derived from the principle that in Christianity there is no difference between noble and ignoble misfortune, whereas Judaism, while relating the two categories to each other, separates them from each other. It is a terrible situation when nature and duty are not one! It is a struggle out of which man cannot rise as a perfect being except by divine grace. This is the riddle of all riddles: If I am to obey nature, I must smash my fellow men to pieces (and without my willing it, this has become the case). If I obey duty, I must smash myself to pieces, must mutilate myself, and allow my spirit and my body to become stunted. What then am I to do? Here Judaism says that the good deed must be performed. If need be, it must be done without joy and in spite of the clear insight that the ultimate power of love cannot here be put to use. What a dreadful seriousness in the statement by Rabbi Tarphon: "It is not given to you to complete the work, yet you must not shirk your duty" (Ethics of the Fathers).

With whining man in mind and with great inexorability, perhaps even with some irony combined with weeping love, Moses himself, that greatest of all teachers, has made the following decision:

> For the commandment that I give you today is not beyond your powers and is not unattainable. It is not in heaven, so that you may say, "Who may go up to heaven to fetch it down for us and announce it to us so that we may fulfill it." Nor is it beyond the sea, so that you would say, "Who would go across the sea and fetch it for us so that we may act accordingly." But this word is very close to you. It has been placed into your mouth and into your heart that you may fulfill it. I call today upon heaven and earth as witnesses that I have placed before you life and death, the blessing and the curse. So choose life, so that you and your children may stay alive. (Deuteronomy 30:11ff.)

Here then is the place of choice, of free and moral decision. Man is capable (it is not beyond his powers) of doing the good deed even against his own inclinations. It would not be, then, the good deed on the third level. It is true that this is not the excess which comes through grace ("it is not in the heaven"), and yet it has its own value as the good deed on the second level, which has been fought for in a hard struggle. There is a deep longing in man's heart. The good things which are against nature should be raised to the sphere of an enthusiasm that sails along driven by divine winds. Without that longing, the good things which have been acquired through spite are likely to harden and become real sins. But the longing for higher things does not prevent us from performing the good things in that lesser form in which it can be done even against our own inclinations. As God said to Cain (Genesis 4:7): "Sin croucheth at the door. Thou art its desire, but thou shalt rule over it." He is referring to murder, which, being a deed, can be avoided—not the desire for murder, over which man has no power.

Many passages quoted in the preceding chapter concerning man's sovereignty refer to the narrow domain of the second level. For as far as man wills the good against his own nature, Judaism not only offers hope through grace (duty coincides with nature) but also a manly and defiant sympathy. "I will not let you go unless you bless me." God Himself smiles at that rebellion against Him. "My children have defeated Me." The Baal Shem Toy, the founder of modern Hassidism, was reminded of the legend concerning Elisha ben

Abuya, the heretic who up to the last day of his life had refused to
repent. When questioned about this, the heretic replied: "I have
heard a heavenly voice proclaim that all men can be forgiven, but
not so Elisha ben Abuya." The Baal Shem said, "How lucky was
that man. As could no one else, he might have served God with a
complete unselfishness."

My fingers tire from writing it down. It is so unspeakably sad.
The garden in front of my house is withering. It is and remains an
impenetrable secret that those humanly graspable and calculable
things—where holiness contradicts man's deepest divine voice—must
be done in spite of the profound "No" which resounds from our
soul. Moses has erected a great image in order to enable us to measure our own suffering by comparing it with his. And yet nobody
seems to have properly interpreted the incident related in Numbers
chapter 4, verses 1ff. This passage presents the innermost meaning
of Moses' character. The people, having reached the wilderness of
Zin, clamored for water. God told Moses and his brother Aaron,
"Gather the congregation, and speak in their presence to the rock."
But Moses hit the rock with his staff twice (as Rashi explains, the
rock wanted to be more obedient than Moses and did not listen to
the first blow), and the waters came forth. Thereupon God told the
two brothers that, as a punishment, they were not to enter the Holy
Land. What a terrible punishment! The goal of an entire life, of the
heroic deed of deliverance, of forty years' wandering in the desert—
all this wasted because of such a small lapse! But that lapse was as
symbolical as the punishment. Moses had obeyed the social duty.
With the utmost speed and without further ado, he wanted to save
the people from dying of thirst, and what he saw influenced him
more than the seriousness of the divine command. Thus he repeated
the miracle in the same form in which it had worked for him once
before (Exodus 2:17) when he had hit the rock. He acted in a more
superficial and reasonable way, since striking is more effective and
tangible than speaking, and thus his inner voice was dimmed. He
disregarded his I, the deeper call of his heart, the divine command.
In order to be quite certain of achieving results, he neglected the
delicacy and the exactness of his soul. His faith was not strong
enough, he did not "sanctify" God. Moses was not to forget that he
suffered for the sake of the people. The punishment did not defame
him. There was no word of anger on God's lips, contrary to many

another case of divine displeasure. He was even allowed to behold the Promised Land, the land of grace, although he could not enter it. And he died "by the mouth of the Lord" (Deuteronomy 34:5), which, according to the Rabbis, means that God kissed him. We may therefore say that, paradoxically enough, Moses had acted in the proper way "at the waters of strife," provided that we assume him to have believed that the literal fulfilment of the divine command would bring about the death of the people from thirst. This confusing feeling must have overpowered him at least temporarily, for more than once God had threatened to destroy His obstinate people. Therefore the leader decided on water at any price, and when this account is reported again (Deuteronomy 1:37), we read, "Also the Lord was angry with me on account of you." With this in mind, we do not have here a real punishment but the stating of a fact, the presentation of the most human tragedy: man who must do the good even against the divine call and who is then excluded from the "Promised Land." Mount Nebo stands for the grace which man has desired in vain all his life and for which he has made the greatest of efforts . . .

"Choose life, so that you and your children may live." This shows clearly that we are concerned with time, with the sequence of generations, which means material and "ignoble" misfortune. Here is where man has to make his choice—in the struggle with ignoble misfortune. This struggle is within the freedom of human choice. This is not the place to talk of inner peace and love. Avoidable misfortune must be avoided at any price, whether with joy or without it. This is the basic Jewish view, as opposed to the Christian one.

It is strange that people who consider themselves endowed with a delicate soul again and again reproach the "Old Testament" for its concern with material rewards for good deeds—the good life, sitting under one's vine, etc. But such accusations merely express the different views of the "struggle against ignoble misfortune." Where there is freedom of choice and hence commandments, success is possible, and the struggle against avoidable misfortune is just that—a struggle against avoidable misfortune. Such simple terms are the only way in which that simple fact can be expressed. It combines two concepts which have become clear to us in the course of this book: good things on the second level, where duty and nature do not coincide, and where commandments are meaningful; and noble misfortune on the second level, and only there are repairs possible. These two concepts are correlated.

The God of Revenge

The other side of those misunderstood promises is a term which has been even more gravely misunderstood—The God of Revenge.

Anti-Semites have constantly made much ado of the fact that our God of Revenge visits the sins of the fathers unto the fourth generation. And yet, anyone endowed with a less hypocritical view must see that this verse is merely the simple and naive reflection of the actual course of things, and it is true in all its details.

Not to eliminate avoidable suffering, which was the task of the fathers, will lead to the punishment not only of the fathers themselves but also of their children and their children's children. "Choose life, so that you and your children will remain alive." The wise lawgiver had foreseen it, and no matter how we react, this is the way things stand. The term "God of Revenge" was not invented in order to terrify people but in order to open people's eyes to the real world order, where sons suffer through their parents' syphilis, where innocently maturing generations are suddenly, and without knowing why, faced with a war which they had known only from hearsay, and which they had hoped would be eliminated once and for all—a war which they owe only to the martial spirit, the annexionism, the heroic deeds of forebears rotting in their graves. One beautiful day in May, we returned from an outing, in an atmosphere of flowers and beautiful books, a little strengthened and comforted in the midst of all the savage things which had happened around us, somewhat rested and hopeful. Suddenly we saw in glaring colors, "War with Italy" new hatred, new war, to be continued and prolonged ad infinitum. We complained, and we accused the Italians of injustice. Did we ever have an argument with them? Did we not love their country more than our own motherland—the row boats on Lake Garda, the grassy mountains around Genoa, the kindhearted and blackbearded, noisy people of the vegetable stalls and fishmarkets, and above all the splendid folksongs! O Italy, O travels to the South! And now war, enmity. We could understand it as little as if it had been a war on the moon, until we remembered Radetski, the white blood-spattered uniforms of his regiments, and the martyrdom of Upper Italy, described so movingly by Ricarda Huch in her *Risorgimento*. We remembered that our grandfathers had "pacified" that Upper Italy by force, and that even then, in small hotels in Milan, faded copper plates were hanging on the walls, depicting a beautiful woman chained to the ground, mourning on her face, guarded by an Austrian soldier with fixed bayonet, and in the background the dome of San Marco . . . When I remembered that copper plate, I understood for the first time: "He who visits the sins of the fathers upon the children, the grandchildren, and the great-grandchildren."

This is the way things are. Fully authorized by the facts, a thousand times supported by history, Moses proclaimed an inspired law of social justice: "When you become rebellious and disobedient, I tell you this day: You will surely perish. You will not live long in the land, which you are now crossing over the Jordan to possess." The proverb well known to the exiles in Babylonia was right: "The fathers have eaten unripe grapes, and the teeth of the children have become dull." The prophet Ezekiel was to speak up against this attitude. It is God's secret. Here, in the field of avoidable and ignoble misfortune, there is, in the proper meaning of the word, "inherited sin"—a sin completely and unwillingly taken over from preceding generations, so that innocent people are hated through inheritance; while the "inherited sin of ignoble misfortune," according to Rabbi Hannina, has a reverse side. There is a "God of forgiveness" for noble misfortune, over which man has no power; and there is a "God of Revenge" for ignoble misfortune, and here man has been called upon to create order at any price, with free choice and even against nature if need be.

Should we then violate nature for the sake of duty? We must not formulate things so sharply. At least, when applying the formula to an individual case, we must be determined to be very careful. Because often duty can be found on the side of nature. And if then we decide against nature, this should be so only in extreme cases, when obedience to our inclination would lead to a violation of duty and to crime; whereas duty shows us a practicable task in the domain of ignoble misfortune.

Contrary to Christianity, in Judaism nature is not something unholy. "He who fasts too much is called a sinner." This was proclaimed against asceticism, and in a devilish humor (for we find humor too in the "pedantic" Talmud) the writer tells us that once the Rabbis succeeded in placing "evil inclination" in a cage, and consequently on the next day no fresh egg could be found in all of Palestine. The decision is thus never made without regarding nature or degrading it. The Talmud often quotes the following saying: "Greater is he who does a good deed because he has been told to do so than he who does it voluntarily." But, as with the statement by Rabbi Hannina, this one must not be interpreted too broadly either. It does not refer to the voluntary doing of a good deed to which one would be obligated ethically, but the meaning is that things done voluntarily have no religious significance. An example would be a blind Jew who fulfills those commandments which do not apply to any people who cannot see. The conflict is here not between the inclination and one's duty, for it is presumed that both are present. Otherwise, a third way—religious consecration—would apply. The statement must not be interpreted to mean that he who does his deed from a sense of duty and against nature, is higher than the one in whom the duty and the inclination come together.

Duty vs nature: the Christian Solution

Judaism and Christianity share the insight that the highest good can only be experienced when, through divine assistance, nature and duty coincide. Contrary to often heard statements, this idea is not the sole property of Christianity. The difference between the two religious attitudes lies in the fact that, in the case of a conflict between nature and duty, Judaism chooses duty—thus avoiding sin— and Christianity chooses nature.

I quote from Ricarda Huch's book *Luthers Glaube*:

> Surprisingly, Luther says that a virgin who refuses to marry because she believes she is doing something meritorious, God-pleasing, and saintly, is actually serving the devil. If, however, she decides to remain a spinster because she does not want to get married and because the duties of married life would prevent her from doing things more important to her, she is a proper Christian virgin. *This means that God does not only not reward those who overcome their natural drives with a great effort, but He even punishes them.*

Matthew 21:31 states that the harlots and the publicans have a better chance to go to heaven than the Pharisees and the scribes, although the latter were pious, honest, and chaste. Luther saw in the Pharisees not simply evil people who disguised themselves, but "pious, honest, and chaste people," whose sin was only that they did not want to sin. Christ did go, as you know, to the publicans and sinners, and he called them his dearly earned property. It is better to sin than to do good voluntarily, for this means wearing a mask, behind which the living face disappears. Luther wrote to Melanchthon: "Be sure to sin, but trust in Christ and be happy in him, for He overcomes sin, death, and the world. We must sin as long as we live on earth."

Not all Christians follow that easy way out. Nor must we allow some paradoxical remarks to furnish a picture of the entire man. Another Christian, Kierkegaard, protests violently against Luther's *"peccandum est."* He too abandons the level of ethics and, in the field of religion and subjectivity, finds himself rid of all duties; but his deeply conscientious concern resounds with great majesty: "In this manner faith enters a rather ordinary society with feelings, moods, idiosyncrasies, whims, etc." Besides inclination and duty Kierkegaard knows a third category, which has nothing in common with inclination and duty, and that is the category of the lonely man. Later on I shall have to say more about this strange construction. But here I am turning against the main trend of Christianity, which has much more in common with the mood of Ricarda Huch than with Kierkegaard. What Scheler had called "relaxation" opens up all its allurements here. The conflict is solved by stating that it makes no sense to do one's duty against sinful nature, but that one must follow that evil nature in order to be guilty of sin, until God will have mercy upon the sinner. The greater the sin, the greater the divine mercy. Because this paradox is very popular, it is on the way to becoming commonplace. "Tension" seems to be eliminated entirely. Nothing is "done" any more, everything has simply "become."

This senseless radicalism and the emphasis on immediacy and man's drives represent some of the strongest aspects of Christianity, thus paving the way for its union with paganism.

It would be good if our Christian writers were to apply the consequences of that attitude to other fields, too; for instance, to the question of nationalism. But here they eliminate nature, which is in strange contradiction to their general view. One must not contrast duty with nature, on one hand, and then posit a non-existent "Catholic" humanity in contrast to natural national differences in order to eradicate all opposition.

We must realize that the attitude of Christianity toward nature is dangerously open to certain contradictions. Nature is recognized, but it is sinful, an excess of sin, against which no human power can prevail. Nature is thus affirmed, but only as something negative. Nationality must thus also be sinful to the Christian. In the field of politics, that "sin" is attacked with the shibboleth of "universalism"— so general as to be unusable and ineffective. But in private lives, where a concrete sin is faced with a similarly concrete duty—which means that defense could lead to results—a "neo-Christian" soft-heartedness leans towards a new Gospel of "enjoyment coupled with an obligatory feeling of guilt." This enjoyment of life in the shadow of sin has nothing to do with hedonism, for it is neither as harmless nor as stupid; nor must it be confounded with Nietzsche's superman combined with a pagan glorification of natural urges. No, it is an affirmation of those urges, considering them at the same time to be unholy melodies, excesses above the pedal tone of "repentance"—a wickedness that rejects all illusions. It is an egosim which detests itself, knowing all the time, or pretending to know, that, barring a miracle, there is nothing on earth or in one's heart except egotism. It is an egotism that would not think of granting the Philistine struggle against ignoble misfortune more than the title of self-deception. They are men who have decided to do evil as long as the miracle has not made its appearance. These brave sceptics face that truth, but about one thing they seem to deceive themselves in spite of all their hypocrisy. Their longing for the miracle and for repentance is perhaps not so great as they may believe. There's the rub. Otherwise they would not succeed so well in refraining from taking one step towards the good. Perhaps he who restrains himself so well has nothing to fall back on. If they would only once make a mistake, become offensive through a decency, through a kind glance . . . If all of life consists of mistakes and errors, why not commit an error once in that direction?

It is true that doing good without being driven to it is a terrible thing and a sin. Luther seems to be quite right in his *Freedom of the Christian Man*:

The commandments teach and prescribe for us many a good work, but this is not the end. They give the right direction, but they do not help. They teach what is to be done, but they do not give the strength to do it. Therefore they have been ordained in order that man may see in them his own inability to do good, and that he may learn to despair of himself. Therefore they are called the Old Testament, and that is exactly where they belong. The commandment *Thou shalt not covet* proves that we are all sinners and that nobody can live without coveting, no matter what he does, and thus he despairs of himself and looks elsewhere for help for being without coveting, and must fulfill the commandment with the help of someone else because he is unable to do so by himself. Likewise all the other commandments are impossible to fulfill.

So far Judaism is generally in agreement with Luther, except for his remarks concerning the "Old" Testament and his reference to "the help of someone else," which indicated the mediation of Christ, whereas the Jew expects to find grace immediately through God. And yet it is clear that Luther only formulates the problem, he does not solve it. The problem is this: What is man to do as long as he does not feel God's grace poured out over himself, as long as he is not without evil drives, which means, as long as his vitality, the fire of his nerves and the energy of his blood, his secret lusts and the thoughts which he suddenly detects in himself—as long as all this does not flow in the same direction as his conscious intention to do what is right? Thus it becomes clear that the one as well as the other is incomplete. Incomplete is the good deed without the vital tone, and incomplete is the dedication to sin by suppressing all feelings for justice. Why then should one be preferred to the other? Ricarda Huch would like man to follow all his drives without restraint, so that he may be ready for sin and to achieve God's grace and repentance. But why then does she exclude the one drive—the wish to be a decent person—seeing that this too is after all a natural drive of mankind. "Those who seek no other reward than to fulfill themselves are, just because they want to be godlike and are so, more ungodly than others." A profound word, and yet it does not go deep enough. For even if we are to admit that self-suffiency is a bad sin, why should only that sin be avoided, if all other sins are potentially access roads to salvation? Only when a murderer feels repentant and becomes conscious of his misdeed does his sin have an immanent meaning.

Similarly, a self-righteous man may be hit by a ray of divine enlightenment, and his ethical superiority, proving to have been a wholesome error, becomes a source of grace. Why should we be more
wary of this source as compared with other imperfections?

At this point we see more clearly than anywhere else that to Christianity only noble misfortune exists, in which we are delivered into
God's hands without recourse. Judaism, on the other hand, knows
also of ignoble misfortune which must be resisted under all circumstances, and here man's moral freedom comes into play. It is, of
course, terrible that this freedom means a conflict with one's nature,
and makes one aware that the good deed has to be done in spite of
oneself, and that one could do it with much greater enthusiasm if his
nature were different. He is then seized by despair, and nothing is
more appropriate to his situation than that very despair that Luther
describes so well, with the true ring of a personal experience. That
despair may well seize the Jew and the Christian with an equal force.
But then they part ways. The Christian does not like to do the good
deed on the merely human level, without a call from God. The Jew
takes upon himself the distress of the good deed, as an imperfection,
as a blemish, as a symptom of his own baseness—but in spite of all.
On no account would he admit that, being without grace, he should
rather sin than act against his own nature. Here we catch a glimpse
into the horrid depth of the moral universe. May we not say that sin
and subsequent repentance is a divinely ordained path towards purification? Is it not man's destiny to weaken, to be defeated, to melt
away in temptation, in order to taste later a true chastisement, repentance, and subsequently the paradise of a personal ruin, as described by Claudel in his incomparable *Partage du midi*? At this
point doubts pile upon doubts. Perhaps we harden our hearts behind
a shield of self-denial; perhaps we should not flee from sin. For thus
we cheat ourselves of the full realization of our baseness and the experience of repentance . . . Here theory becomes all but speechless.
The Christian says, "It is better to sin and to repent." The Jew says,
"On no account must we sin deliberately. If repentance is to come,
it must appear without my active cooperation and only after sin has
really overcome me. I must never encourage sin. I give in to sin only
after it has slain my consciousness." The "fear of sin" is praised as
one of the main virtues of the patriarch Judah, and a sage once said,

"There are five people who cannot be forgiven. He who repents much, which means that he repents again and again after having sinned; he who sins in order to be able to repent; etc." It is true that we also have an opinion that penitents stand higher than righteous people. But this means only that sin has been defeated; it is not meant as an instruction and a rule for life. Luther's paradox "*peccandum est*" cannot be accepted in Judaism even as a paradox.

At this point I may be accused of simply identifying the "Christian" view with the Protestant one and thus disregarding the fact that in Catholicism there is more room left to freedom. But the school argument between Catholicism and Protestantism is not nearly so important as the parties concerned want us to believe. Both of them make much ado of the differences in doctrine. A closer investigation, however, shows that those differences have been highly exaggerated, and today, after the once fiery struggle has subsided, nobody is concerned with it any longer. How do we now stand with our problem? It is true that the Tridentinum rejected Luther's view that "all deeds which are done before justification—no matter in what manner they have been accomplished—are real sins and deserving of God's hatred, and the more we try to be accessible to grace the more gravely do we sin." Yet the same Council declared that such acts must be preceded by grace, and this means that the rejection of Luther was made ineffective. For this reason it was within Catholicism that Jansenism came closer to Luther's heresy. A patchwork construction can never be kept up no matter what delicate means we employ, and in spite of the admirable organization and intelligence of the Catholic Church. The Jansenists found support in an earlier Council decision of the church, which read, "*Nemo habet de suo nisi mendacium et peccatum*"—"Alone, no one has anything but lies and sins." They could also point to the great authority of Augustine, who considered all works done before or outside of faith (opera ante et extra fidem) to be evil or sinful (opera mala, peccata). He expressed this in striking terms:

> How then? May we not place any deed above faith, so that, before having received faith, nobody can be said to have acted properly? This is indeed so. For those deeds done before faith—no matter how praiseworthy they may appear to man—are vain. They seem to me a great spending of effort and a racing along outside of life. The

good done out of man's nature and not out of those reasons which show true wisdom may seem good when judged by the fulfilment of duty, but the aim has been missed, and it is a sin.

The modern theologian (Bartmann) established a principle which has commonly been defended by Catholics: "Fallen man, using his natural means, is unable to fulfill the entire moral law, to perform more complicated good works, or to overcome stronger temptations." This formulation shows that there is no great difference between Catholicism and Protestantism, but only that some means of escape have been left. By virtue of its very essence there is no room in all of Christianity for an independent province, for man's "ignoble misfortune" and his freedom. Because of this Dante placed all pagans, including the revered Plato, Aristotle, and Homer, into the inferno, while a "particularistic," "narrowly national" Judaism has always taught that the righteous of other nations have a place in the world to come.

Both the Jewish and the Christian solution are beset with dangers. If a Christian always escapes duty, he may lose the consciousness of sin. The Jew—and this is perhaps worse—may lose his despair by doing only his duty and thereby ceasing to be aware of the absence of "joy in doing good." The one danger leads to a slackening, the other to a drying out. While the one sacrifices direction, the other sacrifices infinite horizons.

Here we see how important the new roots in the homeland are to Judaism. There the drives of the soul will become more natural. They can no longer be put to sleep by social affairs, kindheartedness, etc. The conflict with duty will sharpen, it will become insufferable and insoluble, and God's grace will be closer. At any rate the possibility of dangers must not dictate the decision. The important thing to the Jew is the consideration of the tremendous heap of ruins of earthly and avoidable misery. Here help must be given as best as can be achieved, under any circumstances, without yielding to the play of the paradoxes, even if confronted with non-fulfilment. "You must not shirk your duty." As the Preacher says, there is nothing left for man but his work, "for this is your share." This is not much, and humility comes by itself. We must only be sincere and unafraid.

The Coexistence of Both Provinces in Judaism

Judaism, then, is that basic religious attitude of the soul that recognizes both provinces, noble as well as ignoble misfortune.

Freedom of the will exists in the field of ignoble misfortune, of avoidable evil. That freedom is something divine, a gift to mankind from Heaven. It is expressed in the consciousness of the motives and in a choice which is not based on necessity. As Felix Weltsch put it, motives are only suggestions to the will. The will may accept or reject them. I would formulate it thus: free will plays on the keyboard of causality. This deliberate free play must not be underestimated (in contrast to Christianity), although it is limited to a minor domain, that of ignoble misfortune, and even here it does not suffice for the highest achievement. There are experiences which take place on a higher level. The soul then stands apart from the keyboard of causality. It has not only the freedom of choosing the key, but entirely new tones are sounded out of light and air. This separation comes about in the unconscious, without human collaboration, and through grace. This too is freedom, yet differing from the freedom within ignoble misfortune with its rather bourgeois appearance in spite of its godliness. Common to both freedoms is the release from the texture of causality, from natural limitation. But the freedom within ignoble misfortune goes step by step. It is a freedom within definite possibilities, a freedom of selection. The freedom which has been received through grace knows no limitation. It is the freedom of creation. It is as if all of nature were concentrated into one point, without being subjected to that natural force. Grace means to be allowed to obey one's desire in freedom, and to be of such a nature that one can yield to oneself while being in full agreement with the good. Thus grace, looked at from the outside, appears like a synthesis of duty and nature. Within man's soul, however, it is a miracle, God's secret. Within the boundaries of ignoble misfortune, there is a freedom of choice. It attains the attainable. It requires an active man. Within its own limits, it is to be respected. But how are things within the boundaries of noble misfortune, when man is faced with the Infinite? Here only the lowest stage, described in Rabbi Hannina's statement, is placed in the light of freedom of choice. To recognize the Infinite in reverence is up to man. It can be done as long as one's eyes are open. But then darkness begins, the realm of humility. Man cannot do anything by himself. He must wait passively. It is unthinkable that man can do anything about loving God. The realm of natural urges is the proper realm of noble misfortune, and here human strength is out of place. Only divine grace can direct man's natural drives towards the divine. Then man loves God, and this is grace. For to love God and to be beloved by Him are one and the same thing.

In the province of freedom there is steady improvement, an eternal approximation to an infinite goal. In the province of grace there is the leap, the sudden return, the immediate and untimely seizure of the absolute. There is politics, the kingdom which is at all times and places invisibly with us, and there is the incomplete God who needs help. Here in Grace is the Infinite, Omnipresent, before Whom we are nothing. There is the "becoming" and a thousand possibilities— man's responsibilities for the course of avoidable misery—here is being and security, inexplicable perfection from times untold.

It is the particularity of Judaism that it has developed these two realms fully, each for itself, and without compromises. (This has led to some apparent contradictions in the literary sources.) Christianity, on the other hand, tried from the very first to ignore the province of ignoble misfortune without being able to withdraw from it entirely. Catholicism arrived at an artificial mixture of the two provinces, and only the one of grace retained an acceptable meaning. With his peasant's fists, Luther fought against the "sophistic priests and scholastics," calling them "stupid and coarse donkeys," but he destroyed completely the domain of freedom

The coexistence of the two contradictory realms led to a deep problem in Judaism. It may be called the problem of "the incompatibility of the correlated."

5

THE INCOMPATIBILITY

OF THE CORRELATED

The Situation

IT IS A BASIC HUMAN FACT THAT THE DEMANDS MADE UPON US BY ignoble misfortune differ from those we encounter in noble misfortune.

These two kinds of misfortune do not run side by side without friction. On the contrary, they must again and again disturb, injure, poison, and cancel each other. Both are necessary, and yet they are incompatible with each other.

Ignoble misfortune requires active intervention, noble misfortune—except for the lowest level—humble waiting. These attitudes exclude each other. He who is eager to interfere soon acquires the wild charge of a Theodore Roosevelt, a sound eagerness for hunting, laughing cheeks tanned by the air of the sea, and the facts of noble misfortune are disregarded. He who in solitude spends his time waiting, neither stoops any longer to affairs of this world nor understands them, sees the entire complex of avoidable misfortune grow pale and vanish in the light of the larger and unavoidable one, just as the light of the stars disappears in the blue sky at noon. Thus the two approaches—intervention and waiting—exclude one another. This might lead to difficulties, but one can resolve them. What confusion would arise if each of the two attitudes made the opposite one necessary and would become meaningless without it! But they cannot commingle without weakening and cancelling each other, and this transcends human understanding.

This is not just a fact. It is the central fact in this world. The foundation on which we live is of such a nature. This is perhaps the only certain and ultimately provable reality, the ultimate bound of experience, short of the metaphysical.

A constant waiting for grace undoubtedly leads to inactivity, which in turn tends toward a loss of sensitivity to human needs, so that people become concerned only about themselves. And yet the truly lonely man longs for human beings. Only in the caricature of the contemplative life does one turn a cold shoulder to others. Such an attitude should be attacked with the dying words of Kierkegaard: "Salute all men. I have loved them all, and tell them that my life has been one great suffering, unknown and incomprehensible to others. Everything looked like pride and conceit, but it was not so . . ." So speaks the true loneliness of the passionate heart. It does not speak with the flippant and precise satire of our small individualists, to whom it is so easy to be haughty, unsocial, unpolitical, and even very proud of being so. An introvert feels the danger of a lack of love in his inactivity. And he who lives only toward others is menaced by the drying up of the stuff his soul is made of. For this reason Rubiner (in *Der Kampf mit dem Engel*) called out with enthusiasm, "No secrets any more. No solitariness. No private life . . . The soul is a killing excess . . ." And yet, true activity can come only from the soul.

Without this foundation on action, everything goes astray, becomes a torture and a technically well-organized nonsense. Thus willingness to act, as it emerges from the province of ignoble misfortune, thrusts itself again and again against the profundity of noble misfortune. The two types of misfortune need each other, or they would both dry up, and yet they cannot exist side by side. And everywhere in life we encounter that impossibility—two attitudes incompatible with each other and yet dependent on one another.

This is the pattern: solitariness in a waiting attitude (the attitude of noble misfortune) cannot coexist with active interference (the attitude of ignoble misfortune). But nevertheless solitariness and waiting, hoping for grace, without actively interfering, is self-derision, and activity without waiting in humility is empty noise. But waiting spoils the *élan* of the deed, and the deed destroys the fruit of contemplation.

Thus two things exist that exclude each other and yet cannot be without one another. This is indeed a mystery and a visible one at that. This mystery is the law of life of all living things. For this "incompatibility of the correlated" is found not only in the mutual relation of the two categories "being active" and "waiting humbly," but exists also in the following groups, which indicate the domains of noble and ignoble misfortune: irrationality—reason; feeling—intellect; self-redemption—redemption of the world; experience—intention; impression through personal example—organization and propaganda; genius—studying with zeal; inspiration—tradition; becoming and growing—producing; conservatism—democracy; nature—spirit; urge—ethos; music—politics; adventure—bureaucratism; presence—abstraction; the individual—militarism, the State, etc.

I am not here concerned with the fact that there are "eternal contrasts." This is a banal truth. What I want to point out is the special character of these contrasts. In other cases contrasts cancel each other or disturb one another, but here strangely enough, although the elements fight each other, they sink into imperfection when they do not disturb one another.

Nor may we say that the "incompatibility of the correlated" may be termed "polarity." Masculinity and femininity, positive and negative electricity attract each other and destroy one another when they clash, and the existence of the one pole depends upon the other, "hostile" one. Nevertheless each pole may exist in itself. It may strive for a unification with the opposite pole, in which it is then extinguished and neutralized, but before that unification, for which it longs, it can exist in full power, in perfect shape, on the height of its reality. It does not occupy a lower level because of the lack of that unification. Thus one half of the paradox disappears, and can be experienced and physically fulfilled. Although no static balance is possible, there may be a dynamic one. All that is needed is that somewhere in space there must be negative electricity. Then there is a potential charge of positive electricity. In order to keep alive, the two electricities must not be integrated. Such an absurd situation exists only in the province of the soul. In the realm of physics there is a tension and the possibility to survive in a neutral state where the tension has not been resolved. But between noble and ignoble misfortune we find from the very first moment a hopeless situation.

The problem cannot be solved on the level of logic, for everything yearns towards an abandoning of that level and towards ecstasis. The two opposite poles long for each other so strongly that it is not enough that one of the two should exist for the survival of the other.

Each of the two shrinks and breaks down if it attempts to maintain itself in a state of purity, if it does not mix with the other. And yet it cannot do that without ceasing to exist.

Experience and Intention

In his essay *Experience and Intention: the Activist and the Romantic Danger* (revised in the author's book *Gnade und Freiheit*), Felix Weltsch traced these relations back to their original psychological foundations. According to him, in every human sentiment—in the will as well as in love—there is a mysterious ray, which, coming from the I, breaks forth into the outer world. It is the miracle of the human heart that it is able to transcend its own circle. Even criticism, scepticism, and idealism cannot change this fact. Weltsch calls that ray "intention" and states that it is directed towards a "reality." Side by side with this dimension of direction every feeling has a dimension of level, which is, so to speak, the transverse section of that ray— the flesh, without which the skeleton would not be able to live. This is the "experience."

Weltsch presents the following example:

> If I love Venice, there are two aspects to that feeling. There is first of all the intention, which is the ray which goes from my own soul to the real, geographical point in the lagoons, to that unmistakable and definite reality to which one wishes to travel, a reality to which our blessings or our curses may go out, a reality which can be damaged or rescued. But then there is also the inner experience of my feeling, my own vibrating, rich, continually changing concept of that city. That concept receives its very pulse from part of my soul, and my fire warms it and keeps it alive. All this is integrated into an experience of a subjective coloring and a determined force. . . . It is interesting to note that these two basic elements of love enjoy a certain independence. They cannot live without each other and yet they can go their different ways. Among human beings there are those who emphasize the experience, and others who stress the intention. This simple distinction leads to many consequences.

Weltsch proves that neither of the two is complete without the other. Intention without inner experience is "the sin of Europe."

"The present time has succumbed to that danger. The true inner experience seems to have died through an over-estimation of its intention and the consequences derived from it, like organization, abstraction, absorption in club life, tactics and local politics." But we must not underestimate the danger inherent in the opposite side either.

[We may] overestimate the experience, thus injuring the intention; the experience may be regarded as an aim in itself, as the highest goal. We do not honestly love the object but rather the emotion of that love. The blissfulness of melancholy, the sweet torture of yearning, the awe of enthusiasm. The object itself becomes irrelevant. It is clear that this overemphasis on one dimension will end up in the death of the entire sentiment. For, whereas intention receives its very life from the experience, intention gives strength and durability to experience. Without the intention, the experience would be short-lived, though brilliant, yet it would slowly vanish; deprived of its support, it would see its own downfall. The connoisseur of the experience ruins his own feeling. He who allows his despair to melt on his tongue cannot be entirely full of it.

The experience thus needs the intention, but at the same time it weakens it. And although an experience without an intention dies away, it is also true that, when the experience is mingled with the intention, it leads to half-truths, to fiction, to weak bungling. I once read a sketch of Trotzky's life, which showed this man, who was so much concerned with deeds, in various milieus, in cities all over the globe, in Siberia, Vienna, Paris, Switzerland. Yet I feel distinctly that the variety of his surroundings, those backgrounds of his activity, hardly affected him. Wherever he was, it was always the same, since he did the same thing everywhere. If he had travelled around with an artist's open eyes, he would not have accomplished anything. I can imagine that the pyramids played the same role while Jeremiah was in Egypt. He raged against his own people, and everything was to him an abomination and a shame. In order to grow into a gigantic task, the intention has to rid itself of all inner experiences. It must become one-sided and unjust. In order to create works of art, experience must eliminate intention and live its own life, outside of space and time. Nevertheless it remains true that intention and experience need each other, although they are deadly enemies, relying on each other without forgetting their enmity. The "incompatibility of the correlated" is in control here without limitations, horrible and unthinkable.

Personal Observations

"IT IS IMPOSSIBLE TO BE A HUMAN BEING. YET
NOTHING ELSE IS LEFT TO US."—*Eine Königin Esther.*

Man is in a tragic and desperate situation. He relaxes a little in his rulership over the elementary forces, in discretion and self-control, and immediately there is a war. Others, however, maintain that war has arisen because, in an artificial intellectualism, people have ruled too strictly over elementary things and have organized away natural inclinations. The terrible fact is that both opinions are right.

Under the bloody and glaring August sun of the first days of World War I, an idea I had known before came into focus: we writers had done too little, we had not been concerned enough about the forces of reality, we had been busy only with sounds and improvements and pricks of conscience, and thus, the demons had caught us unawares; not only that, but we found out too late that our eternal self-centeredness was in part responsible for the world catastrophe. At that time I made a clear distinction between self-redemption and redemption of the world. I fought violently against "egocentrism," in which I saw nothing but a more subtle form of egoism. I wrote outbursts like the following in my diary:

> What is needed is a turning to the outside of morals. For thousands of years men have been busy with nothing but inner details, with cleansing the trinkets of their souls. It is true that the work involved was hard, heroic, and painful and it may have taken the place of the entire world. It may have appeared to be great, even infinite and in need of superhuman powers. But we must break completely with the self-intoxications of those who take their own souls' part, although we may admire their art and even find it ethical to a certain degree. We must not chisel the temple of our own souls as long as mankind dies slowly of grief. First we must make a clean sweep, and take care of the most primitive things outside. I want success, but not the kind from which these cleaners of their own soul have

fled. I want a universal and human success, which brings order into the world, a success which has also been abandoned by them on their flight.

At that time irrationalism seemed to me a crime, and my entire passion turned towards "ignoble misfortune," and its cure—politics. I soon realized the sharpness of the conflict which presented itself on that path. I noticed that a robust aggressiveness, concerned with this-worldly struggles, could drown out the voices of the soul, the lyrical leisure, the scrupulous wish to be sincere, and a conscience sitting in judgment over itself. This has not always been recognized clearly. An entry in Tolstoi's diary tries to see a perfect harmony between these two tendencies of the human heart, self-redemption and the redemption of the world:

We often read and hear arguments and judgments as to what ought to be the purpose of human life—self-perfection or serving mankind, in order to build the kingdom of God. This fight can never be decided, since both parties are right. Man and mankind have been charged with both goals, with neither of them excluding the other, but on the contrary both belonging together and each dependent on the other. What is the mason's goal when he builds a house? Is it the best utilization of his daily work or is it the finishing of the structure? Only if the mason attains the greatest perfection in his day-by-day labor does he have the erection of the structure as a goal in his mind. He can advance the work on the building only if he tries to utilize every day as fully as possible. Only if man has the goal of creating the kingdom of God on earth can he reach the highest perfection accessible to him, and only in this striving does he contribute to the building of the kingdom of God. He who attempts to improve the lot of human beings, to bring about the Kingdom of God, without creating it within himself is as mistaken and removed from his destination as the one who has merely mapped out for himself the aim of self-perfection, without wishing to build the kingdom of God outside his own person. Man's condition requires that he seek his only true, purposeful, and possible salvation in striving for self-perfection. This, however, can be achieved only if man realizes that he is a tool in the building of the Kingdom of God.

It would be convenient if everything were as clear as Tolstoi has sketched it in these words. Unfortunately they constitute only a shallow sermon rather than a reality. Reality is reflected by the opposite observation made by Bernard of Clairvaux:

> I would call that person a saint who can reach such a goal just once in his life. For to lose oneself as if one were nothing, not to feel oneself any longer, to be redeemed from one's self and to be almost annihilated—this is heavenly life and not a human state. And if a mortal being can be transfigured for a moment in this manner, the miserable world envies him, the evil light of day disturbs him, his mortal body weighs heavily upon him, the needs of the flesh bother him, his insufficiency drags him down, and, what is more important, brotherly love calls him back.

To see that the greatest love of man is the enemy of the highest rapture is to formulate the problem honestly, without fear, in its entire horror.

At that time I did not vacillate, but it seemed clear to me that the active love of man, working for the many, was to be preferred to inner enlightenment or to the devaluating of oneself or to solitary flights from oneself, which are but delicate forms of self-adoration. I wrote at that time:

> If need be, it is better to sacrifice my own purity and the straightforwardness of my soul for the love and the redemption of man than to be a saint and leave others to their fate, unless they can be influenced without a lessening of my own ecstasy. For there are two types of ethical men: those who want to redeem themselves, and those who wish to redeem the world. According to Scheler, love is "a feeling with its own value" and not "a factor to be put to use for the benefit of others." This is clearly the love of the self-redeemer. It glows only within and for the individual. It is directed towards an object, but it does not take hold of it with full passion. It is thrust back onto the individual, who then is content that it has only been aimed at the outside. The love of the self-redeemer is satisfied with aiming and not seriously concerned with grasping. It is an egocentric love which I reject because it takes the subject more seriously than the object. Even when it is an act of self-sacrifice, the goal is one's own blessedness and not that of others. "Give all that you have to the poor." But the point is whether in doing so one wants to release one's own burden or that of others...

In many debates with my friends, particularly with Franz Werfel, I tried to dull the sting which had remained in my heart, in spite of my political work and my decision to devote myself entirely to it. The less certain we are, the more do we enter into discussions. I was driven again and again to find new formulations for this conflict. My books of that time—*Tycho Brahes Weg zu Gott, Die erste Stunde nach dem Tode*, and two unpublished sketches—attack mainly the idea of self-redemption. But then I broke down. Experiences proved to be stronger than clinging to a theory that I had come to love. The subsequent books—*Eine Königin Esther, Das grosse Wagnis*—testify to the catastrophe and the change. The one-sided stress on human sovereignty (and, subsequently, the duty to intervene, and the responsibility) had broken into pieces. Impotence and waiting for grace came to be most important.

In order to make clear what is involved here, I have mentioned personal experiences. But even if I must remain obscure, I cannot say more of the terrible states I had to go through in order to change. But I must at least say that I realized it is not enough to have the good will to reorganize the world. It is not the will that decides but the fact that the will comes from a pure and willing man. This can only be reached through self-redemption. He who undertakes the task of serving mankind, and in doing so neglects himself (unless that self-neglect comes from his deepest soul), he who thinks he can simply do away with inclinations which oppose his "sacred duty," tears asunder the work of nature, and who can say in what unnaturalness he will end.

I was terrified to look everywhere at the stony faces of those who worked for the many—and with the best intention. But they had annihilated their own instincts, because their duty had not grown up intimately and side-by-side with their instinct from the very first. Thus their squashed and perverse instincts put all mankind in the straitjacket of a prickly patriotism, again with the best intention. It was the most virtuous men and groups who invented gas warfare, handled machine guns, manned war planes, and preached war from a thousand pulpits. Simple compassion, the original emotion of the soul, gave way to imagined duties to God and the world. Whereas in earlier times I had believed that self redemption and world redemption were at war with each other and limited each other, I now felt strongly that they needed each other for their complement, and that each one by itself remained imperfect and sinful. But I went on believing also that they disturbed each other.

OVERCOMING THE "INCOMPATIBILITY OF THE
CORRELATED." THE CONCEPT OF GRACE. A PROOF
FOR THE EXISTENCE OF GOD

The "Incompatibility of the Correlated" is a particular aspect of
our finiteness in infinite connections. It is in the same category as the
transitoriness of passion, the transitoriness of life, the course of time,
and death everywhere. The clash of "ignoble" and "noble" misfortune is thus in itself "noble misfortune," raised, so to speak, to the
second power. This incompatibility lends the most vivid expression
to "noble misfortune." For it does not reveal itself when one is cold,
but at the point when the heart runs enthusiastically over the heights
of feeling. The god who reveals himself in the brilliance of a yearning which can never be fulfilled is more awe-inspiring than the god
of old men and of the dead.

Now you should apply this entirely to yourself, to the closest,
most personal and most urgent dangers. You are in love, and thus
your intolerably meaningless existence suddenly gains a purposefulness which you feel to be superhuman. For the first time you feel
that there is a foundation beneath your feet. But when you love and
when you take the first step, you must destroy a structure which you
have erected, by defending yourself against "ignoble misfortune."

The urge and duty can coincide. It is true that this is a mere accident. René Chateaubriand is loved by his own sister. Therefore she
becomes a nun. But suppose that a document found earlier proved
that they are not brother and sister, or your best friend, whose wife
you love, dies, and your love becomes permissible. Or, as in the case
of Paul, an old duty is replaced by a newly felt one. Are these mere
cases of accidents from the outside? This is a secondary question.
What is important is to seize that accident with a believing soul. This
process, which must go on inside the person, is much more important; for otherwise the urge and the duty remain separated, and only
the object of their aim has become identical, and even this only seemingly so. This would be of no help, and peace would not be established. If the finding of that document or the friend's death were
only felt to be an accident, the woman would, in the deepest sense,
remain forbidden and the love sinful. But in analogous cases the urge
does not always seem to be sinful, and duty and the urge no longer
enfold their identical object as two different layers but rather they

become identical and are heightened to a new and unforeseen purity. This is remarkable and stands on a higher level than the other curiosities of existence. As a matter of fact, to be frank, it is perhaps the only curiosity on earth.

Suddenly the duty and the urge, lost without each other, and yet fighting bitterly, are in accord. In a certain personal area the impossibility of the world has been cancelled. Life has become possible, unexpectedly and incomprehensibly. Grace has entered life. Only from this point of view can its essence be described. Now it becomes clear that grace is not a trivial "balancing of contrasts," not a "happy coincidence." It is a divine shattering of the law of life, of the "incompatibility of the correlated." It is a new life of its own kind.

Here immediate experience yields the only valid proof for the existence of God. The testimony of real life speaks up. For on the level of this earth it will always be valid that mere fulfilment of a duty leads to a drying out, that mere obedience to one's urge leads one astray. Both attitudes have to be unified, but this unification hurts their very life-nerve. Consciousness of acting dutifully kills the urge, and animal-like following of the urge destroys all restrictions. No balancing is possible, as long as everything runs straight. But this balancing exists in actual experience. Therefore grace exists—the divine power that makes possible within life what life itself can never admit, by virtue of its own laws.

THE HIERARCHY OF "NOBLE MISFORTUNE":
EXCURSUS CONCERNING DEMOCRACY

Now we can view the different parts of the domain of "noble misfortune."

The lowest and least clear region is that of the mere recognition of noble misfortune, the acknowledgment of the fact that we mortals are faced with an Absolute. This "fear of God," this standing in awe of the Infinite which runs through us small and fragile vessels and threatens to burst us at any moment, is accessible to all men. Anyone who directs his attention to it can feel it unless he seeks artificial means of evasion, and this evading is quite in vogue. Stefan George has Dante say,

> When I sat down in trembling at the gate,
> Looking at my beloved; devoured by flames,
> Thought through the bitter nights; the friend

Looked at me with compassion; 'twas through her grace
That I continued breathing, and through my song to her.
People, unshakable, made fun of me
For planning, loving, mourning,
We mortal men, as if we lived forever.

But looking away from the mystery does not mean not seeing it.
The mystery of noble misfortune can be seen by all. Those who are
not "shaken" by it withdraw deliberately from it, yet it is there for
everyone. It is not in heaven's hand but in yours and mine.

At this point we should note that Rabbi Hannina's statement concerning our freedom to experience the fear of God is the only possible beginning place for democracy. All men are equal in their ability to fear God and thus to acknowledge the world of infinity and
of noble misfortune. No matter how much men differ in their intellect and feelings, this one possibility makes them basically equal. For
this ability concerns the most important decision of the individual.
Thus we arrive at the concept of the "dignity of man." On the other
hand, all non-metaphysical and merely political argument for human
equality is nothing but a playing with words. Whatever is noticed
on the level of experience always reveals only the most terrible inequality of human gifts. Equality rules only in the calm of the soul,
and it is only a potential equality.

With this possibility in mind the Talmud says, "The world has
been created for the sake of every individual." If Jews place such a
high value on the individual, it is because the concept of potential
equality for all men is deeply rooted in the Jewish soul. (Non-Jews
often see in this a sentimentality. A Christian lady married to a Jew
once said, "Alas, when one of you dies, you make such a big thing
of it." The more Aryan an author is, the less feeling he has for the
destruction of a blossoming life. It is to him only a natural spectacle,
a grand display, as elevating as a natural law. It is not always because
of their plaintiveness that we Jews object to such presentations.)

Without being mentioned, the statement by Rabbi Hannina stands
behind the entire system of Josef Popper-Lynkeus, in which the
Jewish concept of the infinite value of the individual is brought to its
logical conclusion. Popper himself may not have agreed with the
Jewish aspect or the spiritual stress put on his system. But his basic
thought—that everyone has a claim on the necessities of life, whereas otherwise the inequality of all men is justified—is nothing but a

more recent and more socially inclined interpretation of Rabbi Hannina's statement. But when Popper places the life of every man, even
that of the feeble-minded, higher than all the cultural values of mankind, he removes himself from Rabbi Hannina, whose statement, as
pointed out previously, must not be exaggerated in its meaning. For
although the "possibility of fearing God" is one of the highest spiritual goods, it is not the highest. It has no claim to an unconditional
preference. It does not represent an absolute spiritual value. It excels
by being the common denominator for all of mankind. But it would
mean overestimating it if one were to see, because of the fear of God,
the highest value on earth in the life of the individual, just as the
speed of light is the greatest possible speed. There is an enthusiasm
compared to which the mere recognition of God, which is inherent
in every human soul, is only the beginning. Popper-Lynkeus does
not want to go into this, and thus his books, in spite of their noble
humanity and spirit of simplicity, have a rationalistic aftertaste and
even an appearance of shallowness; but in our time, appearance is
enough to condemn a book altogether.

All other experiences seem to contradict the assumption of a particular "dignity of man." What we see mostly is just the opposite.
But in Hannina's statement dignity is so deeply rooted that it seems
to represent an a priori judgment. It is not surprising that in the
academy of the same Talmudic sages, in which the original freedom
of man was stated, an especially tender feeling for that dignity can
be discerned. Here are two examples from the mouth of Rabbi
Yochanan ben Zakkai. Incidentally, these statements prove that it was
not Christianity that discovered the soul and the significance of the
individual. Even in the Book of Deuteronomy (chapter 20) we find
a regulation, quite contrary to modern means of coercion, concerning draft exemptions. Anyone who had built a new house without
having it consecrated or planted a vineyard without having used it
or anyone betrothed to a girl without having married her and all
those who were fearful could go home. (Only voluntary soldiers
waged war!) Rabbi Yochanan ben Zakkai questions why so many
different reasons were proffered. Apparently it was so that, when a
timid man turned back, people might assume that he had just built
a house, planted a vineyard, etc. Here is an even more delicate branch
of the same democratic feeling: "Exodus 21:37, states that he who
steals an ox has to repay five oxen, but he has to repay only four

sheep if he steals a sheep. The reason given is that in the latter case the thief has to carry the animal on his back, whereas in the former case he can make it walk. Thus the dignity of man is taken into consideration."

But acknowledging noble misfortune is only the first step. What is all-important is to remain alive in the face of eternity, to love God, not to fear Him.

I do not know whether the four worlds and the ten "spheres" of the *Kabbalah* are identical with a metaphysical arrangement of levels. Yet one ought not to see "empty play with numbers" in sacred traditions. They may even have a deep meaning, impenetrable to personal experience.

The most common sphere is the confrontation of time, as the form of human existence, with eternity—the pain caused by transitoriness, forgetfulness, death, weakening of the sentiments, and indecision.

Advancing from form to content, we arrive at the "incompatibility of the correlated," in whose categories an infinite thing (nature, the unconsciousness) clashes with an element of the finite and human spirit. Thus noble misfortune clashes with ignoble misfortune, and activity requires humility for its complement, although it is also rejected as a disturbing factor.

Finally this entire insoluble complex becomes immediate reality in the individual; and, in the form of a clash of urge with duty, it calls for an immediate solution.

Here, at the climax of misfortune, God's loving grace intervenes. It takes place at this instant, in the completely concrete experience, where the conflict is most intolerable. Noble misfortune cannot be cast out by a spell. We always have death vs eternity, the epidermis vs the spirit, etc. But only a calculating reason can view it in this way. To the one who has been favored with grace, whatever had been incompatible becomes, in the warmth of his loving soul, strangely possible and endurable. This idea runs parallel to the paradox that self-redemption and redemption of the world depend upon each other and yet cannot coexist. We say again, "Give your possessions to the poor," but lost is the meaning of the desperate question as to whether I do it in order to help the needy or to unburden myself. I simply do it, and I do it happily for both reasons, which do not conflict any longer. I am conscious, and I am dreaming. I am alive, but I do not hurt anybody. How this is possible is not known to me. But I know that it is possible since I have experienced it. But it was not Tolstoi's moral rule that brought about the harmony. One is not led to it but torn into it, as into a spinning top, which can stand straight only when moving fast.

Man can live only by virtue of the miracle. But there is no miracle without passion.

In the face of the concrete power of the experience, even the most abstract form of noble misfortune, that of time, is dissolved. In a moment infinite duration is reflected, calm in motion, eternity in transitoriness. "Death has been swallowed up in victory."

The Jewish artist: conscious or unconscious?

At this point a short remark concerning the Jewish artist is apropos.

It is known that the Jews as a race have a large measure of consciousness. It is equally certain that great poems are born out of depths where consciousness no longer plays a role. Full daylight, bright rationalism, and a steady lucidity cannot go together with the shaping demons of the instinct. This fact cannot be doubted, although it must be admitted that the creating power is often assisted by a certain degree of thoughtfulness.

Is Jewish art possible then? And if so, how? There are three wrong answers and one right one.

The first wrong answer claims that great Jewish art is impossible, for Jewish consciousness and intention always step between the artist and his work. Compared to "Aryan" works of art, Jewish ones are second rate. Only in antiquity did Jews create great art, because antiquity was more dull and immediate. (Is this really true?) This is the viewpoint of Julius Bab and many non-Jewish critics (Edschmid and others). Jewish "intellectualism" is attacked. The books by Sombart, Rathenau, and their lesser imitators are full of such accusations. The self-hatred of many Jews, which is part of the Jewish character, assists in this degrading of consciousness. Partly through a misunderstanding of Buber's teachings, even some Zionists use such an argument, in which a comfortable motto against the diaspora and its "decadence" can be found. In Palestine, it was hoped, artists would be tied to the soil, become more rustic and primitive, which means less conscious. (May God protect us from such a development.)

The second wrong answer is that Jewish art is more conscious, smarter, brighter, and thinner than non-Jewish art, and this is the distinction of the former. This seems to be the verdict of Kerr, Hiller, and others. But this is not true; for in its best poems Jewish art is as much lost in dreams as all other art and, like all lyricism, transcends well defined forms and limitations.

The third wrong answer, and this is one that I myself have sometimes given, is that Jewish art is a synthesis of consciousness and the lack of it. But this is not unconditionally true. For between the conscious and the unconscious there is the "incompatibility of the correlated." These two cannot coexist in the normal course of things. To attempt a synthesis would mean to weaken both of them.

Here we reach the only possible answer. It is true that a combination of hydrogen and oxygen leads to the formation of water. But this does not happen when we have two equal parts of these elements. Then we get only a heavy gas. They do not "mix" into water, but they "burn" into water if hit by a spark. Only through a miracle is the co-existence of the conscious and the unconscious possible. It is possible, but not on level ground. It comes about only as the climax of human power and divine grace, as something extraordinary, as an exception. This leads to an important consequence.

It makes little sense to distill conscious elements out of a Jewish work of art. For all this proves is that the work was done by a Jew, and this fact had never been in doubt. It does not say the least about the main question, which is whether we are dealing with a work of art. Everything depends on whether the conscious factor and the unconscious one have been forged together in the kiln of creation and have taken on the form of a higher order. If this miracle has indeed occurred, consciousness does not do any harm. If the miracle does not take place, the lack of consciousness does not lead to a work of art.

We must apply a similar judgment to the so-called banalities; for instance, the delicate instrumentation in Mahler's music, that most Jewish document of our time. That aspect of his music is either part of the entire work of art, or it is not. People will feel many different ways about this, but we should no longer use clichés like "what an ordinary march rhythm!" or "virtuosity, brilliant technique!" or again, in the case of poetry, "Look, there is a genuine philosophical reflection in the midst of the dialogue, and here we find problems in the midst of lyrics!" Such remarks are meant to characterize the author as a rationalist or as a non-artist. In one case a brilliant technique of instrumentation—something highly conscious, and a product of study—may be just a clever veneer. In another case it may be the tool in a whirlwind of inspiration. The idea behind a work of art may be in one case the brilliant secondary noise of a life process, without being an important force for its author, and therefore unimportant. In another case it may emerge from the very depth of the artist's inner experience. This fact cannot be sensed on first glance. But we have been blessed with a group of critics who project their own sobriety and pedantry into the work of art that they are supposed to judge. Any reflection, idea, or technical device in a work of art is to them immediately a very evil symptom. For they suspect the artist of being what they themselves are—dry, full of professorial emptiness, having a will but no ability. They accuse the author of their own lack of feeling.

A good critic does not react to symptoms but to the totality of the miracle. Only at the end does he analyze the elements of the miracle, and he is perhaps surprised to find there also some consciousness. Although this does not change his previous over-all impression, it will make him investigate what changes will have been made that nevertheless go along with the rhythm of the miracle. It would naturally be easier to set up a file of symptoms and thus to register a "non-miracle," since the critic's own heart is in no case open to the immediate sensing of the miracle. But it is just this act of registering and concluding that reveals him as being possessed of the very rationalism of which he accuses the author.

Here is what happens with most critics: the reviewer reads and finds in a Jewish work of art some "clever" remarks, some "smart" observations. He does not ask himself whether these "clever" remarks are the only ones, or whether there are also some "unclever" ones, generated by feelings and under the powerful pressure of an experience. Perhaps things are even more complicated. Perhaps those "clever" places are only single bright spots of light which form in a dark passage, just like a whirlpool that forms in a swiftly moving creek and is swallowed up and dragged away by the current. There are even more possibilities where an artist can put his cleverness and his intellectualism to use side by side with his unconsciously creating force. It is true that normally those two forces—cleverness and passionate devotion—struggle with each other and are incompatible. But perhaps a work of art breaks forth like a geyser and the two powers can coexist. Perhaps they strengthen each other through longing and suffering. Perhaps we have a divine game, in which the author tries to get along with both, experiencing and unifying them in their purity. Such questions do not appear in the filing system of the reviewer. He catches the creator in a "clever" instance, and thus the creator is always clever. His work is artificial and unnatural, and even if the critic were to put his nose right up against the work of art, he would not discover in it a genuine and immediate experience. To him cleverness excludes feeling. One single instance of "cleverness" convicts the author of lifelong and exclusive cleverness.

In grace—and real art is revealed grace—the earthly contrast of reason and irrationality has been cancelled. The miracle that connections are created which one moment before the manifestation of grace had been unthinkable is the miracle which basically makes all art possible, since in every artist there are elements of wakefulness and of construction. Jewish art, like any other art, is in need of such a miracle.

The difference seems to be a quantitative and not a qualitative one. While Jewish art seems to come from both sources, the conscious and the unconscious, with approximately equal strength, in non-Jewish art sometimes the sources of the unconscious prevail. (Similarly, Christianity stresses only noble misfortune, Judaism both noble and ignoble misfortune.) But it is not these sources which form the essence of art, rather it is the charm with which the sources are mixed that is decisive. That charm may succeed or fail, independently of the proportion of the forces.

Nor will Jewish art lose entirely the "instinct for instinctlessness" in Palestine. Only the conflict between conscious and earthly elements in our souls will sharpen, and the mystic flame of integration will rise higher.

It is typical of the Jewish artist that not only his instinct but the insufferable incitement of the anti-instinct, of introspection, of the scruples of conscience, drive him into the miracle. He can live only under a hundred pressures of atmosphere. He hardly knows serenity, coziness, or comfort. But this does not mean that he is nervous and hysterical. He experiences an inexhaustible feeling of continual motion or, like Franz Kafka, the crystalline smile, lovely in the midst of horror.

Non-Jewish artists who have to wrestle with a great gift of intellect belong to the same type. One example is Strindberg. Dante's work contains the entire system of contemporary thinking. This does no harm to the work but adds passion to the lyrical paradise. His *Vita Nuova*, the only original European work with any similarity to the Talmud, is a combination of a frigid *ars poetica* (the *Halacha* of the book) and the enchanted *Haggada* of love. Even without the theoretical excursi, his work contains many reflections, which are presented with the greatest naïveté. Dante is apparently not ashamed of this, although a modern critic would not hesitate to describe these reflections as extremely dry, and thus the entire work as something merely thought out. Dante meditates with clear reason: "After I had had the apparition and finished the song with which love had inspired me, many thoughts assailed and tempted me, each of them irresistible. Four of them disturbed the tranquillity of my life." There follows then an exact account of the four ideas, accompanied by quotes from scholastic philosophy. He then adds: "Remaining in this state, I felt like putting it into verse, and I wrote the following sonnet..." Here the modern critic can see vividly the "rationalistic" workshop. And yet, how strange is that unimaginable, non-rationalistic, and divine song of the sonnets! Then Dante says: "This sonnet can be divided into four parts" etc. The honest man is apparently quite cold-blooded. If he had only foreseen how he would someday be "caught."

6

GRACE AND THE

THIS-WORLDLY MIRACLE

Negation—Parsifal, Luther, Quint

JUST AS CHRISTIANITY AND JUDAISM DIFFER AS TO WHAT SHOULD BE done before grace has descended to man, they also differ in their attitude towards the man who has been blessed with grace. Here we find a new form of the basic difference between the Jewish and the Christian approach.

Of him who has become profoundly aware of the "incompatibility of the contrasts" and has been exalted through grace, Christianity demands a renunciation of this world. The Christian thus "reborn" turns away from this world. According to the Protestant view, his good or evil deeds are of no concern any longer, since sin has been removed with faith; the Catholic view has it that, although the good deeds which follow the justification are not insignificant, they strengthen the justification of the past; but this "strengthening" is a self-contradiction born out of embarrassment. The general Christian view is that the Kingdom of God is not of this world. The magic flowers which grow in Klingsor's garden smell of deceit. All sensuality is of the devil. Parsifal, returned to consciousness and no longer "simple," "has drawn the sword in the sign of the cross. As though shaken by an earthquake, the castle disappears. The garden dries up quickly into a wilderness. Faded flowers are scattered on the soil."

Concerning the community, the faithful Christian has only one desire for it—that it begin to see like Parsifal and unmask the hollowness of its earthly striving under the cross. In certain circumstances that wish can become the moving force of a very intensive activity, but aside from such *propaganda fidei* there does not remain, strictly speaking, any activity worthy of a Christian. For why should we fight ignoble misfortune, "oppose evil," if, from the proper point of view of noble misfortune, evil is only illusionary? It makes no sense to fight against earthly troubles and injustice; on the contrary, sufferings caused by man may be part of the divine plan, an educational means to teach us the vanity of existence. Sometimes Christianity thus gives the appearance of a philosophy which sees train accidents as the main purpose and the deeper meaning of railroads.

In practicality Christianity frequently contradicts this Christian theory. Out of the consciousness of being human, new truth emerges again and again. But in the long run a wrong theory can assail that consciousness and lead action astray. It is true that Jesus cured the lame and the blind, drove out demons, and revived the dead. But Christian sentiment does not always applaud this. In his commentary on the Epistle to the Galatians Luther says, "Christ came to us mainly to fulfill the law, not to teach it. Only accidentally does he also teach, just as curing the sick was coincidental to his saving the sinners." Gerhart Hauptmann is even more precise in the words he places in the mouth of Christo Emanuel Quint:

> The Savior did not come into the world to live the life of a reveller or a glutton, or to be a servant to his own body or to that of others. He has come not in order to help us gain the world but in order to overcome it. . . . Why should the Savior have resurrected the man, the youth, and the child into a miserable world which they had overcome already? . . . No, verily I say unto you, the son of God has not reawakened these dead except for the life to come.

Before and after grace Christianity insists on the negation of this world.

The Legend of Rabbi Simon bar Yochai

The structure of Judaism is quite different, as can best be seen from a very strange Talmudic legend. Rabbi Simon bar Yochai and his son were denounced to the Romans because of a statement they made against Roman rule. They fled and hid in a cave. A miracle occurred—a carob tree grew in the cave, and even a water spring was found. They took off their clothes and sat in the sand up to their necks in order not to wear out their garments. They studied the entire day. Only when the time of prayer arrived did they put on their clothes. They remained thus in the cave for twelve years. At the conclusion of the twelve years the prophet Elijah appeared at the entrance to the cave and proclaimed, "Who will tell the son of Yochai that the Emperor has died and his decree has been cancelled?" Thereupon the two left the cave. They saw people ploughing and sowing. They said, "Alas, those people neglect the affairs of life eternal, and concern themselves with life on this earth!" Wherever Bar Yochai and his son looked, everything went up in flames. Then a heavenly voice said to them, "Have you come out of the cave to destroy My world? Return to your cave!" They returned to the cave and remained there twelve months longer.

At the end of this period another heavenly voice called them out. Only at that point had they reached the stage fitting the truly pious and those to whom grace is granted. They did not reject this world any longer but were able to live in it on a higher level. "Wherever the son injured, the father cured." He said to his son, "I and you are sufficient to the world." They were very thirsty. When Simon's father-in-law, Rabbi Pinchas ben Yair, heard of their plight, he went out to meet them, took them to a bath house, and they cleansed their skin. When he saw the many sores on Simon's body, he cried so much that his tears hurt him. "Woe unto me," he said, "that I must see you in such a condition." Simon said, "Happy are you that you see me thus, for if you did not see me thus, you would not see my soul in this condition. Since a miracle has been done for our sake, I shall establish a useful institution." Jacob also, who had escaped to Sichem from Esau through a miracle, established a marketplace there. Others report that he improved the minting system. Still others say that he built bath houses.

In order to appreciate this legend fully, we must put the end next to the beginning, for it was the very same kind of deeds by the Romans for civilization (establishing markets, trafficking in money, and building bath houses) that had been praised in the presence of Rabbi Simon, whereupon he had made those fateful anti-Roman statements and had had to retire to a cave for twelve years. He said, "The Romans did all that only for their own benefit. They established market places so that harlots might congregate there. They built bath houses for the sake of their own sensuality, and bridges in order to collect the toll." (A parallel source is even more explicit and states that bridges were built in order to amass silver and gold.) We may assume that after describing civilization as he did, a description still appropriate to modern Europe and to expansionist politics, Simon bar Yochai was well aware of the dangers of this world. Yet he affirmed it in spite of all. After having devoted thirteen solitary years to study, to the contemplation of God and to noble misfortune, he was purified to the extent that, on a higher level, he could again say yes to the world and fight ignoble misfortune in the area of human institutions. He asked, at the end of this wonderfully clear, precise, and profound story, "Is there room for some improvement?" He decided that a certain place, which had been considered ritually unclean and which therefore had been avoided by priests, should be made clean. The saint lives in the world. He does not reject it. One might also formulate it this way: After twelve years Simon bar Yochai had reached the stage of the Christian saint. After an additional and decisive year, he had reached the stage of a Jewish saint.

If I, like our ancient teacher Hillel, were asked to condense the essence of Judaism into one statement, I would choose the saying of Rabbi Simon bar Yochai: "A miracle has been performed for our sake; therefore I shall establish a useful institution."

Here the ultimate has been expressed: "A miracle has been performed for our sake . . ." At this point we might expect a different continuation, and what the Rabbi does say sounds like paradox and, in the ears of a Christianized world, even petty (although Kierkegaard would have understood it): "Therefore I shall establish a useful institution." This of course does not mean that every heavenly miracle must be translatable into the lower sphere of human relations. But it is definitely stated that work useful to man must not be despised when confronted with a miracle. On the other hand, this does not refer to work that can be done on the level of everyday, practical morality. One must have passed through a miracle if one is to be able to work properly, not simply to be entangled in activities and to do one's job in a routine manner. Here I must add something to what I have stated previously: even in the field of ignoble misfortune extreme achievements are not possible merely out of moral freedom, rather they owe their existence to an immediate "inspiration" by God. Only thus can true deeds of humanity be done in loving warmth. The great and brilliant deed of love is as rare and as much a gift from God as the brilliant intuition of the artist. The analogy is perfect. This insight implies a break with one of my earlier stages, where I was always surprised at the lack of a parallel between esthetics and ethics. In the latter I recognized the freedom of the deed, in the former original inspiration. In the latter "decency" was free to all: everybody was able—and expected—to be good. In the former there was no road for the common citizen, only for a few chosen ones. Today I realize that although these decencies, free to all, must not be identified with esthetic dilettantisms and sometimes may even show some flashes of grace, they are below the realm of grace of "the good institutions that exist because a miracle has been performed"—the same realm of grace that hovers above a poem by Goethe or a symphony by Mahler.

The miracle takes man out of the otherwise insoluble tragedy of this world, and enables him to live. This is what Amos meant: "Thus saith the Lord to the house of Israel: Seek Me and live." The Psalmist sang, "I shall walk before the face of the Lord in the land of the living. I had said in my consternation: All things human are deceitful." Jesus was a true Jew when he said, "By their fruits you shall know them." Ethics refuses to consider success, but the this-worldly miracle acknowledges it. According to the Jewish view, it is life which distinguishes the one who has received grace from the one who has not. This means that the former lives in both worlds, in that of ignoble misfortune as well as in that of noble misfortune. In a mysterious way the latter has been enabled to save himself and others, to be concerned with the salvation of his soul as well as with mundane affairs. Bar Yochai, who had become one with God and burned the world with his glances, had not yet reached the stage of full grace. (That is, according to the Christian view he had reached it, but not so by Jewish standards.) He must return to his cave and purify himself to be able to stand on the highest rung—to feel the miracle and the human cares at the same time, to acknowledge the smallness of life before God and live it nevertheless, outwardly with the same seriousness as before, inwardly in a new and purer and freer condition of the soul.

The emphasis that Judaism places on this world has often been recognized, but it has almost always been misinterpreted. The this-worldly life of Judaism is not that of the pagan world, which is simply given and affirmed; but it is, so to speak, this world behind the miracle, a world which has first broken down in despair and then been reborn in grace, a gift of God, and felt by man to be such. With supernatural forces and through the miracle, such a world eliminates the "incompatibility of the correlated." Neither a pagan affirmation of this world nor a Christian negation—Judaism is the religion of the this-worldly miracle. All religions recognize that man can be possessed of heavenly powers. According to the pagan view, man utilizes these powers in order to continue in this world in a straight line, ending with the heroic life of a demigod. The Christian view maintains that those powers enable man to break the line and to step out of life. According to Jewish feeling, the God-intoxicated man sees in this world and its task—which he had already given up in his despair, and which he had already destroyed—something new and yet miraculously unchanged. Along with and through God, the powers can go on—thanks to the absurd, said Kierkegaard. It then becomes possible to fight ignoble misfortune, without injury to the salvation of one's own soul. That one can be "sly as the serpents and without deceit like the doves" (which is one of the most beautiful of the sayings of Jesus that are of the Jewish spirit) is only possible through a miracle. This miracle of the lost and regained world is central to Judaism, just as the concern for a lost and regained world in eternity is central to Christianity.

The miracle of this world does not mean a reshaping of this world. Such a reshaping is entirely in the sphere of ignoble misfortune, and we have already spoken of the influence of grace on the lower sphere. No, the this-worldly miracle means that the reshaping of this world becomes possible on a higher level, in a nobler atmosphere, in conjunction with a becoming one with God. It is a concern for the world and, at the same time, a forgetting it. But if, contrary to reason and experience, the two spheres are no longer incompatible, the ultimate degree of humanity has been reached. We cannot go any further. We cannot mix the two spheres nor "realize" God in this world. This is what I discussed under the heading of asymptotism. One cannot realize the absolute in the relative, or the world beyond in this world. Every step into the human sphere would lower divinity and postulate an impossible compromise between infinity and conditionality. This is not the way to think of the this-worldly miracle. Divinity never descends into our sphere. It is enough that earthly conditionality can be raised, if not into the immediate vicin-

ity of the absolute, at least to a place where it can miraculously exist
next to the absolute, "in the face of God." Relativity becomes strong
enough nearly to approximate infinity. The body, an abomination to
the spirit, maintains itself next to the spirit thanks to the grace it has
received. (See the Song of Songs.)

Is politics possible?

Changing this world is the real mystery of Judaism. This has been
expressed with great, perhaps too great a boldness in the Sayings of
the Fathers: "Better one hour of bliss in the world to come than all
life in this world. Better one hour of repentance and good deeds in
this life than all the bliss of a future life." "Repentance and good
deeds"—the coexistence of noble misfortune (repentance) and ignoble misfortune (good deeds) could not have been expressed more
pregnantly, nor could it have been stated in a more paradoxical way
that this stage of immediacy in this world can only be reached after
the emptiness of this world has been tasted to the full.

There are many evidences in our literature to prove that this world
and its joys are offered anew to the saint, and that a state of resignation, of "no exit" must have preceded it. The latter is shown in the
majestic book of Ecclesiastes with its ever recurring "vanity of van-
ities, all is vanity." This statement, made by the Psalmist "in his consternation," rules here without restriction, it tears open its horrid
intestines, the intestines of decay. Wisdom and love of pleasure grow
pale, and are frightened by this scene. Our sages showed their brilliance by admitting this nihilistic and honest book, written without
consideration for a happy ending, into their holy canon; although,
like its counterpart, the Song of Songs, it does not seem fitting for
pious writings ("pious" in the stereotyped European meaning of the
word). But Biblical criticism offers a complete explanation. Supposedly the name of King Solomon at the beginning of the book—he
is of course not its author—gave it authority and protected it from
being rejected. But this leaves the question unanswered as to why it
was particularly this book to which tradition gave the name of Solomon and preserved in it that way. Thus it is the religious genius of
the Jewish people which here, earlier or later, pronounced an astounding and proper judgment. A saying from the Tractate Erubin—

in consideration of the renewed world—comes from the same depth: "For two and a half years the schools of Shammai and Hillel debated whether it might not have been better for man not to have been created at all. At last they agreed that it would indeed have been better if he had not been created, but once he has been created he should examine his actions carefully."

The crisis leads to a new life in this world. Nothing was of greater consequence for the Jewish soul, and nothing is more incomprehensible to the rest of the world. The world knows only of two categories—rejection of this world (Christianity) or its acceptance (paganism). The world does not grasp the Jewish miracle of this world. Thus Judaism is forced into one of the two systems and misinterpreted either in a pagan or a Christian sense. Some Greeks saw in the Festival of Tabernacles in Jerusalem, which was a thanksgiving at the end of the harvest, a festival of Dionysius. What joy was in this festival! "He who has not seen the happiness displayed with torches has never seen real joy." The most pious and dignified rabbis took part in torch parades. Some of them threw as many as eight torches into the air and caught them again. The great teacher Hillel balanced torches on both of his thumbs. In general our literature presents quite a different picture of the Pharisees. Jewish literature is characterized by its opposition to asceticism. Just as pearls are produced through irritation by a foreign body, this attitude has been instigated by the book of Ecclesiastes. We read in the Tractate Sabbath, "The Divine Presence does not rest on a man who is in a sad, lazy, scornful, frivolous, talkative, or leisurely mood but only on one who is happy in the fulfilment of divine duties," as it is said (Kings II, 3:15), "Now bring me a singer; and when the singer sang, the hand of God came upon Elisha."

Here is another formulation of the consequences of the "affirmation of this world on the second level" (the reshaping of this world). Even a saint can busy himself with politics. This, however, does not mean that he *must* do so. It is certain that there are purely contemplative natures who, even on the stage of their highest maturity, cannot be expected to be concerned with affairs of earthly life. But even the possibility for such involvment is extremely important, especially if we give our statement a more precise formulation: "Only the saint can occupy himself with true politics in its deeper sense." From this point of view politics shares in the sphere of holiness, "the fight against ignoble misfortune in this world" has been sanctified. We say that the fight has been sanctified, not this world in its entirety, which would again be the pagan attitude. In Christianity, on the other hand, that fight, together with political interests in general, is out of place. The concept of giving to Caesar what belongs to Caesar and to God what belongs to God has been expressed even more sharply by Paul, Augustine, and Luther. When Bernard of Clairvaux's disciple Eugene was made pope, the older man wrote to the cardinals, "For heaven's sake, what have you done? You have called back into the world a man who had renounced it. He had retired from all cares and business, and you have thrust him back into cares and business." This must again be contrasted with what Rabbi Simon bar Yochai had said: "A miracle has been performed for our sake; therefore I shall establish a useful institution."

Politics is then only possible through a miracle. It is true that there exists a day-by-day politics which manages to concern itself with the removal of ignoble misfortune. Nobody should object to that as long as it is honest. But it will always collide with the sphere of infinity and be in danger of devoting itself to acquiring petty earthly advantages and ignoring immortal values. Nevertheless, according to the Jewish view, it must not be neglected. With an acceptance of dangers and despairing of human achievements, one must continue. One must do one's duty even when, and as long as, grace is absent. This is the first Jewish "in spite of all." But then, when grace does appear—when the soul inexplicably open itself to the glory of the absolute and to earthly sufferings—politics has become possible again, the politics of the mystic Bar Yochai, the alleged author of the book Zohar, the basic work of the Kabbalah. This is a politics which stands on the miracle like a turning top on its point. Here is the second Jewish "in spite of all": having victoriously overcome the world, man turns again towards it, from a higher and more transfigured rung, but with the same carefulness and effort as before.

Theodicy

From here we gain some views on the ultimate problem of faith. Why did God create the world? Why did the sphere of the absolute not remain unmoved within itself? Why did the sphere of the absolute descend to reality, into the "deeds of the beginning?" Why did it appear to the Gnostics as a demiurge, as divinity on a lower level? This mystery can be somewhat enlightened by pointing to the man who has received grace. Man who has been chosen by the miracle receives charisma to deal with the human affairs from which he had been removed and, again to view human affairs as important, so that he works with them without losing his state of grace. Similarly God has become creation without losing divinity—"Out of love," as the Kabbalah puts it.

The old legal argument between God and man, the theodicy! If God is absolute, and perfect within Himself—the God of grace, Who does not need man—why all the sufferings of creation, why sin and temptation, since by overcoming them man does not mean anything to God? Man does not help God, nor can he become creative in view of God's omnipotence. If the Absolute has been perfect from the beginning, man's life and sufferings are meaningless. Then God could be an evil demiurge and the world one of his bad whims, perhaps His "fall." Why should man "purify himself"—if this is the meaning of all suffering in the world—only to enter a sphere that was already perfect and complete without him? In other words, man's existence must mean an enrichment to God, something without which the absolute sphere would not be complete.

But is this even conceivable?

By considering man endowed with grace and the this-worldly miracle, we may come a little closer to understanding. The man who has received grace is perfect. Yet the incomplete world is not meaningless to him. What is incomplete enriches what is complete. The real miracle of the world is that earthly things do not fade into nothing when hit by the ray of infinity. They have a value of their own. Thus the body means not merely a degradation of the soul; it also represents a new dimension of the soul that can only be attained through material things. A bodiless soul would have a greater value, but in a certain sense also a smaller value, than the soul which is held prisoner in the body. Who is bold enough to understand this fully? The consequences are beyond grasping; however, we may add that, similar to the miracle of this world, creation may have a meaning to God—that the absolute, in spite of being absolute, is enriched by what is limited and faulty, that the coexistence of the absolute and perfect world, together with the created and developing one, is more than the absolute alone.

The saint can do without this world. But he turns to it again, and after having been blessed with the miracle, he loves the world. Through love, the world looks different to him. In spite of its unimportance it is important. It can be lived in, in spite of its dichotomy of body and soul, in spite of the "incompatibility of the correlated." Thus God too can only be imagined as a God of Love.

Only he who loves understands God. And perhaps God understands among all His creatures only him who loves.

Material Interests in Judaism—Nationalism—Socialism

One might argue that the fact that some exceptional men have been granted the ability to concern themselves with politics, due to the miracle, does not have anything to do with the average politician. This makes sense, and yet it is wrong. The Christian objection to politics stems from the attitude that politics even at best is entirely hopeless. By expecting the politics of the miracle, at least in exceptional cases, the Jewish attitude clothes even politics on the lower level—good intentions, but without grace—with a different meaning. If the sun can be found nowhere and never, the fight of the night beacons against the darkness of the sky has no significance and is even grotesque and ridiculous. But if day is possible, a night light has meaning, and the illumination of a small room becomes the symbol for the universal illumination of the heavenly sphere. This has often been regarded as Jewish optimism and Messianism, although the description almost always goes astray into wrong categories; for instance, pagan continuation of this world, or asymptotism.

Grace may be compared to the wind, which blows into the sails and drives the boat in the direction of its destination. The freedom of the will and political intention are intense rowing. Progress is being made, yet it is certain that in this way the shore cannot be reached. This is man's strange situation, and still he must go on rowing. If the wind stops—utter hopelessness—man must row on in order to gain at least a little advantage, and although he cannot reach the coast, at least he can touch important islands, perhaps those which the ship driven by the strong wind of grace would never reach. This is not much of a consolation, and yet it is not worthless. If then the wind starts blowing, the Christian allows the oars to idle—they had never really been used seriously—and allows himself to be driven entirely by the wind. The Jew also permits his boat to be driven in this manner, but just because of this he gains the strength to use the oars joyfully. For even though the boat may hasten towards the coast driven solely by its sails, the oars become the steering wheel and maintain the particular direction in the all-dissolving multiplicity of infinities.

Viewed from the highest sphere, no fact of this world can ever become irrelevant to the Jew. Not one material factor or hue of man's immortal soul may be neglected. Armed with this insight, we may interpret properly the strangest and only slightly understood phenomenon—the metaphysical emphasis with which the national and social problem is dealt with in Judaism, which is without a parallel in the vast realm of Christianity. With its universalism, Christianity even tries to eliminate nations altogether, as if facts could be wiped out by a decree. It is very strange that in the conflict of urge and duty Christian theoreticians side with nature, stress man's sinfulness and need of grace, and defend themselves bravely against a false harmonization. Yet in the area of national differences they agree in an inadmissible manner and believe that those differences can be dissolved if all of mankind is covered with a jelly layer of Catholicism. In the first world war, it became evident what value must be placed on such a jelly layer. Judaism is quite different. Judaism, too, is basically universalistic and does not restrict itself to one nation. It is entirely wrong to maintain—even Jews are sometimes guilty of this false assumption—that Judaism is against proselyting. Only because of certain circumstances was the Jewish mission among other nations stopped. As long as there was a Jewish center in Palestine, many people from alien nations were converted to Judaism, and great teachers of the Talmud rose from the ranks of the proselytes. But it is characteristic of Jewish propaganda that delicate this-worldly differences were always taken into consideration, even within Judaism itself. The attitude, which has never been fully resolved, was that the nations that had been converted to Judaism without becoming part of the Jewish people went on developing their national powers in special groups, under the influence of the Jewish religion. Whereas to Christianity, all nationality—like everything else in this world—is sinful, Judaism sees nationality transformed into a non-material religious sphere, although this is only possible through a miracle. Paul's disregard of earthly boundaries, and his dislike of national frontiers. "Circumcision" caused his rejection of Judaism, and not his belief in grace. He did not assail circumcision because it was a Jewish custom but rather because he saw in it a manifestation of the formation of natural groups and earthly differentiation. If Paul had fought against the difference between Germans and Romans, he would thus have abandoned the Jewish view in the same way as was the case concerning Jewish identity. Judaism believes that all differences can coexist with unity, and that difference is divinely ordained, whereas in difference Christianity sees earthly things, the fall, and evil. In consequence of the rejection of nationalities by Christianity, there arose a complete falsification of the concept of nationality that continued to cause trouble in dark and repressed countries. It took terrible forms, and at the same time the fiction of overcoming nationalities was maintained by Christianity like a beautiful dream. This two-sided morality, which I will deal with in detail in the eleventh part of this book, as the third and crudest Christian-pagan amalgam, is typical for Christianity. Christianity's ideals are so high that nobody really tries to attain them. At the same time politics is left to itself and is of no interest to Christianity—left entirely to material concern, which means left to the devil. The most pious Christian rulers and statesmen, such as Bismarck and certainly lesser spirits, were slaves to that duality. I shall never forget a sermon in a small North German church, which began with turning the other cheek, and ended in a praise of Hindenburg, "who taught the Russians that we are not to be joked with and drove thousands of them into the Masurian swamps." For politics and religion are two different things.

The same holds true of social life. By its very essence Judaism must fight for social justice. But in a letter to the city council of Danzig (dated May 5, 1525) Luther advocated a strict separation of things spiritual and economical: ". . . but the Gospel is a spiritual law which cannot be the foundation of government . . . Therefore the spiritual rule of the Gospel must be differentiated from worldly rule and must not be mixed up with it. The Gospel rule must be adhered to only in the sermons of the preacher and must not disturb anyone's desires. He who wishes to follow it may do so, and if not, he need not." This means that Luther allows earthly things to take their course. Thus he cannot forbid usury, although he disapproves of it. When a nobleman turned to him with the question of whether it was right to oppress the peasants, Luther calmed him with the ugly statement that has become famous: "If oppression is of long standing and has been practiced by your parents and grandparents and has not been introduced by you, you have no reason to be alarmed about it." His reasoning is even uglier: "The common man must be burdened, for otherwise he might cause trouble." Compare this to the glorious social legislation of the Book of Deuteronomy and the following Talmudical statement: "Be very careful with the children of the poor, for Torah will come from them." Luther, who was so courageous in matters of conscience, became a slave to his prince when political questions were involved, as in the insurrection of the peasants. Out of the spirit of his teaching, and not in the manner of a compromise, which was always alien to him, he maintained that it agreed with the "freedom of a Christian man" to obey senseless orders of the authority "although the tyrants are wrong in demanding such things." Thus Protestantism was partly responsible for the rise of "the respect of what has become historical", and for the strange apolitical German concept of freedom and the submission of subjects. All this has been frequently pointed out (see, for example, Mehring's *Lessinglegende*).

Max Weber

Max Weber wrote a brilliant essay, *Die protestantische Ethik und der Geist des Kapitalismus*, on this position of Luther, who was so disinterested in this world. Seemingly without intending to do so, Weber has stated the most disturbing accusation of the Christian idea. The essay is extremely important to all those who wish to go to the heart of the matter and has indeed aroused great interest, but not a sufficient amount. It stimulated the book by Sombart, who tried to hold Jews responsible for capitalism and thus constructed an absurd image of Jewish religiosity. It also inspired some essays by Scheler, who attempted to purge at least Catholicism. But how high Max Weber stands above his followers! It is his essay which ought to be read. There arises, out of Weber's great knowledge of literature, that pernicious Christian concept of the irrelevance of all things material, that concept which created the capitalistic spirit and thus the main source of all ignoble misfortune, amassed through man's own guilt. Max Weber put it this way: "Luther could never entirely rid himself of the Pauline indifference to the world, and thus he could never arrive at ethical principles for action in the world. The world had to be taken as it was, and this alone was religious duty." We see thus that in Protestantism the spirit has abdicated as a guide for this world, and free play was given to economic egoism. This represents only the first step of corruption. A second idea, developed by Luther and Calvin, had to be added in order to establish hell on earth. They objected to the Catholic view that there is merit in retiring from the world. They held that good deeds—including the monastic life— were worthless. Because man was placed in this world as a punishment, he had to work without enjoyment, and this drudgery was really his "calling"—a word that, according to Weber, originally had a religious connotation. This acceptance of the world as it is is the exact opposite of the Jewish changing of this world, the this-worldly miracle! It is quite understandable that people of such a fanatical mood of self-hatred became, precisely because of their sober piety, the best victims for exploiters as well as mindless machines. This is demonstrated by Weber through facts in the history of economy (the rise of industry through Huguenot emigrants, the prosperity of Puritanic England and of those sects in the United States). Referring to the delicate differences within the various Protestant sects, Weber shows the first psychological foundations for the capitalistic employer—the concept of "chosenness," *certitudo salutis,* the certainty of salvation,* the rejection of all values of the senses, the acceptance of solitude and constant self-control, steady self-intoxicating labor, the concept of this world as a vale of tears. It is strange and paradoxical that it was this very rejection of this world which raised the demon of this world, Mammon. Yet it is not so strange after all, for what men neglect grows more luxuriantly in secret, and what is stringently objected to gains gigantic powers. This was cer-

---

* According to the formulation given by the Tridentinum, this certainty leads to the forgiveness of sins. In spite of his own weakness, man must be absolutely sure that sins have been forgiven—thus the belief in infallibility.

tainly Freud's opinion. Thus has capitalism become the revenge for the rejected world, directed against a mankind spiritualized by Christianity.

Judaism beyond the Alternative; Troeltsch, Cornill

Max Weber does not know of the this-worldly miracle. For him there exists only complete retirement from the world, the meditation of the monk, or the Protestant return into the world as it is, with the effect of pagan affirmation of the world. This last is all the more dangerous, for here the Yes is proclaimed not out of joy but because of nonchalance and ascetic conscientiousness, which really implies a No.

At any rate, even to Weber's criticism there is only the choice between this world and the world beyond. Christianity and Judaism are related to each other because both of them pose that alternative. In spite or because of their complete opposition, there exists the possibility of injurious synthesis. Paganism affirms this world, and does not know of the world beyond. Christianity affirms the world beyond, and rejects this world, except as sin or punishment.

After two thousand years of having been indoctrinated with this single choice, everyone has become used to it—everyone except a small remnant which remains loyal to the basic Jewish attitude. This attitude seems to be incomprehensible to the rest of mankind.

"A miracle has been performed for our sake, therefore I will establish a useful institution." This is the very clear distinction of Judaism, yet in comparison with the crude Christian-pagan alternative, it is delicate and complicated. In this immortal formula it sounds simple, perhaps even too naive, but if followed up through all its consequences and applied to all the phenomena of the world, to life and art, neither misused for a degradation of the miracle nor for the lowering of the deed, it is boundlessly deep and incomprehensible that the improbable should have become true. With this unbreakable formula, Judaism has defended itself energetically against the alternative of the would-be moralists who, like brigands, lie in ambush at the roads of mankind and, calling out, "This world or the world beyond!", pull out their revolvers. Though Judaism has defended itself and is still doing so, it has always been forced into that choice.

Those who are more or less interested in Judaism see in it, depending on their own caprices or aptitudes, sometimes a lifeless specter and at other times an over-fattened massive materialism. But its essence is that it is neither of the two, nor even a synthesis of the two or a golden mean between them, but something incomparably new.

It is not only the lesser minds who make the mistake in their investigation of first distilling out of Jewish complexities whatever is Jewish and then labeling the mangled remains as pagan or Christian—for they do not recognize a third possibility—but even in the books by leading minds I find everywhere this grotesque misinterpretation.

In an essay entitled "Das Ethos der hebraeischen Propheten" (*Logos*, Volume VI, Book 1) Ernst Troeltsch undertook to free the Jewish ethos of that blossoming period of all "abstract interpretations" and attempted to interpret it as "the ancient law and the ancient custom of the peasant clans," as though in analogy with German-pagan concepts. He maintains that we do not find there any universalism, but only a non-urban traditionalism, a provincialism which was in accordance with the historical circumstances. Of course the grand views of the prophets concerning universal politics do not fit in this system. Troeltsch finds a very simple solution: the prophets were not politicians but utopians, who "rejected the course of cultural development and the course of political necessities. Their passionate faith in God did not have room for either." But it is quite clear to me that even as a mere politician Jeremiah was great and venerable and that, for instance, his opposition to the war with Babylon testified to his God-intoxication and also—because of its absurdity—to his sound realism. This is the this-worldly miracle and deeply Jewish—what is impossible on the level of the every day is made possible through God; namely, the integration of the most unearthly inspiration with sober reasoning. (Another figure of that type was Joseph Karo, the author of the *Shulchan Aruch*. For 32 years he worked on that code of rituals and laws. But does that mean that he was a dry religious legalist? He was just the opposite. He was a cabbalist enthusiast, a mystic who believed that the completion of his work would bring about the beginning of the Messianic time. For forty years he was entangled in visions. The Mishna, personified, appeared every night at his bed and whispered revelations into his ear. And yet—or perhaps just because of this—when he was awake, he formulated, with a keen mind, the smallest details of the daily laws.

A mystic and also a man of order. Similarly Ezekiel was a visionary and an organizer. Isaiah found himself in a whirlwind of God, and yet he was a politician). But Troeltsch seems to think that every peace-loving statement must be a document of political immaturity. "The utopian character is seen from the description of the remnant and their fate. They will be an ideal of religious and moral perfection, without suffering and war" etc. Then follows Isaiah's vision of peace, to which Troeltsch adds, "These prophecies have accordingly never been fulfilled." Of this we are well aware. But was it not enough to set up that ideal, the lowest stages of which are humanly attainable? Here we see clearly that the pagan-Christian alternative cannot understand the Jewish mind. It must be composed of two halves—a banal and this-worldly one and an inefficient one, concerned solely with the world beyond. Troeltsch fails to understand the specific type of Jewish politics, which, looking down from the spheres of the miracles, is concerned with material things. "Above all we miss any idea of the state and what goes with it. This is the opposite of Greek and Roman ethics and legislation, which start with the polis and end with the imperium." It is true that the Jewish ideal of the this-worldly miracle has nothing in common with the politics and theory of state mentioned by Troeltsch as the only possible one. But this does not mean that it has become utopian and non-political. We leave it to non-Jewish historians like Benzinger to praise as "real politicians" Ahab and those kings against whom our prophets arose. Their wars of conquest seem to have merited such praise!

Whereas Troeltsch, from his pagan point of view, would like prophetism to be a little more pagan in order to be viable, the Christian-spiritual Cornill (see his book *The Prophets of Israel*) is disturbed by the undoubtedly existent share of tangible interest in the state and reality, which characterizes the religion of the Jewish prophets. He would like to come to their assistance through an injection of some Christian negation of this world. He expresses this in the following way: the development of the Jewish prophets points to Christianity as the crowning and conclusion. (We are well acquainted with this very popular hypothesis, which has not been doubted by anybody.)

Reading the two works of Troeltsch and Cornill in close succession, a smile appears on our face. There is an insoluble remainder, which the learned gentlemen have not understood and which they would like to take from Judaism. It is just this neglected remainder which is truly Jewish, and which can be changed into neither a pagan nor a Christian concept. Cornill is quite Christian and aware of only the two choices if he wants to discover in Jeremiah a progress in the direction of "subjectivism and individualism, a separation from the community." In the Book of Deuteronomy, which according to Biblical criticism was written towards the end of prophetic times, he sees a separation of Church and State, of laymen and clerics, of spiritual and temporal powers. "It is true that Deuteronomy still had to reckon with the State and with national life as concrete powers and important factors, but one has the impression that these are embarrassing, an obstacle in the realization of ultimate goals, which are of a purely clerical and religious nature." A profound and hopeless misunderstanding of everything Jewish speaks out of this statement. No wonder Cornill greets the destruction of the Jewish State as the elimination of the last obstacle to the Jewish world mission—Christianity—and congratulated Judaism on its political *capitis deminutio*. Ezekiel, the man of moving loyalty, the "guardian over the house of Israel," the great organizer of the exile and the one who prepared the return, is supposed to have harbored such wishes or premonitions. What the genius of the Jews has felt about this and subsequent events has been preserved for all time in Psalms 126 and 137, in the Lamentations, in Deutero-Isaiah, and in Ezekiel's chapter of the valley of the dry bones. Cornill does not understand that national restitution is compatible with a divine world mission and even may be a condition for it—the this-worldly miracle. He finds the later prophets decadent, and also Ezra and Nehemiah, who fulfilled the prophetic phrase, "little sympathetic," although he is forced to admit that it was they who protected the Jewish spirit from Hellenism and thus indirectly made Christianity possible. This clear proof that sometimes political means are needed for salvaging the vessel of the oncoming spirit is wasted on Cornill. He is unaware of the fact that not Paul but Yochanan ben Zakkai is the legitimate heir of prophetic politics, which again and again establishes a Yabneh when Jerusalem falls. This book shows us how a scholar trained in the Christian spirit remains alien to the Jewish character even if he wants to be fair, and even if he is not hostile to Judaism.

7

LOVE AS A

THIS-WORLDLY MIRACLE:

DANTE, KIERKEGAARD

"Trust my experience: If man, steady in his inclinations, were to find constantly new nourishment for a renewed feeling, undoubtedly
his solitariness and the power to love would
make him like God. For those are the two
eternal joys of the highest being. But man's
soul quickly becomes pale and dull, and it
never loves one and the same object with the
same fire."—Chateaubriand: *Atala*

THE DUKE: Will we love each other forever?
Do you bring me love eternal?
THE QUEEN: If this existed among men,
what need would there be for God and
heavens?—*Abschied von der Jugend*

BUT THERE IS A VAST COMMUNITY OF SPIRITS WHO, ALL BY THEM-
selves, come close to the inner essence of Judaism, without a dogmatic bridge or a knowledge of the facts, remote from any intention,
and perhaps directly opposed to that relation. They are the great
lovers. For the essence of the great love is a "this-worldly miracle"
in its boldest and purest form.

Two great lovers, Christians of the very first order, come close to
the Jewish attitude towards the world, as far as their experience is
concerned. We shall still have to investigate their particular attitude
to the Christ-idea as the cause of that strange spiritual relationship.
We are talking of Dante and Kierkegaard.

In anticipation we state that it was not their belief in Christ but
their love blessed by grace which decided their entire being.

Love as a Miracle

It is a commonplace to state that of all passions love occupies a special rank. Is this because of degree, a maximum of intensity? That would be shallow and insufficient. It is by its quality that love distinguishes itself from all other passions.

For all other impulses are found either in the sphere of noble misfortune or in that of ignoble misfortune or, at least, mainly in one of these.

The desire to eat, for instance, is concerned with nourishment; and, in a finer form, the gourmet wants to titillate his senses. At any rate it is something finite and physical. Therefore it is a removable and ignoble misfortune. Even if we see a social phenomenon in the urge to eat, that is, the obligation to feed all the world's hungry mouths—which would touch the problem of justice—we undertake a difficult task; and yet it is statistically conceivable; hence, not at all an infinite task. The problem can be fully solved.

Other desires are directed towards infinite aims. The urge to know, the love of God, evil lust for power—in such cases there are only temporary stations, whereas the final point remains at an infinite distance.

Yet both classes of desires are alike in that they are pretty well confined to one of the two spheres—noble or ignoble misfortune. Love alone roams through both realms. Without a doubt it is directed towards infinity. Although it cannot express its intention and meaning perfectly, it is centered on an eternal, absolute, inexhaustible, and unchangeable feeling, which is concentrated solely in one person as its focal point. For this reason the true marriage is the natural and only possible form of love, if this be possible at all. Who would be so woefully low as not to find infinity in the meaning of love, and in what loving hearts feel? Even if such a one were to dismiss all "illusions," he would still retain (see Schopenhauer) the possibility to honor the infinity of love as the "genius of the species," as meta-individual Eros, who loves in the beloved something as yet unborn, unknown, not yet existing, the infinity of future generations with all their possibilities, among whom may also be the Messiah. But it is utterly superfluous to use physiology—the "metaphysics of sexual love"—in order to smuggle in infinity. In the immediate phenomenology of feeling, and without any side glance as to consequences, the entire depth is present. The loving heart clings to a safe point which does not originate in a human sphere but in the realm of the unchangeable, limitless, faultless, exclusive, absolute. Little man becomes only the cause of a glowing, swelling tide which engulfs him and in which he disappears.

But now it is horridly strange that, in that same love whose flames swallow man up entirely, there is also room for the entirely human rhythm of need and fatigue, titillation and wear, yearning and fulfilment, hunger and satisfaction, for the strong spice of change with all its lamentable physiological weaknesses, for cooling off after enjoyment, for the well-known *tristitia*, for curiosity and surprise, for a wholly calculable mechanism which sounds through again and again and shares somehow in even the most exalted passion, the mechanism which runs like this: "When you love me, I do not love you, and when you do not love me, I want you." In short, there is room for all the suffering and all the shame of the material world, of finite ignoble misfortune.

Thus does love drive man forcibly into the storm of infinities, but then it presents to him what he seems to have wished as something quite limited. Its meaning is "unattainable and limitless" but the facts are "edible and digestible." In other words, "the incompatibility of the correlated," elsewhere found only between inclination and duty or between two urges, is here experienced within one and the same drive, as if condensed within a very narrow space, more concentrated than ever, more insufferable than ever, but also more undeniable and inescapable than ever.

If elsewhere the impossible is required of man—to combine the attitude of noble misfortune with that of ignoble misfortune—here impossibility reaches its very apex. In one and the same feeling we find noble and ignoble misfortune, both relying on each other and destroying each other. A solution seems to be so impossible that it can only be found in the fact that man was created in the image of God. Compare the two quotations at the beginning of this chapter. This is the same as saying that in the real sense of the word love is only possible as a divine act of grace, which means disregarding a thousand love affairs and choosing the one inalienable faithfulness. This choice is not only based on reason but it is felt as the one possibility, as a real necessity. In the last instance reasonable choice and sentiment, logos and eros, are one. We are moved by Dante's report in his *Vita Nuova*, that, after the death of Beatrice, another beautiful woman caused him to fall in love, and then he continues,

> When I wrote the sonnet which begins with the words "Oft comes to me a lovely thought," I said "lovely" because I talked to a lovely woman, which in itself was evil. One day, at the ninth hour, a mighty apparition arose against that adversary of reason [*contra questo avversario della ragione*]. I seemed to see the beautiful Beatrice, clothed in the red garment in which she had come to me the first time . . . Immediately I started thinking of her and to review the images of time past one after the other. I bitterly repented the wish by which I had been dominated for some days against the steadfastness of reason. After I had driven out that evil wish, all my thoughts turned again to the blessed and lovely Beatrice.

Not being much of a systematician, I cannot maintain that all highest grace must carry along the this-worldly miracle. Most probably in those exalted regions too there is a variety of shapes. I am satisfied to know that there is a kind of highest grace which reflects its rays back into this world. Thus there is also the type of lover endowed with grace, to whom love is the this-worldly miracle. For it could be deemed necessary that since the value of the beloved is esteemed so highly as to reach infinity, that value would swallow up all finite and visible values, including even the earthly figure of the beloved. But according to the heavenly order of things this does not have to be the case. Let us remember that Simon bar Yochai gained the courage to do a good deed out of a miracle. After all material things had been eliminated by the absolute, he could, from a higher point of view, sense both side-by-side. Similarly an inexplicable share remains in all individual aspects of the beloved, in her conditions of life and, beyond that, in life in general; although all of this has stepped behind. In true love, small and earth-bound things do not lose their significance next to heavenly ones but become important again.

I have spent much time considering the following problem: How is it that the one who loves happily is not burned by that love, but that it is just he who is able to live in simple earthly joy, burning in a relatively calm fire, and doubling his energy for good works in the world? What links connect a passion which remains inextricable as long as it maintains itself on the level of reality and therefore categorically demands to be transferred to the beyond, with the interest in a reality which had been rejected and made impossible by that very passion? I believe that the this-worldly miracle effects this transformation of a mind directed to the beyond into a new interest in the world. The spirit of love is touched by the heavenly boundlessness of the beloved one as well as by her earthly limitations. Thus it receives a true view of boundaries and variety, a view which has beheld unity and, strengthened by this light, goes back to our own darkness. That view has rid itself of loveless systematization, the tendency to generalize, and transitoriness. The lover sees the germ of love in whatever is natural and in the state of development. He sees. No one else does. Thus does politics get its meaning from the meaning of erotic love, which leads to the love of one's neighbor, altruism, in short, all good deeds. It is not true that, in the love between a man and a woman, feelings of friendship play an essential role. But love is a breaking-in of the miracle. Because of that miracle, everything else—even friendship and noble humanism—becomes possible.

> Being together is intoxication of the heart and weeping humility.
> Being together means help to each other. And where there is such help,
> there is a coming together. Being together leads to the farthest distance.

Dante

A new, recaptured worldliness is thus the highest form of love. This is an astounding result, considering that the "infinite" component of love is directed towards the Platonic realm of ideas (*Symposium*), thus abandoning reality. And even the "finite" component of love, which reminds us of Don Juan, is utterly unfit to attain worldliness, which means the worldliness of the this-worldly miracle. Fatigued after possession, and incited to new desires, vacillating, always unsatisfied, it can only lead to a worldliness which is right at hand—disillusion, skepticism, and disgust with the world. But out of the clash of the two components, should there not arise a faith which lies behind "infinite resignation" (Kierkegaard), a faith which, "thanks to the absurd," takes hold again of the reborn worldliness in the glow of the morning's dawn? Here an objection occurs, which I am tempted to disregard, since it sounds so primitive, so terribly humdrum, that perhaps nobody would raise it. If I were to write this book in a "noble style," I would be better off not to mention that objection altogether, since this would then be "below my dignity." Whenever a thought is developed, a counter-idea appears to everybody, but the author may pass it by silently, as if it were not worth dealing with. The reader, in whose mind that counter-idea arises, is ashamed of his ridiculous thought, which the author has apparently neglected because it can be so easily proven wrong. In this manner objections are not clarified but psychologically strangled. I do not wish to be so "noble" and conceited. It is better to lose face than the inner truthfulness that dictates this book. Therefore I adopt the reader's simple and trivial question as my own: Did Dante love his Beatrice with such an infinite and transfigured love for the sole reason that this love was an unhappy and unfulfilled one? Was it the grace of his love that Beatrice died on time? This question transcends matters of love. It concerns basically our entire attitude of life. Can we have a pure relation to the things of the world only by renouncing them, or do particular circumstances allow us to become engaged in them without a blemish? Is the very breath of life impure? Does even honest possession pollute the proprietor?

If this question is decided on the basis of distance, Christianity is right. If it is affirmed on the basis of "concern with things," paganism is victorious. If this concern is understood on the basis of a miracle, the worldliness of Simon bar Yochai, one is close to the Jewish approach.

In these three attitudes of the soul, longing has a different role. In paganism it really plays no role whatever, it is rather a bothersome obstacle, a necessary evil before fulfilment. This holds true of many erotic poems of the Greek Anthology. In Christianity longing is everything, it is the indispensable motor which, in an infinite tension, keeps the spirit awake (every fulfilment means the end of the spirit). It is the motor that transfers the energies of the soul, which have no object of their own, onto substitute objects—mankind as a whole, pious deeds, the universe, God. Thus Dante's way would be an eternal search for Beatrice, and since he cannot find her in the body any longer, he looks for her in scholastic philosophy, in the church, in faith. The passion he had devoted to her he transfers to other objects, and in that fire they glow as never before. If he had found Beatrice in this world—what a thought! In the problem of love, the question of Judaism is posed quite concretely and inescapably: Does love lead to resignation and to an abandonment of the world, or does it lead, through infinity, back into a renewed world? Does love necessarily remain unfulfilled or can it be, perhaps only miraculously, compatible with fulfilment?

The degree to which a man is perturbed by this question and driven to despair shows how much he is immediately and essentially interested in Judaism. That despair comes from the need of his body and his spirit and not from some national vanity or religious piety. This should be seriously considered by those who talk so glibly of how "bitterly seriously they take their Judaism."

Christian love exists, although there is an emphasis on its being unattainable. Neither this fact nor that of its nobility, exaltedness, and rarity can be denied. It is not only rare, but love as a this-worldly miracle—that ideal of the Jewish attitude—is mostly encountered in mere allusions. For we must not forget that we are dealing with miracles in the strictest sense of the word, and miracles are not common occurrences. I emphasize this so that the reader should not identify just any cozy side-by-side-living, friendly cordiality and helpfulness, a sentimental relationship of the souls, with the "miracle of love." My words should not be lowered to such a level. The highest degree of love is an exceptional case, something hardly to be hoped for, a happiness hardly to be imagined. Dante experienced it. His love was that of the "this-worldly miracle," not that of Christian resignation. Here it is not so important that, as he seems to allude in Chapter 29 of his *Vita Nuova (lodatore di ne medesimo)* and in Chapter 37 (appendix), it was returned. What is decisive is that this love filled him with happiness and joy and not solely, in the manner of the Christian knights, with anxious yearning. This positive factor is the true sign of his blessedness. This becomes especially clear when we confront his love with Petrarch's similar situation. In the prologues to Petrarch's sonnets (and elsewhere) he speaks of sighs ". . . with which I nourished my heart, as long as the first youthful error lasted," an error which was to end in bitterness.

> And now the only fruit of my stupidity
> Is shame, repentance, and the clear insight
> That joy is as disappearing as a dream.

This is a Christian insight. Dante would never have spoken like this. He has nothing to be sorry for, nothing to hide in shame. To him love was not vanity or "youthful error" but the highest form of truth. In spite of his great grief he did not complain, as Petrarch did (in the horrid descents of sonnets 310 and 311), of being "tired of life, but not satisfied." When Petrarch surveyed his life—twenty-one years of useless wooing, ten years of weeping after Laura's death—he came to the conclusion that his life had been "empty and wasted." He regrets this, and feels his life should have been better spent. "I know my life and cannot pardon it." It is in this very contrition that he found the strength to turn entirely away from "the deceit of life" and to devote the rest of his days to the glory of God. Thus his love led him to the Christian negation of the world. This is the Christian way. Out of the renunciation of the beloved, the renunciation of this world blossoms forth. To an unfulfilled longing all longing seems to be unattainable, all striving vain. (We have the same basic attitude in Flaubert's *Education sentimentale*.)

When Beatrice died, Dante's feelings were quite different.

"After that sonnet I had a wonderful vision, in which I saw things which made me decide not to say anything more of the beloved one until I would be more worthy to speak of her. In order to attain that goal I strive as hard as I can, as she must surely know. If it is the will of Him through whom all things live that my life should last a few more years, I expect to tell of her what has never been said of anybody. Then may it be the will of the Lord of grace that my soul depart and behold the glory of its mistress, namely that blessed Beatrice, who, transfigured, looks into the face of Him *qui est per omnia saecula benedictus*. Amen."

Here speaks apparently a different type of love. It was not a painful disappointment that dictated those lines, in which the plan of a tremendous work (the *Divina Commedia*) is foretold, but eternal gratitude, gratitude to the beloved, being inspired by her, new potentialities for the years ahead, and the hope for a blessed death, which means a renewal of the entire world, an opening up of eternity, and an added importance to things material—a this-worldly miracle.

That Beatrice is Dante's guide in the Beyond would be understandable even according to the Christian attitude ("Eternal longing. Substitute objects.") But it is as a living being that Dante passes through hell, purgatory, and heaven. He himself emphasizes again and again that particularity, and describes repeatedly the surprise of the shadows who see suddenly among themselves a man of flesh and blood. It is not after his death that this pilgrimage through the lower and upper spheres starts but rather "in the midst of the path of our life." Strangely enough, this is hardly ever mentioned by the commentators. Yet for an understanding of Dante it is of the greatest importance that he experiences the miracle of his purification through grace and that this does not mean the end of his role in life. There is still left the second half of his life, and in it he has a mission to fulfill. Many instances in the "divine" poem allude to the fact that, after having concluded his wandering and even after having merged with the light of divinity, Dante will have to accomplish many important political deeds. This is perfectly analogous to the way of Simon bar Yochai. For Dante was indeed a politician and stood up for a very concrete political program—the unification of Italy and Europe and the establishment of a universal monarchy under the German-Roman Emperor. It is true that his was not a program to the taste of Troeltsch but very much in line with the Jewish prophets of utopia. It was the program of an everlasting kingdom of peace on earth! Into the very heavens was that great Florentine followed by his wishes for his homeland, its national emergencies and painful upheavals, hopes and curses. Never did he see in such concerns for this world a pollution with too much materialism, as it would have to seem to a consistent Christian. Thanks to Beatrice and her miracle of love, he can point out the proper ways to be followed "here and now," even when intimately merged with his God. It is as if Beatrice warned him (and she proclaims indeed those glorious words): "Not in my eye alone is Paradise." In the fifth circle of the blessed world, on a star beyond the galaxy, the poet is thus addressed by one of his ancestors, Cacciaguida, in order to praise the good Florence of former times and to contrast with it the decay of Dante's time. To those who have been transfigured in the Beyond, nothing has become irrelevant or unimportant. Ignoble misfortune has not lost its meaning in the noble one. This deepest of all mysteries appears at the end in the divine vision, whose center bears a human countenance. Relative things have not been lost in the Absolute; they have not been swallowed up in the glory of infinity. They go on living as the miracle of this our world. Only love can accomplish this highest grace, and therefore this last glance tears the poet out of his last moving and conscientious surprise, towards the highest joy—love.

> Eternal light, at peace now with thyself,
> Knowing thyself and known by thee,
> Smiling and happy with thyself,
> When to the circle which I saw in thee,
> Like light reflected, I did turn my eye,
> Following it with my glances—
> There was a painting in the center,
> The colors were our own, it was our image,
> I could not take my eyes off it.
> The scientist will try in vain
> To find the laws for measuring a circle—
> Thus did my eyes attempt to understand
> How the image fit the circle,
> How its features merged into the light.
> But my own wing could not attain such heights.
> My spirit was then pierced by a lightning
> Which gave it what the soul had longed for.
> Defeated was the power of fantasy,
> But like a wheel, in even motions,
> Did the desires follow love,
> Which moveth sun and stars.

It would of course be easy to see Christ in this man who appears in God, and undoubtedly Dante did not have any other intention, if we remain with dogma, but this is not the point. We are concerned with the particular personal form which the Christ dogma has found with Dante. Then it becomes clear that in the *Divina Commedia* Christ as the Savior, the giver of grace, plays a very subordinate role—not in the poet's intention but in the execution of that intention. Whether it has previously been mentioned by others or not, Christ is hardly ever mentioned in the poem. The only time when he steps into the foreground is in the vision of the griffin, who pulls the wagon of the church—an artificial, frigid, impersonal image (*Purgatorio*, 29th song). We are hardly touched by the fact that the union of God and man is alluded to in the allegory of the griffin. At any rate, in this instance as in others, Christ is outshone by the apparition of Beatrice, who always appears—if not literally, at least by implication—as the one who brings salvation, who is the agent and the redemptress. Dante's honesty teaches us with convincing force that the road to grace is different for every man, and that the pattern of redemption laid down by Paul—that all men are redeemed through Christ—is nothing but fiction. To Dante, grace was represented in his unchangeable love for Beatrice, which allowed him to experience all earthly and heavenly things, politics as well as poetry, in a divine dimension. In his *Vita Nuova*, the real account of his rebirth, Christ is not even mentioned. Everything appears as the work of love. As this love also enabled him to experience the entire dogmatics of Christianity on a highly personal level, it became the agent between him and Christ (and not vice versa!), and it finally created the superhuman and inconceivable structure of his *Commedia*. Such a Christianity does not take its departure from the theoretically impossible foundation of dogma, but it becomes the last goal based on a deep personal experience. It turns Christ's vicarious death into a mere symbol, but otherwise the only agent between man and God is the personal experience of grace. Such a Christianity without Christ will of course always be possible, and the Judaism presented in this book is really nothing else. But Christ's agency is incompatible with individual grace. Therefore Dante is very much concerned that there should be no agent, no third power between the blessed of the heavenly rose and God (*Paradiso*, 31st song). It is true that angels fly to and fro between the flower and the divine light, "but the glance of the Exalted One and the brilliancy of the rose were not diminished by the winged throng. For the highest light, which sends forth its rays according to merits, is so penetrating that it cannot be interrupted in the entire universe."

Would this not have been the proper place for the teaching that one can come to the Father only through the Son? Dante does not mention this here nor anywhere else. It is through Beatrice that he comes to the Father. A little more, and she would become a divinity. This is the way I explain a stanza (*Paradiso*, end of the 32nd song), which has been variously interpreted. There it is Saint Bernard who, instead of Dante, prays to the Savior's mother. What Mary was to Bernard, Beatrice is to Dante—the one worshipped in divine love. This is also the reason why, in the entire poem, Mary is treated with much greater warmth than Christ. But Dante is reluctant to express that last deification of his beloved. He gives us only allusions.

He would like to replace Mary with Beatrice. But since this is impossible—only Mary can be worshipped—Dante does not pray but St. Bernard replaces him in prayer. Dante keeps silent as an act of superhuman chivalry towards Beatrice. I do not know whether Dante has escaped the papal index. But soon after his death the papal cardinal legate of Ravenna wanted to disinter his body and have it burned as that of a heretic.

Kierkegaard

The concept of the this-worldly miracle, formulated here as the core of Jewish feeling about the world, is nowhere as clear as in Kierkegaard's *Fear and Trembling*, nor has it been expressed with so much clarity anywhere else.

With one minor exception, Christ is not mentioned in that essay. As in Dante's *Vita Nuova*, everything is based on immediate personal experience. In Dante's case it was Beatrice. With Kierkegaard, in the main theme as well as in reports of a secondary nature, the subject is Regine Olsen, although she is never mentioned by name.

The main theme concerns the faith of Abraham and the sacrifice of Isaac, which in the literature of Jewish legends is also considered an act of sanctification. But even as far as experience is concerned, there is a great difference between Kierkegaard and Dante. Beatrice died while still young and left the poet with a perfectly pure memory, to which he had only to cling in order to be exalted. His state of grace consisted in the fact that he had the power to retain that memory. But Kierkegaard left his fiancee under circumstances that, viewed from the outside, appear like injustice, although Kierkegaard himself sees in them a divine call. But the loyalty with which he afterwards held fast to Regine in secret is of the same degree as Dante's loyalty, and the transfigured form of the beloved to whom he dedicates his entire work and for whose glory he claims to have written everything, is the guide to heaven, just as was the case with Dante. Therefore, in one of his pseudonyms he rightly states: "That an unhappy passion is being honored and that it can make one happy in the highest sense—this is an inspiring task to him who can be satisfied with the idea, with himself, and with heaven's share in his knowledge. Thus something that in other cases has no meaning can be clothed with a beautiful meaning." But the origin of the grace in which Kierkegaard found himself could not be denied. It had some elements of magic, of illusion, of egoism and was at any rate much more problematic than with Dante. That grace does not lead to the this-worldly miracle, although from the very beginning it seems to aim at the this-worldly miracle, and although nobody has excelled Kierkegaard in the theoretical definition of that complexity. I for one must admit that only by reading his formulations (in *Fear and Trembling*) have I received a clear notion of what I have always considered the third factor besides Christian negation of this world and pagan continuation of this life. Thus it is to Kierkegaard, who so strongly objected to disciples and followers, that I here owe every-thing, although perhaps in a meaning that was quite outside his in-tentions. I use him thus only as a Socratic "cause"—and this is what he has demanded—and not as a "teacher," a role which he ascribed to God alone.

Kierkegaard asks: "What is so great about Abraham?" Abraham had faith. He was the father of faith. Through faith he had retained his hope for a son even in his old age, at a time when clinging to such a faith may have seemed to be almost ridiculous. At last that son, who is tied up with the divine promise of chosenness, was born to him. But then, after the temptation of long waiting, comes the second temptation, even more horrifying. God spoke to Abraham: "Take Isaac, thine only son, the one whom thou lovest, and go to the land of Moriah, and sacrifice him there on one of the mountains which I shall show thee." With an unsurpassed exactness, Kierkegaard dis-covers the awesome and tempting aspect of that unheard-of com-mand. It has often been stated in moralizing sermons that the tempta-tion lay in the fact that Abraham was expected to give up that which was dearest to him. But according to Kierkegaard the decisive thing was that in the name of God Abraham is required to commit what is, ethically speaking, a crime—murder. The demand of religion is thus in strict contrast to what is commonly valid. Clearly the sacri-fice of Isaac by Abraham was to Kierkegaard the symbol of the sacrifice of his own fiancee. This, however, is not to be taken as if a poet were in search of a symbol and historical examples, so as to be able to express himself in a better and more naive manner, but rather as if he placed his own burning suffering into other people's fate. It is like a lamp placed into a hollow glass column, so that the column now becomes clearly visible in the night, together with all its details. Ever since that great experience, it has remained Kierkegaard's grief that he is alone with God, responsible only to God—an individual man who cannot make himself understood in the category of commonly valid things and of duty, a man who cannot "be revealed." But he does not look down on duty in a haughty manner like Luther and many Christians of today (Ricarda Huch). It is with pain that he loves the moral law, and it causes him terrible pain that he cannot fulfill it.

> He whose soul has been deep enough to grasp all morality with infinite passion and duty and the eternal validity of common things, to such a one there cannot be anywhere—be it in heaven, on earth, or even in the netherworld—a terror like the one of a collision, when morality itself is on the defense. And yet that collision confronts every one, at least in that he has to have a religious attitude towards the religious paradigm, which must be irregular and yet a paradigm, or else the religious paradigm does not express common things but individual and particular ones (visions and dreams etc.) and is still supposed to be a paradigm. In Abraham's temptation he was not opposed to morality. He could have realized it well, but was prevented from doing so by an absolute value, which placed the voice of duty on the defense. [See Kierkegaard's *Unscientific Postscript.*]

Here we have Kierkegaard's signs of faith: soulfulness, subjectivity, solitude, and not being able to make oneself understood. Later on he was to identify that faith with "religiosity A," which means religiosity outside Christianity. It is not the particular faith in Christ but faith in general, the faith in a personal experience, which appears in life as a divine command, incompatible with any duty. What is decisive is how Kierkegaard describes that faith and where he finds the advantage of that feeling of faith, as compared to other exalted and great feelings. Here we have the instances which so completely reveal the essence of Judaism but which, as will be seen later, are not properly followed up in Kierkegaard's work. For, as is well known, he later turned towards the most radical Christianity in the sense of the negation of this world. But here he is entirely wrapped up in Abraham's this-worldly miracle, and no one has understood it as well as he did.

> Abraham believed, and he believed for *this* life. For if his faith had been directed towards a future life, he would have more easily

thrown everything away in order to hasten away from this world, to which he did not belong. But such a faith—if it exists at all—was not the faith of Abraham. For a faith which imagines its object on the outer horizon but is separated from it by a yawning abyss of despair is not faith at all but the very opposite. Abraham's faith was centered on this life, he believed that he was to live long in the land, honored by his people, blessed in his generation, unforgettable through Isaac, in whom he saw his most precious jewel. [*Fear and Trembling*]

It is thus not true that, because of the miracle of faith, man is directed to the world beyond; but rather it is through faith that one regains this world. Only through a faith which is meant for this life can man truly live. If Abraham had not had that firm faith in God's love, if he had resigned himself and prayed that God Himself should take Isaac away if He wanted him, he would not have renounced eternal bliss. Kierkegaard says: "I am thoroughly convinced that such a man is not rejected, that he can be saved for all times like anyone else, but he is not saved in this world." Abraham did not give up Isaac. This is evident above all in the fact that, once God has miraculously released the sacrifice at the last moment, Abraham could again rejoice in his son. This is a particularly beautiful discovery by Kierkegaard, and it seems to me to be incontestably true.

If at the moment when Abraham sat down on the donkey's back, he had said to himself, "Now Isaac is lost. I could as well have sacrificed him at home and saved myself the long trip to Moriah," I would not need Abraham; whereas now I prostrate myself seven times before his name, and seventy times before his deed. But he did not say so, as is seen in the fact that he was very glad to have Isaac back. He needed neither preparation nor time to collect himself for this world and its joys.

Faith is therefore preceded by a movement of infinite resignation. "Only after the individual has exhausted himself in infinity has the moment for the breaking forth of faith arrived." He who stops in this infinite resignation is a "tragic hero." He is great and admirable, but he is not yet "the knight of faith." It is of the latter that Kierkegaard sings,

In an infinite measure he renounced everything, and thus he took hold again of everything, thanks to the absurd. . . . To turn the leap in life into a walk, to express the sublime in every day—this is what that knight is able to do, and only that is the miracle. . . . He knows the bliss of eternity. He has felt the pain of renouncing the most valued treasure in the world, and yet worldliness tastes as good to him as to the one who has never known that higher value. . . . It takes a purely human courage to resign from all worldly things in order to gain eternity . . . ; but it takes a paradoxical and humble courage to grasp the entire worldliness through the absurd, and that is the courage of faith. It was not faith that made Abraham give up Isaac, but through faith he gained him.

These profound remarks by Kierkegaard throw a light on the legend of Bar Yochai. When the two teachers emerged from the cave, when they despaired of this world and burned it with their looks, they were "knights of infinite resignation"; and, in order to attain the highest rung, that of faith, they were sent back to the cave for one more year. Thus they regained worldliness and could tolerate life. They could rejoice in the gift of Isaac and move about in earthly things "thanks to the absurd." Simon bar Yochai could say: "A miracle has been performed for my sake; therefore I will establish a useful institution." This is exactly Abraham's situation. The knife has fallen from his hand, but he does not lose his mind nor does he argue with God. His mind unbroken, he embraces his son, and jointly they walk back into life.

Whereas the ideal of Christianity is that of unending resignation, that of Judaism is the this-worldly miracle, the worldliness regained through the paradox. As is well known, Kierkegaard's further development did not follow in the direction of the this-worldly miracle. It is true that in his diary there is a very touching passage, in which he gives a resumé of his entire relationship to the lost fiancee, as if it were the application of the Abraham legend: "My sin was that I did not have faith in God's omnipotence, but where is the boundary between such a faith and tempting God? . . . If I had had faith, I would have stayed with her. God be praised and thanked, now I have found the right way." But this passage is an exceptional one, he was not permanently able to retain the idea of the "guilt," an idea in which he could perhaps have regained this world. By and by his inner attitude turns to the opposite, and the pivotal point of his faith is not any longer that he should have stayed with her but that he left her. He rids himself of his guilt, but at the same time everything becomes negative, and life becomes resignation and suffering.

To be beloved of God and to love God means suffering. . . . If the pagan poet says that sorrow is seated behind the horseman, the Christian says that it is seated in front, and man forgets about what is behind him. . . . Life is of course pleasant, and dying is a terror. But alas if the command is to live like a dying man, then life in this world is a terrible torture. Dying becomes a blessing, an unspeakable and indescribable blessing, it means returning to the proper element.

I shall explain later why the belief in Christ as the only way of grace must lead to the devaluation of this world. As the example of Kierkegaard teaches, the direction is reversible. The devaluation of this life, which had been achieved for other reasons, creates the possibility of the belief in Christ, for which one would look in vain in Kierkegaard's first works. Those books were written under the immediate depression of the unhappy betrothal, and they are full of the most personal experiences. In them there is no room for the Paulinian fiction of universal grace, but the way of grace is described as an entirely independent and personal affair. Christ the Redeemer is hardly mentioned at all. In the later works his role is much greater, for in these Kierkegaard undertook to renew the strictest Christianity. Here we are more and more disturbed by a tendency that I would like to call *argumentatio ex negativo*. In order to prove himself right, Kierkegaard justifies himself before his own conscience by pointing to his suffering, to the fact of being misunderstood and lonesome, and to the fact that he causes offense in the eyes of the world. Like Paul before him, he considers alternate possibilities of action but "where would the offense then be?" Unless he hurts others, he believes he has acted wrongly. Now it is true and based on a deep feeling that in ninety-nine out of a hundred cases he who does good must suffer and come to grief. Nevertheless the one percent, the recognition of the good deed, must not be neglected as a possibility; and, even in case that this should be considered an objectionable optimism, it is clear that the statement "all good things create offense" must not be turned into its opposite, as if all things offending were good. Negative things, like suffering and hurt, must therefore not be used as an argument. The good must be proven to be so because of its own value, and not because of its hurtful effect. The *argumentum ex negativo*, a typically Christian way, is the exact opposite of the this-worldly miracle, for it presupposes that this world is necessarily damned and to be rejected, that this-worldliness cannot be attained even through a miracle, and that it is the highest fruit of faith to turn one's back to the world so that, after having been admitted to the higher order, one need not be concerned with the lower one any longer.

Here arises a very complicated and difficult question: How could Kierkegaard forget so completely his first feeling for the constitution of this world, and end up so far away from his point of departure? This question becomes the more complicated if we admit honestly that we may indeed detect connections between Kierkegaard's starting position and the final point and that, in this infinitely delicate and superior spirit, all things melt into each other.

We can easily see that Kierkegaard's change has to do with his central experience, his betrothal. He himself repeats often enough that everything in his life and in his work is connected with that event. It is decisive that Kierkegaard annulled that betrothal, which had been based on deep love. The reason he gives is his incurable melancholy. But we may never be able to discern the deepest reasons for this; for, if I know how to judge these conflicts, the deepest reasons are at the same time the most concrete ones, even physical ones; and this is exactly what Kierkegaard wishes to treat with silence. He wraps this in poems and does not even reveal it in his diary. "I will not put down in writing the more concrete explanation, which I am hiding in my innermost soul and which contains what is most horrifying to me." One of the editors of Kierkegaard's works maintains that the reason for his melancholy was that he could not confess his past to his beloved, that he might have had to admit the loss of his sexual innocence and the very remote possibility of the existence of an illegitimate child. The *tertium comparationis* between this novelistic episode and the main diary of the "stages on the path of life" seems to be the almost senseless insecurity, the fear of the possibility of having committed a crime, but not the crime itself. At another place Kierkegaard himself expresses it thus:

> How am I being punished? By charging my conscience with that possible murder. . . . What does my reason have to say about this? That the worst is not really very probable. What does that mean to me? Nothing at all. My ethical obligation is not exhausted by a calculation of probabilities, but it requires me to feel responsible for any possibility whatever.

Many statements made by his fiancee and her family should have made Kierkegaard believe that the annulment of the betrothal might mean her death, her fading away. This is the "possible murder." Kierkegaard compares with this "murder" the account about a "bookkeeper" who once, in a state of intoxication, visited a brothel, and in his old age is tormented by the thought of neglecting his paternal duty towards his child, whom he cannot find in the great number of children in Copenhagen. "To feel responsible for any possibility whatever" is the point of comparison, and not the visit of the brothel.

Abraham receives a divine order which, humanly speaking, makes him the murderer of his own child. Kierkegaard, too, heard a divine voice which told him that he could serve God only in lonely melancholy and in being shut up. He was told that he would not be allowed and that it would even be impossible for him to tolerate a female companion on his way. By satisfying the divine command, he had to be cruelly unjust to his beloved, whom he abandoned. For many years—potentially forever—he made her unhappy, in addition to the fact that the annulment of the betrothal to the rich and brilliant young man necessarily looked like an abasement of the girl. Kierkegaard tried desperately to prevent such a consequence by taking all guilt upon himself. In his *Diary of a Seducer* he attempted to present himself as being guilty to such a degree that even the girl would believe it and lose her taste for him. In that manner he hoped to soothe her pain, but it is almost certain that his comedy, fantastically constructed and executed with many scruples of his conscience, was unsuccessful. At any rate his doubts concerning this tortured him greatly and clarified for him the entire dubiety of his situation. His thoughts were disturbed by the problem that the divine command, addressed to an individual, could call for something that goes against duty, against common human life—a crime. Where then could certainty be found? Might not the divine command that makes an end to duty be a mere devilish illusion, the mask for a base human desire? A mask for egoism? Then everything would be a lie, and everything would be lost.

Kierkegaard had to find above all a safe place where he could stand up against this possibility, and thus arose his strange system in which the divine command is characterized by negative signs. It turns against duty, and also against egoistic desires. Here is the root of the later *argumentum ex negativo*.

In order to secure the proper distinctions, Kierkegaard erects a mighty foundation, his book *Either / Or*, which deals with the fight between esthetics and ethics. Ethics here stands for what is commonly valid, the domain of duty, esthetics for the subjectivity of enjoyment, sensuality, variety, seclusion, individuality, imagination without real existence. In this fight the common things are victorious, duty defeats desire, and the defender of the happy marriage defeats the loving illusionist.

In subsequent writings by Kierkegaard the common things are opposed by religious things. It is again subjectivity, the soulfulness like the esthetic things which had been overcome long before; but this subjectivity is of real existence, it is the most real thing imaginable—truth and divine grace. Grace is opposed to what is commonly valid (duty), since it is attainable only by the individual in his most quiet solitude, and he can give only himself an account of whether the voice he has heard in his innermost soul is a divine command or not; but by being of an essentially higher order, grace differs also from desire (inclination, esthetics). Hence, according to Kierkegaard, grace is the opposite of duty and inclination. It is indeed the lack of both, whereas, according to my own view, it is characterized by the wonderful coincidence of duty and inclination.

And yet we must remind the reader that even according to my view not every coincidence of duty and inclination raises man to the "third level of the good." Such a junction may be a mere accident, and religiously ineffective. For supernatural grace, which overwhelms man, is completely free. It is not supported by any causal order, and thus it cannot be derived from any preceding state. (To have recognized this and to have defended it energetically against the Pelagian and other heresies is one of the great merits of the church.) My definition of grace—the coincidence of duty and inclination—must therefore not be misunderstood as an explanation of grace, but only as a description of its effects. For grace is of course neither a desire nor a moral duty nor their coexistence. It is always a new, third, and supernatural element, but as a secondary phenomenon—only possible in grace and not in man's creaturely state—the cancellation of the "incompatibility of the correlated" and the junction of inclination and duty becomes typical. Incidentally, this is not only the Jewish view but also corresponds to a beautiful definition given by Augustine, who sees in grace a divine assistance, "connected with nature and doctrine through burning and glowing love" (*adjutorium bene agendi adjunctum naturae atque doctrinae per inspirationem flagrantissimae et luminosissimae caritatis*—where *natura* corresponds to the inclination, and *doctrina* to duty). Is grace always tied up with this secondary phenomenon? Or is it possible for grace to emerge from the level of inclination and duty by containing neither of them and thus living at a distance from them? Who would dare to make decisions in this area, where everything depends on personal experiences, and laws and calculations fail? Since grace is always free and undeserved, such a possibility cannot be entirely excluded. The question is only whether this is the case with Kierkegaard.

Kierkegaard's polemics are convincing when he proves that neither inclination nor duty alone constitutes grace and the divine command. Concerning inclination, Kierkegaard points out—contrary to Luther's "*peccandum est*"—that the "ordinary society" of inclinations, feelings, moods, etc. has nothing to do with faith, which must be preceded by "a motion of infinity." Only then, after a complete resignation, can faith enjoy this world, thanks to the absurd. In this sense he also emphasizes that his opinion, which, seen from the point of view of God, leads to the individual's freedom from the moral law and to an apparent irresponsibility, could become a trap to the weak. In the following remark he rejects such a misinterpretation: "If the entire weight is placed on faith (where it belongs), I believe I can speak freely of Abraham. For as far as faith is concerned, our time is not extravagant, and only through faith, not through murder, can we approximate Abraham." Kierkegaard is as clear in his emphasis on the difference between unconditional fulfilment of one's duty and the grace of faith. He dedicates the largest part of his work to that distinction. He establishes the category of the tragic hero, of which he speaks with trembling. (This too in opposition to the neo-Christian tendency, which identifies fulfilment of duties with Philistinism, and which dares to leap into grace without having a notion of the dread of the lower rung, the painful adjustment to what is commonly valid.) Kierkegaard thus honors Agamemnon, who sacrifices his daughter publicly for the benefit of the common weal, yet he places him below Abraham, who, in his solitude, is faced with an irrational divine command—Abraham who cannot be understood by anyone, who cannot express himself in generalities, and to whom there is consequently left only the way into faith or the rebellion against God.

We may therefore join Kierkegaard in believing that grace is neither identical with the inclination nor with duty. But does this mean that grace is remote from both of them? It is strange how eager Kierkegaard-Abraham is to make a distinction between his situation—he admits that it goes against duty—and a situation where the opposition to duty may have arisen out of creaturely desires. It is as if he defended himself against the accuser in his own soul and covered himself with the pain caused by his own decision; for it is this very pain which proves that the neglect of duty was not based on egoism or the following of common advantages but rather for the sake of God. If the proof is faulty, Abraham is a murderer, and Kierkegaard a seducer of girls (in the spiritual meaning of the word). This then is the situation: duty can be violated in two ways—on a lower level, if morality is neglected because of desire; and on a higher level, if duty is suspended because of the salvation of the soul. Only the individual's conscience can decide whether he has violated ethics through an exalted or a base motive. The deed itself is neutral in this respect. Kierkegaard always stresses the horror and the terrible pain inherent in the circumstance that this decision is made without any control by the world outside, without any communication with it. "The individual can only communicate within himself as to what must be understood as Isaac." The individual makes his decision against his own inclination, and he does not even have the satisfaction of knowing that he does so for the sake of the others. In a higher sense he makes that decision only for his own sake, for that of his metaphysical I, for God. This makes it even more important that he should not have any doubt, but must be convinced of not having yielded to his physical *I* and even of having caused it pain. This pain, this *argumentum ex negativo*, is absolutely necessary for covering up the violation of duty. This explains certain statements Kierkegaard made in his diary:

> Now, at this moment I really feel the blessedness and the comfort of knowing with God that I left her while suffering, and that just that was suffering. How this adds to my strength! If I had left her out of egoism, in order to take hold of more brilliant things, then my life would be certain despair. But now I am very calm. Whereas, in

the opposite case, I would say: I have lost, I say now: I have been victorious.

Such outbreaks must lead to mistrust. I am always skeptical if someone uses his suffering as an argument. For we can never know how much pleasure is hidden in a suffering which has been thought through so clearly. Only dull suffering is absolute suffering, entire suffering. To put it more exactly, Kierkegaard could not know whether perhaps deeper and repressed drives shaped the decision made against the drive. It is here that *Fear and Trembling* starts. We have strange instances to prove this. At one time Kierkegaard admitted that he could love only from a distance. But did he not create that distance artificially? (Grace is hurt by man's having a share in it; therefore, Dante's grace was so much purer.) We detect this in a strange entry in his diary, which contradicts the one quoted above: "But although, under those circumstances, I had to say that in suffering I could be happier without her than with her, she had touched me, and I would have liked to do everything." Another entry describes the special character of his love: "Although I have perhaps never loved her erotically, I can truthfully say that the kind child has moved me most beautifully." At this point we should remember how intensively the little episodes in the *Stages* concern themselves with the father-son conflict ("father complex"); for instance, "silent despair," "Solomon's dream," "Periander." Particularly the last mentioned is a very moving description of the implacable hatred between father and son, with all the signs which call for a Freudian psychoanalysis. The conclusion of the story can indeed be felt as a symbol of a "forced repression":

> He wishes to die, and yet he was afraid lest after his death he would be put to shame. Then his wisdom found a meaningful exit from life. He showed two young men a hidden passage. He told them to go there the next night, and to kill the first man they would meet and to bury him immediately. When they had left, he told four other people the very same thing—to wait in that passage, to kill two young people they would meet there, and to bury them at once. Then again he told that to eight more people—to kill the four. Thus Periander himself appeared at the appointed hour, and he was killed.

This leads us to conclude that Kierkegaard's abandoning his fiancee was considered as self-punishment in his subconscious, as an atonement for the dead father, and as an atonement for repressed evil thoughts concerning his father, whom, incidentally, he had loved with an extraordinary respect. Such phenomena are known to psychoanalysts as over-compensation. Compare to this the curious and enthusiastic dedication to his father, and his strange relation to Bishop Mynster, a relation mixed of respect and wild rebellion, "my melancholical attachment to the pastor of my deceased father." (See also the entry in his diary on July 9, 1838, and numerous other instances.) In addition to the religious call, which retains its own value independently and must under no circumstances be reduced to something psychological, there existed, at least in Kierkegaard's subconscious, deep motives against getting married. These are also present in Kafka's powerful novel, *The Trial.* "I shall sweep your fiancee away from your side, you will not know how." These are the words which the ghost of the angry father addresses to the son. And we have not even taken into account more conscious reasons, some of which are mentioned by Kierkegaard, either to be rejected or to be utilized further; for instance, the fact that he had abandoned his sweetheart for "esthetic" reasons, because of poetical fancies, etc.

Kierkegaard himself presents his situation as pure pain. But if he were so firmly convinced or, at least, had convinced himself that he was not driven on by urges but acted exclusively by divine inspiration, there would be in this much comfort and security. In order to preserve that security, he was bound, from then on, to see in his urges the exact opposite to what was divine, and thus he, who had taken his point of departure from the this-worldly miracle, had to end up by rejecting this world. In his later writings we even find gross misinterpretations of Judaism, due to a typically Christian approach, although originally he had seemed to be predestined as no one else to understand Judaism. He had to pay a high price for his peace of mind and his inner security. That price was the fundamental rejection of all potentialities of this world. God had to be removed from his drives so that the violation of duties could appear as being of divine origin and not as a confirmation of his urges. If the this-worldly miracle had been considered in the sight of God a *post-factum* justification for his desires, a clear definition would have become impossible. Thus to Kierkegaard the abyss between God and nature became more and more frightening. If he had not sought and found security in this, he might have been assailed by a much

more painful doubt. Suppose that the divine command ran parallel
to the sensual urge, both of them directed against duty. Suppose that
the violaton of duty could not be praised as a violation of one's desires. Suppose it were pleasant and generated sensuality and in spite
of all this were considered to be divinely ordained. In this terrible situation, André Gide places these horrifying words into King
David's mouth: "Now, Joab, I ask God this question: What is man
to do if God hides behind each of his desires?" *(Bathsheba)*. It would
then be possible that, when God told Abraham to kill his own son,
he did not talk to an Abraham who loved his son but to an Abraham
who hated his son, and who, even before having received a divine
command, would have liked to rid himself of the bothersome son.
What a horror to realize that an earlier, animal hatred was identical
with, and yet different from, a supernatural command! Let us take
another case. A man loves his best friend's wife with all of his physical and mental powers, and her husband needs her as much as does
the lover. The lover knows that living with the woman would mean
a purification and an improvement; but that purity, commanded by
a divine order, contradicts his obligations as a friend and as a human
being. Fatefully enough, the command runs parallel to his purely
physical mating urge. If he does not obey the command, he betrays
God and can never become a whole man; and, if he does follow it,
he will always be suspected of not having obeyed God but rather his
own flesh (This is approximately the situation of Doctor Askonas in
my novel *Das grosse Wagnis*.) The *Christian* Kierkegaard escaped
that tragic situation by fleeing into the negation of this world. The
situation was much more desperate than he admitted. He knew that
he had violated his ethical obligation. But since he believed he had
made a decision *against* his inclination and since he felt certain of the
conflict between his desires and the law of God, he felt quite sure
that he had decided for God. Only that conflict made his pain and
the suffering of subjecting his urge worthwhile. The rejection of his
drives and the subsequent most radical rejection of this world, a rejection identical with Christianity, was his only way out of the
dilemma. In this sense he was possessed of grace—the certainty of a
divine command. Subjectively he had that certainty; and, compared
to it, the objective skepticism mentioned here is of no importance.
At the same time, we see that the granting of grace has an entirely
individual character. Thus it is one of Kierkegaard's main theses that

the entire truth lies in subjectivity. It is with this in mind that I shall try later on to analyze his faith in Christ.

There is yet another reason for dwelling on Kierkegaard's case. It is one where the Divine Presence—the brilliance of the this-worldly miracle—appears temporarily but then is swept away in leaden grey clouds, in pain without measure. Kierkegaard says something about the extraordinary rarity of the this-worldly miracle. And this is indeed the way it ought to be understood. If I were to believe that people could live a comfortable life, that their healthy stomachs could swallow the conflicts of life, that such people could claim this book for themselves with its this-worldly miracle by utilizing the Jewish teaching presented here to cover up their ruthless this-worldly appetite—I should not have written this book. Such people are neither Jews nor Christians but simply pagans. The danger is obvious. Since, at the end, all the affairs of this life are taken care of, "thanks to the absurd," anybody who turns to the affairs of this life can claim to do so, "thanks to the absurd." But Kierkegaard's "infinite resignation" must not be merely an empty phrase. It would be a thousand times better to founder in that resignation—as was the case with Kierkegaard and Flaubert—than not to have gone through it at all and to profane God's name by calling a miracle what was done in the course of nature.

Jewish legend has it that in any one period there exist only thirty-six righteous people. Nobody knows who they are, and yet the entire world is based on them. If one of them should be recognized as one of the thirty-six, he would die immediately. This story shows how exclusive the folk belief is. But it is comforting to know that "the world is founded on them," although the whole matter is very sad. In other words, although grace, which blesses and affirms life in a form visible to us, is so extraordinarily rare and concealed, its very possibility transfigures our life and its meaning. And even if we may not maintain that we live and love properly, even if we do not go far enough in resignation and in good works, we know that this is not the fault of life as it is but our own fault, our very own. In spite of the view of Christianity, this life is not self-contradictory and basically evil. But we must wait and hope.

8

LOVE AS A

THIS-WORLDLY MIRACLE:

THE SONG OF SONGS

Christian Love

LOVE AS A THIS-WORLDLY MIRACLE, THE DIRECT LOVE BETWEEN MAN and man and for man's sake is alien to Christianity. It knows only the love of God (noble misfortune), and only through that agency does there exist "Christian love of one's neighbor," which, assisted by Charles Dickens for instance, people like to imagine, and not without reason, as being something weak, boring, and of little effect.

For love is impossible without a positive attitude towards this world, as it is viewed by Judaism, at least potentially. Without that positive attitude each one of us is tied to God with a wire, and we act without being connected with one another, in an ethical puppet theater. To the consistent Christian, a direct feeling between man and man is in itself too worldly, too material. An immediate share in the fate of an individual or a group becomes impossible. Remember, however, Jeremiah's roaring outburst, "My bowels, my bowels! I am pained at my very heart; my heart maketh a noise in me; I cannot hold my peace, because thou hast heard, O my soul, the sound of the trumpet, the alarm of war. Destruction upon destruction is cried. . . ." (IV. 19) But Christian love is abstract and directed entirely towards the world beyond. Thus ignoble misfortune has no place, nor has man's care for his fellow man. The Jewish concept of love has been beautifully illustrated in a legend concerning Rabbi Moshe Leib of Sassov, which Martin Buber (*The Tales of the Hassidim: the Later Masters*, p. 86) tells like this:

Rabbi Moshe Leib told this story: How to love men is something I learned from a peasant. He was sitting in an inn along with other peasants, drinking. For a long time he was as silent as the rest, but when he was moved by the wine, he asked one of the men seated beside him, "Tell me, do you love me, or don't you love me?" The other replied, "I love you very much." But the first man replied, "You say that you love me, but you do not know what I need. If you really loved me, you would know." The other had not a word to say to this, and the peasant who had put the question fell silent again. But I understand. To know the needs of men and to bear the burden of their sorrow—that is the true love of men.

Christian love, on the other hand, transpires entirely between the I and God, and it fastens on other objects only through an agency. Thus Scheler believed that one could also demonstrate one's love of an enemy by killing him, as long as the latter's metaphysical I is preserved. This means he must be killed in a gallant manner, in an honest struggle, without hatred or resentment. Such is the logical extreme at which we arrive if we consistently carry through Christianity's unconcern with this world.

Here is one of the main areas where Christianity and paganism merge, that cancer on Europe's Christian-pagan civilization. To make it quite clear, the Christian unconcern with material needs, the avoidable misfortune of one's fellow man, is equivalent to the one-sided pagan emphasis on one's own strength, which can be found, for instance, in Gomperz's concept of freedom (in his *Die Lebens-auffassung der griechischen Philosophen und das Ideal der inneren Freiheit*): "Yielding oneself out of inner strength, sufficient to itself, and not considering it a catastrophe when an individual goal is not reached." What is the "inner freedom" which represents the principle of classical, Indian, Christian—hence non-Jewish—ethics, and, according to Gomperz, that of ethics in general? "Inner freedom means a power, not determining outer fate in an arbitrary manner, but rather a power that determines one's inner fate independently of the outside world." This is only possible if we have within ourselves "an excess of strength," which goes forth in "loving devotion" or in "creative productivity":

> Here the deed is not performed in order to arrive at a certain goal, but it is an aim in itself, and the effect is of secondary concern. If fate obstructs one activity or one effect, another deed or effect can do the same service . . . Regardless of the means, the discharge and

the joy connected with it remains the same. In any case, there is the possibility of the fulfilment of the wish. Thus man becomes independent of fate, a free man within himself. His situation is similar to that of a child playing. The child, too, is interested only in spending an excess of strength in play. If one toy is not available, another one will do. If he cannot throw his ball to the right side, he will throw it to the left. In either case he can be satisfied, happy, and contented. He can also be serene, knowing that he is independent; for every consciousness of one's own supremacy is accompanied by serenity. But if the child were interested in reaching a certain effect etc.?

Compare also Max Scheler's view: "The Christian symbol of the halo ... illustrates the idea that the goodness and beauty of virtue do not rest in acting for others but primarily in the exalted being and essence of the soul. Only incidentally, as an example, is it important to others" [*Abhandlungen und Aufsaetze* I: 4]. If we apply to this the terminology of Felix Weltsch, we arrive at the conclusion that pagan and Christian love are experiences without an "intention." Under these circumstances the commonly accepted statement that Christianity has discovered the soul and the I takes on an unwelcome meaning: Christianity has initiated the onesided emphasis on egocentric love by rejecting this world and by ascribing an importance only to the place where that negation takes place, the I. We may say that Christian love is spiritual egoism.

It goes without saying that erotic love, too, the love between the sexes, without any positive attitude to this world, is unattainable in Christianity, be it as a fact or as an idea. The fact itself is accepted half-heartedly. It can only be a "necessary evil." Paul said: "It is better to marry than to suffer heat." "If they cannot abstain, they may marry." "When a virgin marries, she does not commit a sin. But it is an affliction of the flesh." It makes one sad to read the definition of the sacrament of marriage, offered by official Catholic dogma: "The Christian marriage is a sacrament, through which a man and a woman come together in an undivided union for the purpose of reproduction and in which they receive God's grace to fulfil the particular duties of their estate." Theologians disagree concerning the holiness and the sacramental quality of marriage. Some find it in *remedium concupiscentiae*, others in its permanence. Nobody seems to have thought of love.

The Song of Songs, an Interpretation

It is the tremendous achievement of Judaism—an achievement which sends its rays across millennia—to have seen in love, not in a spiritually diluted love but in the erotic relation between a man and a woman, the this-worldly miracle, the purest form of that divine grace, the flame of God. This has been expressed by the admission of the Song of Songs into the canon of the Holy Scriptures. The great Rabbi Akiba declared the Song of Songs to be the holiest book of the Bible. According to an oral communication received from a Hassid, Rabbi Pinchas of Koritz (a disciple of the Baal Shem) used to say: "Nobody can understand the Song of Songs. For all other holy scriptures are a bridge from this world to the higher spheres, but the Song of Songs is a bridge from the highest sphere to God Himself."

Without a doubt the Song of Songs is a folk poem—according to the Talmud it used to be sung in taverns—and that originally it was meant to describe a very simple love story. But we would utterly misunderstand that marvelous work if we were to turn up our noses at that "very simple love story," and see, in the establishment of a natural meaning, a strict refutation of later interpretations. For later on the "song" was interpreted spiritually, a glorification of the spiritual relationships between God and the human soul (or Israel). But it is important not to see in the original meaning of the Song and its symbolic interpretations two different conceptions; for the significance of its entire action lies in the unity, in the relationship, and in the fact that such a relationship was at all possible. For here is the deeper meaning, by means of which our fathers, who cannot be praised too highly, accepted the song into the canon, albeit not without hard struggles. In them lived, consciously or unconsciously, the basic Jewish view of the potential sanctification of the most earthly things, so that in their flexible and blossoming souls they could see a description of physical passion under the aspect of a divine service. This may indeed be unique in world history. Inclination and duty were integrated, and the grace which led to that unity pointed the way, not out of existence but back into life, into the joy, the beauty, and the purity of this world. It is therefore meaningless to maintain that the symbolic interpretation of the Song of Songs saved it from rejection by the Rabbis. For this does not explain how the most exalted and divine things could be described in a style which utilized, in unveiled sensuality, all the charms of the human body, all *ecstasis* of physical surrender. This very possibility contains the greatness which interests me. Today, in a world corrupted by the pagan-Christian attitude, such an interpretation would be utterly impossible. I would like to see the college of cardinals or rabbis who would dare to explain that the verse, "A bundle of myrrh between my breasts is my beloved one" (i. 13), refers to God as the beloved man, Israel the beloved girl, and Moses and Aaron the two breasts! He who dared such an interpretation for the first time, and felt it honestly, must have experienced love, an entirely physical love, in a sphere of dignity, cleanliness, and purity, which must be called *the* miracle. Without that experience, without a ready and understanding response to that experience, not even the claim of Solomon's authorship could have saved the book from reprobation and from being forgotten.

By going a little deeper, we see that the relation to infinity and to God has not been created for the first time by the symbolic interpretation. The interpretation rather worked out what was already contained in the Song. We have said that every love has in it two elements: one perishable and finite, and one that points to eternity. We stated that only grace can overcome the conflict between these two elements, and that such overcoming is a highly concentrated form of the this-worldly miracle. The Song of Songs testifies best to that form of the this-worldly miracle. This love does not evade physical enjoyment, it throws itself passionately into the transitory appearance and disappearance of all caresses, and at the same time that love is experienced as something eternal, "strong as death, seriously weighty as the netherworld," as "the flame of God," unquenchable, not to be compared to any earthly good, and hence far removed from the sphere of the "ignoble" and the measurable. Therefore, although animal drives claim their full right and are fulfilled, there are, between the lovers, those high points of human relations which make us cry when reading the Song, those soulful exclamations such as "my sister, my bride," or "my friend, my pure one," or the heavenly tender call of longing "O, if thou wert like a brother, sucking my mother's breast. If I were to find thee outside," etc. At the end, as in a feverish dream, erotic images of the girl come again to the fore ("there thy mother lay in travail")—images that seem to express simultaneously a longing for motherhood as well as the most innocent and loving absorption with the childhood of the beloved. In a wonderful way everything is here intertwined, and out of the heart of the lovers, who feel that their material being cannot be exhausted in all eternity and can indeed coexist with infinity, there bursts forth a light which penetrates the entire world—the landscape, spring, the foreign "daughters of Jerusalem," even the appearance of the king. Everything is immersed in the grace of love, everything is given a fragrance and a color by that love, everything is filled with love. The whole world is love! This insight makes of the Song of Songs the climax and the most precious possession of Judaism and of mankind in general. Here is the mysterious talisman which, through the millennia, has saved Judiasm from becoming petrified, and here will begin the renascence of Judaism, not in the sense of a political movement but as a rebirth of the Jewish spirit!

There is indeed a charm about the Song of Songs. This charm is, in its dreaminess, more effective than all the silly business of industry and commerce, as it races noisily through our days. If it were at all possible to prove the reality of miracles, this would prove it. At least here it is accessible to the dullest mind. One can read in Max Weber's essay how strongly the stream of feeling* which emerged from the Song of Songs has defied the difficulties connected with the Christian faith and that within Christianity, on a foreign soil . . . and certainly so in Judaism. The orthodox Jew of eastern Europe has retained to this day the instinct for the mystical double meaning of the

---

* As a parallel, I shall quote a few lines from the *Sermo in cantica canticorum* of Bernard of Clairvaux. The soul turns to Christ. "Non quiesco ait, nisi osculetur me osculo oris sui. Gratias de osculo pedum, gratias et de manus, sed si cura est ulla de me, osculetur me osculo oris sui. Non sum ingrata, sed amo. Accepi, fateor, meritis potiora, sed prorsus inferiora votis: Desiderio feror, non ratione . . . Vernalis suavitas et spiritualis amoenitas . . . Flabat spiritus et fluebant aquae et erant mihi lacrimae illae panes die ac nocte." After having finished this book, I found some excellent observations about the relation of mysticism and erotics in Meir Wiener's *Die Lyrik der Kabbalah*. He writes, "The English nuns, the great Catholic mystics of the twelfth and thirteenth centuries, the Spanish mysticism of the sixteenth and seventeenth centuries, German mysticism, the Jewish Kabbalah, and Persian Sufism utilized the symbolically understood terminology of the Song of Songs for their teachings. There must therefore have existed important historical connections between the branches of that teaching, which have not yet been fully investigated."

Song of Songs. He recites it on Friday evening, at the beginning of the Sabbath, and while immersing himself in the symbols of Israel and the unbounded love of God, he also prepares himself for the only night in the week in which he is physically a man. In Hassidic circles in particular, the Song of Songs is experienced as an expression of the unity with God. One can read in *The Golden Chain* by Perez of the beginning of the eternal and universal Sabbath, of the dance of the enchanted Miriam with the old and sainted rabbi, and then the words, "Let him kiss me with the kisses of his mouth."

Reconstruction

Without a doubt the Song of Songs has come down to us in a ravaged and confused state. Even the Talmud mentions that many verses have been lost.

For many years every time I read the Song of Songs I felt like reconstructing it. But this had to be done without forcibly changing the magically clear chaos in which the Song is found today. Such mysteries cannot tolerate a rough hand. But the more often I read it, the more clearly did the parts fit together into an entity, as it were without my assistance, all by themselves.

Of course I did not want to change the text. Who would dare do that! There is no surer sign of an incurably Philistine mind than such an unbelievable profanation, which unfortunately is committed so often, and which ought to be punished by flogging. Any addition to or change in the atmosphere of that poem is simply a slap in one's own face. Therefore I did not want to change any words but only to rearrange the verses. In doing so, I decided not to make use of any literary criticism offered previously but to read up on those results at the end. All I was after was a "poetical probability." If a rearrangement—no additions, no omissions, no "emendations"—created a meaningful unity, one might have approximated the original form. We would then have to explain for what reasons that original form was changed into the one we have now. This is my hypothesis:

An unbiased reading of the Song of Songs creates the feeling of an opposition to the king. If we connect the verse towards the end "If a man were to give away the best things of his house for love, they would only despise him" with the exclamation, "My vineyard

is mine, thou O Solomon mayest keep a thousand pieces of silver"—
this can only be interpreted as a protest against royal power. We
must find the same meaning in the description of the heroine's attempt to flee. She wants to be united with her lover, but is stopped
by the city guards. This incident is related in two chapters and has
perhaps deliberately been camouflaged in this manner. On the other
side, there is not one verse which clearly contains the heroine's declaration of love to the king, but there is many a statement in the
opposite direction, and an unfulfilled longing for a shepherd. In general, the contrast between two milieus, Jerusalem and the country,
can hardly be overlooked. If the poem was originally a song of pastoral love between a shepherd and a shepherdess—a love which is kept
alive against the king and his harem—we may assume that someone
who wished to preserve the song wanted to hide the anti-royal tendencies by rearranging the verses, and perhaps he even wanted to
reverse those tendencies. For that reason he may have ascribed the
work to the king. Towards that purpose he would then have divided the poem into larger and smaller fragments, in the process of
which the action was completely shattered, and the offending phrases
would have been weakened. According to my reconstruction the
editor divided the work into 29 fragments, although it is also possible
that the first editor is only responsible for a few changes, and once
the process of masking had been introduced, other rearrangements
may have followed by accident. We must not think that the editor
had evil intentions or was only interested in the royal court. He
simply wanted to rescue the poem, and for this we are grateful to
him! He had a fine feeling for lyrical values, and never interfered
with them. He merely divided the epic elements, the descriptions of
the rape, the flight, etc. These he separated into small fragments and
kept them as far from each other as possible. Thus, according to my
hypothesis, the second verse of the song goes together with the very
last one. They were separated by the entire breadth of the poem, for
if they were read immediately after each other, they would produce
the situation which the editor tried to avoid. This situation, incidentally, remains the same even if the poem should have arisen after the
reign of King Solomon, for even later such an obviously anti-royal
poem would not have passed the censorship unharmed. The people
even liked to think back fondly to King Solomon, the greater the

disparity became between the politically corrupt present and that period of ascendency.

Here I have already entered the field of learned investigation, and I must admit that after my first attempt at reconstruction I have lost my scientific innocence and purity, by looking up what the professionals had to say concerning the Song of Songs. What I then learned—or, better, suffered— belongs to the saddest by-products of my love of that poem. All I can say for my own consolation is, that the more light we have, the more shadow. I was told that side by side with the religious-allegorical interpretation—which is quite proper if integrated with the literal meaning, as already observed by Rashi— there are two "secular" types of explanation: a royal hypothesis and a pastoral one. The former disregards all the passages directed against the king and sees in the poem a description of a love affair between King Solomon and a shepherdess. My own attempt falls thus within the category of that pastoral hypothesis, first established by Ewald in 1826, and subsequently elaborated by different authors. All of them follow the sequence of the text, except for minor rearrangements, and at the same time they try pedantically to interpret the obviously disconnected text as a real drama, with stage directions, notes concerning the place of action, and a superfluous number of dramatis personae. This enterprise must be held together with the equally brilliant counter-criticism, which points out that the Hebrews of old knew neither a stage nor a drama and that the 116 verses of the poem can hardly be subdivided into ten to fifteen independent scenes, the longest of which takes no more than two minutes of slow reading, so that the ancient Israelites can hardly have turned to such presentations (D.C. Siegfried). Thus, unbelievable though it seems, the text and its sequence are slavishly adhered to, but otherwise it is unscrupulously mistreated. My own attempt differs in two points from others known to me. It rearranges the verses for the first time radically (for this the hypothesis of interpretation is of a secondary concern, everything depending on the poetic probability of the newly constructed poem). Furthermore, I do not think at all in terms of a strictly dramatic form. The poem is a lyrical one, written from the point of view of Shulammith. The insertion of small dialogues and scene-like visions does not alter that basic character. The fact that the action is erratic is typical for all lyricism, which flows from man's soul. Here everything depends on the tremendous feeling, which floods the entire world. Facts are coincidental here and appear in a trembling, blurred, and unclear light. One might call this expressionistic art.

But the accomplishments of the Biblical critics do not exhaust themselves in such a Shakespearean dramatization of the Song of Songs (according to Oettli there was a second stage in the background!). The main part is still to come. The "right" interpretation—by which we mean the one accepted nowadays by the school of professors of theology—goes back to Wetzstein's essay concerning the Syrian threshing plate. I am quoting from D.C. Siegfried's commentary,

> As Wetzstein's interpretation shows, the indispensable harvest instrument of the Syrian peasant—it was often his only piece of furniture—was the threshing plate, and it played a special role at weddings. It was the seat of honor for the newly-weds. It was placed on a high scaffold, after having been decorated with multi-colored pillows by the bride's maids. The bride and the groom sat on that "throne," honored as a king and a queen. Thus the wedding week was also called the royal week, and it lasted a full seven days. Although the bridegroom may have been a poor peasant or shepherd, he was treated as a king during that week and praised as such in wedding songs offered in his honor. It was only natural on such occasions that the poets utilized descriptions of royal affairs, as known in Israelite history. The poor peasant who later will find it difficult to support his one wife and his family, is here given an entire harem, as Solomon had. We must not think that his young wife was offended by such songs. She would be very happy if her new husband could afford such an institution.

This style is varied through unbelievable distortions. It is true that in our song the bride is never referred to as a "queen," which would be in accordance with the custom of the threshing plate. That does not matter. We simply change Shulammith into the Shunamite woman of the Book of Kings, Abishag, who had an affair with an Israelite king. Of course that king was David and not Solomon, but a poet may be generous when it comes to a little incest. In this manner King Solomon and the shepherd are forged into one, and both of them are but conventional masks of the same irrelevant bridegroom, who, at his wedding, is serenaded by some songs, provided that he can afford to pay the players. His actual life is of no concern. Fortunately we can prove that the Syrians did sing at their threshing plate weddings (which did not have to be proven in the first place) and that on such occasions there were sword dances, hymns to the bride and the bridegroom, etc. More fortunately still, those Syrian hymns were called "wazfs." I believe that this exotic and Bedouin name did something to the professors of theology. Without it that strange hypothesis could not have acquired citizens' rights. The "wazf" was decisive! Who could withstand the temptation of decorating his Biblical commentary with such an exotic, ethnographically genuine jackal howl as "wazf! wazf!" a howl that suggests a trip around the world? When Siegfried thus adds headings to the individual parts of the poem, he mentions "wazf to the bridegroom in the form of a story," "wazf to the bride with the concluding enjoyment of love." Wherever we look, there is a wazf. The entire poem is a collection of wazfs. This does not mean that the author of our poem may not have used popular wedding songs. Possibly individual verses have their parallels in popular Arabic poetry. But out of such material the poet obviously created something new, an independent masterwork, high above the level of such folkloristic suggestions—high in its meaning and in the details placed into that meaning through conflicts and solution. But that conflict would be eliminated if we were to assume that Solomon and the shepherd are one and the same person, and both of them are a poor peasant. But how are we then to deal with those passages which mention longing and the flight, the wish to escape from the harem in search of pure love, the search of the one and only for the one and only, the rejection of the king and his wealth? Such difficulties call for serious thinking! After all, the wazf-omania is too harmless for Christian commentators, and they are happy to see the conflict eliminated. Let us listen again to Professor Siegfried:

> The Semites lacked individualism and the idea of moral freedom connected with it. That an individual should attain a moral aim by struggling with the powers of the world, as Shulammith fights for the possession of the truly beloved, is unthinkable to the Semites, and they would not be able to comprehend it. We do not there find individual action separated from the forms of society and accepted customs.

Now we have finally reached the theory of "forerunning." Judaism is but a forerunner to Christianity, and it was the latter which for the first time discovered the soul! *Hinc illae lacrimae!* Now we suddenly understand the Syrian threshing plate and the canine bark of the wazfs! Judaism should speak of individual love. This must never be. Away with the literal meaning! Let us instead have some Bedouin dances! But with what Bedouin dances would those gentlemen get rid of the fourteen years Jacob courted Rachel, or the story of Thamar and Amnon, or that of David and Bathsheba, or, since the entire idea of moral freedom is supposedly alien to Judaism, of Moses' individual call, his reluctance, his acceptance, or Jeremiah's chapter 20, or even the Ten Commandments? If it were not so sad, it would be funny. But we find here a systematic attempt to undermine the highest values of Judaism. This systematic misinterpretation is little interested in the fact that, *en passant*, and to the higher glory of Christianity, the most precious poetry given to mankind is made meaningless and unpalatable and worthless. "We know quite well how in the Orient and particularly in Israel a man acquired a wife. At any rate the girl had no say in the matter etc." (Siegfried). He thus imagines that all the immortal verses which describe the seeking and finding of the two lovers in the open spring landscape, the longing, the rebellion, and the happy reunion after considerable troubles deal with "fictitious scenes," told by a paid singer to a conventional couple, who of course never heard of such a thing! What a situation! Things which cannot happen at all, which are prohibited by custom, which neither the newly-weds nor the wedding guests nor the poet can have experienced—such things are praised in song and presented as an ideal, and none of those present is hurt by the hypocrisy. Nobody asks how anyone could imagine such fiction and why it was supposed to flatter the young people—all this plain invention! To these uncorrupted children of nature it is as incomprehensible as it is to us that poetry, even folk poetry, has nothing at all to do with life; and if they were to detect that, it would sound to them like savage irony. Nobody can have a lower opinion of the essence and the deeper roots of poetry than that Protestant professor and his ilk. But if it is a question of "expurgating" a Jewish value, and of preserving the priority of Christianity in the field of the individual love of the soul, one takes apparently many things in one's stride. It is the same intention which always changes "love" into "enjoyment of love."

This fits in better with Jews and their wazfian *Weltanschauung.* "The continuation of the wazf up to the call for the enjoyment of love and to its consummation . . ."—a few more funny headings like this, and everything becomes clear. Thus the erotic factor in this most sacred love idyll is indecently coarsened. Everything means "enjoyment of love," even the lyrical verse "I went down into the garden of nuts to look at the green plants of the valley." The savage professor of theology races through the lines and finds in almost every word allusions to the ultimate in sexual relations. Apparently he does not know that there exists a very tender secondary erotic aspect —perhaps the sweetest thing in love—say, an erotic experience of a landscape, which, viewed jointly with the beloved one, opens entirely new vistas. It becomes close and familiar, as if unmasked and clarified from the inside by love. Every description of nature, every naive joy in odor and blossoms, every walk in the gardens is to the simpleton a paraphrase for coitus. And yet the Song of Songs is so full of a charmingly seductive landscape of the heart that it ought to impress even the dullest of minds. But one must not lock oneself up deliberately and lower everything to the level of a coarse lasciviousness, as is done by the Bible critics. Then we understand well why suddenly, and apparently without rhyme or reason, there breaks forth, in the midst of the enthusiasm concerning the girl's beauty, the great and heroic description of Lebanon and Hermon (Chapter 4). To the one who is filled with the happiness of love, the world becomes too narrow, the pastoral atmosphere too orderly. The heart, romantically savage, goes out to the "lion's den and the mountains of the leopard" (4:8) to an all-encompassing survey of the whole country. Here the symbolically religious interpretation is intuitively right when it explains such passages of wild grandeur as referring to God and not merely to human behavior. For love is God, and its enchantment transcends the boundaries of what is merely human. But how does all that look to our pedantic professors behind their theological counters?

As has been stated previously, this is an annotation based on a terrible misunderstanding committed by a latter-day reader. The "mountain of myrrh" and the "hill of incense" (v.6), and "the smell of the garments like that of Lebanon" (v.11) made that reader think that the lovers spent their honeymoon there, although the place is not only unfit for this but also a most dangerous one, in view of the wild animals mentioned in verse 8. It is quite clear that the boy must have asked his beloved to leave that place.

Can such things be tolerated? May such shallow talk be called scholarship? May it be allowed to soil the most heavenly province of our soul?

Now it cannot be denied that individual parables have to do with the full possession of the beloved; but others, in an air purified by the satisfaction of natural desires, in an atmosphere comparable to that after a thunderstorm, without mugginess and lust, far away from professorial desires, look up innocently to what mankind possesses forever—a happy immersion in the beauty of nature. Intoxication which makes one lose one's mind and deepest calm, safety in the midst of intoxication—these are the two basic chords of the Song of Songs. These chords sound from sexual passion, yet they make the landscape, God, and the world vibrate together with it and make them audible. Thus the joy in the Jewish beloved leads to the joy in the Jewish soil, in a verse familiar to the modern Jew and greatly appreciated by him. "The time for pruning the vineyard has come, and the voice of the turtle dove is heard in our land." (2:12). According to Budde, of course, "in our land" was stricken out. Shulammith is called Barah (chosen), and *Tamati* (my pure one). Our lascivious commentators cannot stand for this. This is what Siegfried has to say: "Barah. In Psalm 73:1 this word refers to moral purity. Such a thought is out of the question in the Song of Songs. Like *tamah*, it can only refer to bodily features" etc. In her feverish vision Shulammith says: "Arise, my beloved, let us go to the field, let us spend the night in the villages" (7:12). Our good professor does not understand this. To him this is not erotic enough, since "erotic" must mean the ultimate, a dirty joke must be implied. Since the Hebrew for "villages" and for "cypress blossoms" is similar, Siegfried suggests the reading "cypress blossoms" and sees therein an allusion of an erotic character, just like the vine and pomegranate blossoms. After having worked through the Song of Songs in such an indecent manner, he is struck with the verses 6 and 7 of the eighth chapter—"in a modern sense the first and only decent word we hear in that song about love." It is very kind of him not to cut these verses too into shape through some cypress blossoms. He does not tell us how these two verses fit into the work, which, according to him, is of a quite different style.

The public is unaware that through such commentaries, which are little read, the Jewish spirit is degraded. Just because these "accomplishments" by Christian scholars are hardly noticed, it is important to make them public. In the obscurity of the universities, an infinitely scholarly machinery lays the scientific foundation for the contempt of the Jewish character, and through a thousand thin canals the result of such "critical investigation" penetrates general civilization, literature, and public opinion. This applies to not only the Christian world but the Jewish one as well. Influenced by the trend mentioned above, "Jewish" comes to mean something obscure, incomplete, permeated by half-pagan sacrificial rites, barbaric, and of the lowest sensual order, whereas "Christian" of course means the glowing truth of feelings. I am trying to shatter this view, which seems to have been commonly accepted, or at least to cast some doubts upon it, and perhaps to make it appear possible that in the hierarchy of concepts "Jewish" and "Christian" may stand for just the reverse. We must admit without reservation that Christian theologians and Bible critics concern themselves patiently with all the details of things Jewish, that many of them do not believe in ritual murder and have publicly protested against the blood libel. Such acts are brave and decent and based on an honest and humane mind. The good intention of many of these scholars should not be doubted. But why should our Jewish experts prostrate themselves reverently before a good intention, which should be taken for granted, a good will which is expressed in the studies of our literature and in the recognition that we are not cannibals? Why do our rabbinical seminaries see in the mere good will of a Christian colleague something to be worshiped and revered? And why do they praise again and again such unheard of objectivity when the great university professor sees in the Psalms a worthy precursor of Christianity, and finds the entire "Old Testament" worth reading? We ought at last to find the right approach to that proselytizing "scholarship," whether it is done consciously or unconsciously. With all the respect due to the zeal and the goodwill of these gentlemen, we must state that many of them have no feeling for the living spirit of Judaism, because they consider Judaism to be dead, that it has finished playing its world-historical role and has been replaced by Christianity. He who believes this is bound to see everything in the wrong light. Such assumptions poison the best of intentions. Yet to many a Christian theologian, it is indispensable and an essential part of his scholarly outfit. It is his professional sickness. I must in all truth admit that I owe much to the books written by Christian theologians, that I read them passionately, and that I admire the wealth they have to offer. I am sorry to have to be so outspoken against an entire class of men, whose seriousness I do not doubt. If only we did not find with them that wrong assumption, that theory of "forerunning" and all that depends on it. It is terrible to read what Siegfried has to say about the "beloved." In Chapter 1, verses 7 and 8, the beloved is a shepherd. In Chapter 6, verse 2, he is a gardener who is careless enough to allow his flock to graze in his garden. This is the interpretation of "My beloved went down to his garden, to the bed of spices, to gather lilies and to feed in the gardens." "Chapter 3, verse 2, and Chapter 5, verse 7, presuppose that he roams the streets of Jerusalem by night, with no concern for his flock." It must not be admitted that he went to Jerusalem in order to free his beloved from the royal harem, for, according to the professors of theology, the beloved and the king must be one and the same, or else what would become of the wazf?

But enough of such discords.

Here follows now the Song of Songs in the rearrangement of verses that I suggest. Although, by clinging to my principle, an improvement might be possible, I do not flatter myself that I have arrived at the proper reconstruction of the original poem; yet I would be happy to have succeeded in approximating it with poetic probability. This then is my scheme:

1) II 8–14	4) IV 1–16, V 1
2) VIII 13	5) II 15
3) I 16–II 3 (half)	
6) VIII 11 and 12	11) VII 1–11
7) I 7 and 8	12) I 9–11, 13 and 14
8) III 6–10	13) I 2
9) VI 11 and 12	14) VIII 14
10) VIII 5 (half)	15) VIII 8 and 9
16) III 11	19) I 5 and 6
17) I 3, 4, 12	20) II 3–7
18) VI 3–10	21) V 8–VI 2

22) VIII 10	23) VII 12–VIII 5 (rearranging 4 and 5, omitting the first half of VIII 5. See no. 10)
24) III 1	27) V 7
25) V 2–6	28) III 4
26) III 2 and 3	29) VIII 6 and 7

As can be seen, nothing has been changed. I have only subdivided two verses, I have repeated one half verse (II:3), and several verses which are repeated in the original appear only once in my version.

Without any force we have arrived at a fourfold division, in beautiful rhythmical relation to each other: first and third part—calm; second and fourth part—motion. First part—calm in happiness; third part—rest in misfortune. Second part—motion from fortune to misfortune; fourth part—motion from misfortune to fortune. My hypothesis—the deliberate masking of the tendency by rearrangement of the parts—was inspired by a factor of dramatic composition. For the beloved girl is serenaded twice, in the fourth and in the seventh chapters. No matter how hard the editor tried to harmonize the entire work in order to eliminate the conflict, he has not succeeded in erasing the difference of mood, which can still be detected. In the first one a deep soulfulness is apparent, which is missing in the second. I assume that the first poet's original intention was to contrast the shepherd's chaste and tender declaration of love with the harem king's insulting manner of wooing. To the shepherd the beloved is a "sister" and a "bride," and here are the glorious verses about the Lebanon, then those of love, of the "locked garden," etc. The king's sexuality has a very general character, and we hear only of the body. It is typical that the king's praises start with the feet, the shepherd's with the hair and eyes. This alone characterizes the subtle sensualist, and in addition to this his praises reveal a clumsiness in a way which would never have occurred to the shepherd. To call a tanned guardian of a vineyard "daughter of a nobleman" makes just that impression on me, and appears to have been used by the author in an ironic way, like so many other phrases. This also holds true of the ostentatious statement "the king chained in thy curls," which must be taken together with Shulammith's immediate reply: "I belong to my beloved, and for him do I yearn." Although the current opinion discourages the assumption of conflicts in the poem, the difference in tone—not weakened but stressed by repetition—disproves that theory.

As far as details are concerned, my reconstruction speaks for itself. Only a few more observations: The erratic verses about the foxes (II:15) are meaningful at the end of my first part. Prepared by the climax in V:1, which raises the lover to the climax of his happiness—he seems to talk to his friends as if he were intoxicated by his happiness—these verses express the high spirits in which the lover feels himself ("our vineyards are blossoming"); but they also hint to the fear of evil in this world, a fear which may well overcome man in his happiest moments, a premonition which serves as an introduction to the second part.

This scene starts out in the style of a story, mentioning where the action takes place, and it makes good sense to utilize both meanings of the word "vineyard." Everything connects well with the concluding verses of the first part. At the same time a slight protest anticipates what follows. This shows how much that great poem can express within narrow confines. This is true of every work based on inner and condensed feelings. "One step leads to a thousand connections." We must imagine here that King Solomon is visiting one of his possessions in Baal Hammon. Close by he meets Shulammith, "leaning on her beloved." From a distance a chorus of peasants watches the events respectfully. The king is surrounded by his retinue. In accordance with the style of the poem, a style which receives its motivation from a personal observer, all these events are merely alluded to and shadowy, called to life by the streams of the moving sentiment, only to disappear again. Thus the appearance of the king in his sedan chair is seen from the point of view of a peasant girl, legendary, superstitious (a masterpiece in itself). Jerusalem and its daughters and heroes like a fairy tale, its sword "against the terrors of the night"; all this in a pious and reverent awe of the anointed of the Lord. In a moving contrast to all that, we have the sensual call which comes from the flunkeys of the court: "Turn around, turn around, O Shulammith, that we may see thee." And then comes the innocently charming and modest reply of the shepherdess "What do ye wish to see in Shulammith? Is it perhaps the martial dance of the soldiers?" She does not know what she could offer to such noblemen besides national warriors' dances. She is fast instructed by the king's reply, which I have characterized above. The masterful presentation shows how the king becomes more "royal," making his words clearer and clearer, words taken from the terminology of the harem. It is hard to understand why Pharaoh's chariot should create difficulties for the commentators. In I Kings Chapter 3 we are told that Solomon married a daughter of Pharaoh, and here, where the king is supposed to be presented with little sympathy, that unpopular circumstance is recalled, thus contrasting rural Judaism with manners of the Egyptian court. In that light we also understand the change of pronoun in I:2: "Let him kiss me with the kisses of his mouth." Here Shulammith still speaks to the king and as previously she refers to her beloved as someone absent, but suddenly when a decision seems to be at hand, she cannot tolerate the disguise any longer, and in a careless upsurge of love, she addresses unexpectedly the shepherd himself: "For lovelier than wine is thy love." She immediately calls on him to take to flight, while she is being led away by the king's men. All that the powerless shepherds who are left behind can do is to weep (this is the proper place for VIII:8 and 9). At the same time they praise Shulammith and approve of her proud defiance. "If our child should be like her, standing fast like a wall, we shall crown her. But if she should yield, we shall lock her up." This too is a clear protest against the royal kidnappers of girls.

The third scene is in the harem. The odalisques serenade Solomon, flattering him slavishly. They welcome the new girl according to his wishes and also show some jealously, perhaps in order to flatter him even more. Each of them wants to have the king for herself. This piece is confusing and has perhaps deliberately been provided with fragments of genuine declarations of love (between Shulammith and the shepherd). In quite modern style Shulammith appears with a declaration of loyalty. Unrealistically and turning everything upside down, her loyalty has turned into a refrain, it does not change any longer, nor does it need or tolerate any shadings. It is a rigid form which expresses a strong and very intensive passion. The king is terrified by the looks of the abducted girl, "terrible as an army with a banner." "I abjure you, O daughters of Jerusalem. . . ." The king leaves, and Shulammith has been seized by a feverish vision, thinking of her beloved. The women of the harem hear for the first time the magic saying of a love which has been decided upon once and for all. Is it fitting that when Shulammith wants to present her

beloved to them, she takes her parables from the precious *objets
d'art* of the palace, her new surroundings, instead of using the rural
metaphors which are elsewhere used in the book for a description of
physical features? We have hardly any words to express our admir-
ation for what Shulammith says further, and which is inspired by
the genius of true love:

How, in captivity, she feels closer to him than ever before—

how she feels him to be her brother and, as a sister, recalls to
him the first scene—

how, in an ecstatic daydream, she roams with him through the
beloved country

how the innermost memories, of her own mother and of the
shepherd, share in her feelings—until the king interferes and calls
for quiet—

how, in the fourth scene, the beloved first appears in a vision,
and she acts in an affected manner, half asleep—

how she is terrified, then remembers, and then understands the
situation, and duped by the vision she decides to flee, and then, as
though by magic, the beloved becomes reality (he had looked for
her in the streets of Jerusalem, they have been attracted to each
other, and now they cling to each other)—

how all this ends in a jubilating call of love and in contempt for
all other goods—

Truly here I must apply what, according to our sages, some disciples said after hearing an exalted teaching: "If we had been born
only to hear this secret, it would have been enough." Well, if I had
been born only to see through the mystery of the Song of Songs, it
would have been enough!

The Song of Songs

I. *In the Country*

The voice of my beloved! Behold, he cometh, leaping over the
mountains, skipping over the hills!

My beloved is like a gazelle or a young hart.

Here he standeth behind our wall, looking through the windows,
peering through the lattice. My beloved spoke and said unto me:

THE SHEPHERD

Arise, my beloved! My beautiful one, get thee up!

For the winter is past, the rain is gone away.

The blossoms are seen in the land. It is time to prune the vine, and the voice of the turtle dove is heard in our country.

The fig tree putteth forth its fruit, and the grapes with their blossoms give forth their fragrance. Arise, my beloved! My beautiful one, get thee up!

My dove in the rocks, hidden in the clefts, let me see thy countenance, let me hear thy voice. For thy voice is sweet and thy countenance is lovely.

Thou who dwellest in the gardens—friends hearken to thy voice, let me hear it!

SHULAMMITH

How beautiful, my beloved, how lovely, how fresh and green our couch.

THE SHEPHERD

The beams of our house are cedars, our furnishings made of fir.

SHULAMMITH

I am the lily of Sharon, the rose of the valleys.

THE SHEPHERD

As a rose among thorns, so is my beloved among the maidens.

SHULAMMITH

As an apple tree among the trees of the forest, so is my beloved among the young men.

THE SHEPHERD

How lovely, my beloved, how lovely! Thine eyes like doves from behind thy veil, thy hair like a flock of goats, descending from Mount Gilead.

Thy teeth like a flock of newly shorn sheep arising from the water, each of them having twins, and none barren.

Thy lips like a thread of purple, and thy mouth lovely. Thy temple as a pomegranate from behind thy veil. Like the Tower of David is thy neck, standing like a bulwark. A thousand shields hang there, shields of the heroes. Thy breasts are like two fawns, twins of a gazelle, feeding among the roses. Until the day cools and the shadows flee, I will go to the mountain of myrrh, to the hill of incense.

Thou art perfectly beautiful, my beloved, there is no blemish in thee.

Come with me from Lebanon, my bride, come with me from Lebanon! Look down from the top of Amana, from the top of Senir and Hermon, from the lions' dens, from the mountains of the leopards.

Thou hast robbed me of my mind, O my sister, my bride, thou hast robbed me of my mind with one of thine eyes, with one strand of thy necklace.

How sweet is thy love, my sister, my bride, much more precious is thy love than wine, and the fragrance of thine ointments sweeter than the odor of balsam. Thy lips drop honey, my bride, honey and milk are under thy tongue, and the odor of thy raiments is as the fragrance of Lebanon.

A locked garden is my sister, my bride, a locked garden, a sealed spring.

Thy shoots are a grove of pomegranates with precious fruit, blossoms of cypress and nards.

Nards and crocus, calamus and cinnamon, myrrh and aloes, with all spices.

Thou art a fountain of gardens, a spring of living waters, descending from Lebanon. Arise, O North wind, arise, O South wind, breeze through my garden, that its fragrance may flow out.

SHULAMMITH

Let my beloved come into his garden to enjoy its precious fruit.

THE SHEPHERD

I am coming to my garden, my sister, my bride. I gather my myrrh and my fragrance, I eat my honeycomb with its honey. I drink my wine and also my milk. Eat, O my friends, and drink abundantly!

Now catch for us the foxes, the little foxes that destroy the vineyard, for our vineyards are in blossom.

II. *The Rape*

Solomon had a vineyard in Baal Hamon; he left the vineyard to the guards. Each one was to give a thousand pieces of silver for its fruit.

My vineyard is mine. Keep the thousand, O Solomon, and two hundred for those who guard its fruit.

Tell me, thou whom my soul loveth, where wilt thou be with thy flock at noon? Why should I stand sadly with the flocks of thy friends?

THE SHEPHERD

If thou knowest it not, thou most beautiful among the women, follow the tracks of the sheep, and watch thy goats by the tents of the shepherds!

I have gone down to the garden of nuts, to see the fresh shoots in the valley, to see whether the vine is green, and the pomegranates in bloom.

But my soul led me to the chariot of a nobleman and to his men.

What is rising from the desert like a pillar of smoke, with the fragrance of myrrh and incense and all the spices of the merchant?

It is Solomon's chair, surrounded by sixty of Israel's strong men. All of them have swords and are experienced in warfare. Everyone's sword by his side, against the terrors of the night.

Solomon's chair is made of wood from Lebanon.

Its pillars are made of silver, the ceiling of gold, the seat of purple, it is furnished with the cushions of love of the daughters of Jerusalem.

"Who is she who cometh from the wilderness, leaning on her beloved?

Turn around, turn around, O Shulammith, turn around, turn around, that we may look at thee!"

SHULAMMITH

What do ye wish to see in Shulammith? Is it perhaps the dance of the warriors?

THE KING

How beautiful are thy feet in the sandals, O daughter of a nobleman! The curves of thy hips are like a necklace, a work done by artists' hands.

Thy navel a round bowl, not lacking wine. Thy body a sheaf of wheat, surrounded by roses.

Thy breasts like two does, twins of the hind.

Thy neck like a tower of ivory, thine eyes like ponds in Heshbon at the gate of Bath Rabbim, thy nose like the Tower of Lebanon looking down on Damascus.

Thy head crowns thee like the Carmel, and the hair of thy head is as purple—the king chained in thy curls.

How beautiful art thou, how lovely, beloved one, in thy enjoyments!

Thou art shaped like a palm tree, and thy breasts are like grapes.

I think I shall go up on the palm tree and take hold of its branches. May thy breasts be like grapes on the vine, and the fragrance of thy nose as apples, thy palate like good wine which flows over the lips and the teeth of the beloved.

SHULAMMITH

I belong to my beloved, and to him is my longing.

THE KING

To a mare in Pharaoh's chariot do I liken thee, O my beloved. Thy cheeks are lovely with circlets, thy neck in beads. We will make for thee golden circlets with ornaments of silver.

SHULAMMITH

My beloved is like a bouquet of myrrh, lying between my breasts. My beloved is like a cluster of cypress in the vineyards of En Gedi. O that he kiss me with the kisses of his mouth— For thy love is more pleasing than wine. Flee, my beloved, like a hart or a young doe on the mountains of balsam.

THE REMAINING SHEPHERDS

We have a little sister, without any breasts. What shall we do to our sister when people will speak of her?

If she is a wall, we shall build upon her a silver crown. But if she is a door, we shall shut her up with an iron lock.

III. *In Solomon's Palace*

WOMEN'S CHORUS

O daughters of Zion, step forth and look at King Solomon, see the wreath with which his mother has crowned him at his wedding, on the day of his heart's joy.

Precious is the fragrance of thine ointments. Thy name like oil poured out. Therefore do the maidens love thee.

Draw me after thee, we will hasten. The king took me into his chambers. We will jubilate and be happy with thee, and praise thy love more than wine. Those who love thee are right.

As long as the king was on his couch my nard gave off its fragrance.

SHULAMMITH

I belong to my beloved, and he is mine; he feedeth among the roses.

THE KING

Beautiful art thou, my beloved, like Thirza, lovely as Jerusalem, awe-inspiring like men in arms.

Turn away thine eyes, for they frighten me . . .

I have sixty queens and eighty concubines, virgins without number.

But one is my dove, my pure one, the only one to her mother, the chosen one of her who gave her life. The maidens saw her and praised her, the queens and concubines glorified her.

CHORUS

Who is she who breaketh forth like the dawn, beautiful as the moon, brilliant as the sun, awe-inspiring like men in arms?

SHULAMMITH

I am dark but lovely, ye daughters of Jerusalem, like the tents of Kedar and the carpets of Solomon.

Do not look at me that I am so dark, the sun has singed me. My mother's sons scolded me, they made me a guardian of the vineyards, but mine own vineyard have I not guarded.

As an apple tree among the trees of the forest, so is my beloved among the young men. I wished to sit in its shade, and its fruit was sweet to my palate.

He took me to the tavern, and his sign above me was Love.

O strengthen me with raisin cake, refresh me with apples. For I am sick with love.

His left arm under my head, and his right arm shall embrace me.

THE KING

I adjure ye, O daughters of Jerusalem, by the hinds or the gazelles of the meadow, do not disturb the beloved one, neither arouse her until it please her.

SHULAMMITH

I adjure ye, O daughters of Jerusalem. When ye find my beloved, what will ye tell him?—That I am sick with love.

CHORUS

O thou most beautiful among the women, what is thy beloved more than another one, that thou adjurest us thus?

SHULAMMITH

My beloved is white and red, excelling above tens of thousands.

His head is like pure gold, his curls rolling down, black as the ravens.

His eyes are like doves by the springs of water, bathing in milk, sitting by the edge.

His cheeks are like beds of balsam, towers of spices, his lips roses, flowing with myrrh.

His hands are golden rings with precious stones, his body a work of art made of ivory, covered with sapphires.

His thighs pillars of marble on golden sockets, his looks that of the Lebanon, chosen like cedars.

His palate is sweetness, and he is entirely lovely. This is my beloved and my friend, ye daughters of Jerusalem.

CHORUS

Where did thy beloved go, thou most beautiful among the women? Where did thy beloved turn, that we may seek him?

SHULAMMITH

My beloved hath gone down to the beds of balsam, to feed in the gardens and to gather roses.

I am like a wall, my breasts are like towers. Then I was in his eyes like one who findeth favor.

Arise, my beloved, let us go out to the field, let us spend the night in the villages.

Let us arise early to go into the vineyards, let us see whether the vine is in bloom, whether the blossoms have opened up, whether the pomegranates have budded. There will I give thee my love.

The violets send forth their fragrance, and at our doors are all manner of fruit, fresh and old, which I, my beloved, have kept for thee.

O if thou wert only my brother, sucking my mother's breasts. If I found thee outside I would kiss thee, and no one would be allowed to put me to shame.

I would take you into my mother's home, the one who hath raised me, I would give thee spiced wine and the juice of the pomegranate. (His left arm under my head, and his right arm would embrace me.)

Under the apple tree I would awaken thee, there did thy mother give thee life in pain.

The King

I adjure ye, O daughters of Jerusalem, by the hinds or the gazelles of the meadow, do not disturb the beloved one, neither arouse her until it please her . . .

IV. *The Flight*

On my couch in the nights did I seek the one whom my soul loveth. I sought him but I found him not.

I was asleep, but my heart was awake. The voice of my beloved knocketh. "Open the door for me, my sister, my beloved, my dove, my pure one. For my head is full of dew, and my curls of the drops of the night."

I have taken off my raiment, how could I put it on again? I have washed my feet, how could I soil them again?

My beloved stretched out his hand through the window. My soul went out to him.

I got up to open the door to my beloved, and my hands were full with myrrh, which was flowing on the lock.

I opened the door for my beloved, but he had gone away, disappeared. My soul was frightened at his words. I sought him, but I found him not. I called him, but he answered not.

I will get up and roam the city, the markets and the streets. I will seek him whom my soul loveth. I sought him, but I found him not.

The watchmen, who roam the city, saw me. "Have ye seen him whom my soul loveth?"

The watchmen, who roam the city, saw me. The watchmen of the walls beat me and wounded me, they took off my veil.

As soon as I had passed by them I found him whom my soul loveth. I held him tight, I did not leave him, till I had taken him to my mother's house, to the chamber of her who had given me life.

Put me like a seal at thy heart, like a seal at thy arm. For strong as death is love, heavy as the nether world is passion, burning like fire, a flame from God!

Many waters cannot quench love, floods cannot take it away. If one were to give away the best things in his house for love, he would but be despised.

9

THE FAULTY FOUNDATION

OF CHRISTIANITY

"God Himself will come and save you. Then
shall the eyes of the blind be opened, and the
ears of the deaf shall be unstopped." (Isaiah
35:4f.)

I AM NOT CONCEITED ENOUGH TO BELIEVE THAT IN THE PRECEDING
eight chapters I have succeeded in presenting all that Judaism has to
teach. But perhaps I have presented a path towards the Jewish feeling
concerning the world, or, at least, the path that I have taken.

These are the elements of Judaism which we have uncovered: the
distinction between noble and ignoble misfortune, the call of man to
face both complexes with the proper attitude, conscious of his moral
freedom as far as ignoble misfortune is concerned, and, aware of his
shortcomings, humbled in the face of noble misfortune; we have
noticed the conflict which arises out of the simultaneity of these contrasting approaches, the "incompatibility of the correlated"—divine
grace overcoming that conflict—and the recapture of the lost world
on this earth by means of grace, the this-worldly miracle.

In almost all these aspects, Christianity differs essentially from the
fundamental feeling of Judaism. So far I have limited myself to occasional allusions. But now, once we have covered the entire distance,
it may be possible to encompass in greater detail the differences between Judaism and Christianity, and to determine the common
source that appears to be responsible for those differences.

That common source is the view that there is only one grace for
all men and that that grace must consequently be characterized in all
cases by one and the same predetermined fact—the belief in Christ
and his vicarious sacrificial death, suffered by an incarnate God in
order to save mankind from original sin.

Judaism, too, knows that it is not by his own strength that man can
rise above the conflict of sins and truly live, but only through the

power of divine grace. But, according to the Jewish view, divine
grace does not depend on any other condition. There is no fast
marching route towards grace. Grace can be offered throughout the
entire breadth of life. God alone knows in what form grace is granted
to the individual. I believe that in everybody's life at least once—
possibly more often—grace does appear, and man has only to accept
it. In this area nothing can be proven, since generalizations are impossible. For the same reason there are individual differences in the
form of one's life after one has received grace. Nor are there commonly valid principles as to whether grace, once granted, can be lost
again, whether it may be enjoyed a second or a third time, or whether
everyone is potentially ready for grace. No rules or laws are applicable here. Only the inner experience is decisive, an experience in
which God meets individual man; but that path is not a leisurely
walk, where two or three men can be found side by side. It is rather
a narrow track which everybody must go alone, with no pattern or
example to follow, and no assistance at hand.

In contrast to this, dogmatic Christianity establishes the following
plan: the belief in Christ is valid for all and redeeming for all. In this
connection my term "dogmatic Christianity" is narrower than would
be "official Christianity." In this sense Kierkegaard, too, belongs to
"dogmatic Christianity," although nobody will call the raging opponent of "a thousand officials hired for the prevention of Christianity"
an "official representative."

Here is what a teacher of Christian theology, Bartmann, writes,
and he could hardly have done otherwise:

> If we can obtain grace by our own strength, we can also get salva-
> tion ... But in that case, as Paul has already written concerning the
> Judaizers (Galatians 2:21) Christ would have died in vain, or, at
> least, we would not owe our salvation mainly to him. A supernatural
> salvation would turn into a natural one, and the boundary separating
> the two would be gone.

It is typical that Bartmann does not take into consideration the
possibility of a different approach, where man, though not saved by
his own strength, would indeed be saved directly and immediately
through God and through individual grace, granted throughout the
entire breadth of life. Then, too, Christ has died "in vain," in the
theological sense of the miracle, not in that of the heroic-human one,
in which his death will be a tremendous example for all times. But
the religious Christian cannot be satisfied with Christ as an example,

st means denying a dogma indis-
Savior. It is this dogma of agency
of a supernatural salvation. For
nediator is no less supernatural.
rence between Christianity and
of the former, in exactly that
:ommon! That common point is
ıe grace, without which there is
e Christians nor to the Jews. But
ıe construction of supernatural
nd for all. Not quite two thou-
as a sin offering in the form of
do is take hold of that gift of
ıough Catholics call in addition
riew has it that the form of sal-
idually, and in a form which is
mple is Kafka's story "Before
n *A Country Doctor*. A man
per of the gate stops him. The
our of his death arrives. In his
the gate, "Since everybody
, ___ .. ._ .. ɯaɩ ın all these years no one but me
has asked for admission?" The keeper of the gate exclaims in a terrifying voice, "No one else could ask admission here, for this entrance
is meant for you only. Now I am going to close it." God can only be
experienced individually. The religious "forms" of the Jews refer
mainly to ignoble misfortune—danger to mankind—which is, however, in close connection with noble misfortune, due to the this-
worldly miracle. Although the form can thus appear potentially in
many variations, this must not be confounded with pantheism, which
would like to experience God in nature, which means at all places
and at all times. According to the Jewish view, God can potentially
be experienced everywhere, yet it cannot be stated in advance where
He can actually be experienced, in which of the thousand daily possibilities He really meets man. He comes in the storm of the unexpected. The call may come on the race track or in the desert, by
watching a leaf driven by the wind, by listening to a tune. It may be
in a request, a glance, the trouble of a painful situation, or the shock
of a surging enthusiasm. In all of these God *can* appear. Then He
raises the situation in which you experience Him high above all

previous feelings. We must admit that the pantheist is correct in stating that, on a lower level, God is present everywhere in nature, and He is felt in the regular course of laws and necessities, but not exclusively so. Suddenly, like a lightning, the miracle flashes through the mist of necessities, and those are the moments of God's appearance, and it is those moments with which we are here concerned. Only they cancel the natural "incompatibility of the correlated." The situation is quite clear. Finding God everywhere, the pantheist finds Him nowhere, since he cannot recognize a distinguishing revelation, which is exactly what interests the Jew as well as the Christian. To the Jew, that revelation is basically possible everywhere and in all forms of experiences, although it is realized only on rare occasions. The Christian imagines a fast marching route. He expects the appearance of God only from a certain direction and in a certain form—in the belief in Christ.

The faulty foundation of official Christianity is that, out of all possible experiences, only one appears to be worth experiencing— faith in Christ. This has led to tremendous and far-reaching consequences. Next to that unique value, nothing can be of any value. The devaluation and emptying out of is this world is the necessary consequence of the belief in Christ. Let us note the following statement by Kierkegaard: "That eternity is present at a certain moment in time means that existence has been abandoned by the hidden immanence of eternity." "There is no immanently basic relationship between temporality and eternity, since eternity itself has entered time and wants to establish the relationship there."

In his Letter to the Galatians, Paul said, "If justice could be obtained through the Law, Christ would have died in vain." But it is not only in view of the law that Christ would have died in vain. This would also be true if justice were obtainable immediately through God, through an individual experience, or by means of supernatural grace, granted on an individual basis. By Christian standards, in all of life and existence there cannot be an immediate encounter with God, anywhere or anytime, for otherwise Christ would have died in vain. This fear is the secret motive of all Christian speculation. In order to point out the need for Christ's atoning death, man's fall, which preceded it—the original sin—is painted in the most horrifying colors. Catholic dogma naively reveals that the theory of original sin has been worked out *ad hoc*, to create the space needed for Christ's deed. Thus, for instance, Bartmann states: "Original sin must not be viewed by itself but only in the light of all theology. Adam's sin and its effects are not a final point in the development of mankind but a disturbing interference, which must be overcome." Thus speculation stresses the proof that this terrible original sin cannot be atoned for through a direct, lightning-like encounter with God but only in the historical form of God's incarnation and crucifixion in Jerusalem at a certain time. It is true that Anselmus (*Cur deus homo*) still taught that the incarnation was not the only possible means of atonement but merely the most perfect one. However, the modern theologian (Bartmann) comments, "God's justice had to call for a full atonement for the offended honor; but that atonement could not be achieved by sinful man, who stands far below God, and therefore it had to be done by a divine man who represented mankind." Here it is quite clear that the devaluation of human existence is an unintentional consequence of that construction.

Original Sin and Grace

Here is, for instance, one Protestant definition of original sin:

It has been maintained that original sin is not only the terrible lack of all good forces in spiritual things which refer to God but that the lost image of God was replaced by the innermost, most evil, deepest, most abysmal, inexplorable and ineffable corruption of the entire nature and all forces (*ineffabilis corruptio totius naturae et omnium virium*), but in particular that of the higher and dominating powers of the soul, and that this corruption clings to man's reason, heart and will. Thus, after the fall, man inherits from his parents an evil power, impurity of the heart, evil lust and inclinations.

According to some Lutherans (Mathias Flacius) original sin has become man's essential core, his very "substance."

In one point Catholicism agrees with Protestantism: through Adam's fall man has lost his supernatural powers. But whereas, according to Protestantism, the natural gifts have been turned into their opposite, into poison, Catholicism maintains that original sin only "wounded and weakened greatly" man's natural qualities (*Homo spoliatus gratuitis, vulneratus in naturalibus*).

As always, Catholic religious thinking excels that of Protestantism by one distinction, but it makes hardly any use of it. The Catholic wants to respect human freedom. But as soon as it becomes possible for freedom and human dignity to follow up that courtesy and occupy their proper place in the system, Catholicism retires as if caught committing a misdeed. No, man cannot do any good works by himself. The only valid distinction in this area—that between noble and ignoble misfortune—is not made. Catholicism is satisfied with paying compliments to the "exalted" concept of human freedom, with illusionary concessions, with words, with a fine distinction, which, however, leads to the same result, which is the same as the one adopted by the simpler, less frightened, and more honest Protestant—man is eliminated in the face of his divine-human Redeemer.

Since Catholicism assumes that man's good and natural disposition is preserved even after the fall and only his supernatural power has vanished, one might suppose that "good works" are here admitted and that, although they are on a lower level, they are possible without grace and well within the human condition. Catholic doctrine does indeed mention *opera honesta sive ethica bona*, and the opposite ideas—represented by Bajus, the Jansenists, Luther—are considered heretical. But this does not mean that we have here a parallel to the "ignoble misfortune" of Judaism. In the *Lehrbuch der Dogmatik* by Dr. Thomas Specht (Regensburg 1907), we find restrictions which counteract the Catholic progress. Only the label "freedom" remains, since without it nobody could go to hell. Therefore all theology is in great need of freedom.

> Fallen man cannot fulfill the entire natural law without grace. This follows . . . on the one side from the weakness of the will caused by sin and, on the other side, from the difficulties of many prescriptions within natural law. . . . This is confirmed by personal and objective experience, particularly in view of the moral aberrations of paganism.

We find here two errors at a time. *First* there is the basic Christian error that the only way to grace must come through Jesus, for which reason all pre-Christian times and peoples have no way to God. Judaism—supposedly particularistic and not universalistic like Christianity!—teaches that "the righteous of all peoples have a share in the world to come." This is an immediate outcome of basic Jewish concepts, which do not know of any fast marching route. Noble misfortune is shared by all men, and therefore it can be cancelled at all times and places through immediate divine intervention. God can be found wherever and whenever He pleases. In Catholic dogma, paganism is immediately characterized as a lack of grace, whereas I am sure—if a judgment is at all possible in such things—that Socrates lived in God's full grace like the best Christian or Jew. Not in Christ's grace, it is true, but in God's grace. And this is all that counts.

The *second* error is that Specht does not believe human power to be sufficient for fulfilling the natural law. Now when confronted with God, man is indeed powerless (except for Rabbi Hannina's statement), and noble misfortune makes him doubt himself and delivers him up to grace. But as far as ignoble and avoidable misfortune is concerned, his own powers are sufficient. Here he is autonomous and has a free will, and only the highest achievements also require grace in this area. What then is the advantage of the Catholic distinction? It is true that without Christ man still has a free will, but the fall has weakened and injured it so gravely that it is hardly of any help at all. If he remains in that state and does not reach Jesus, all his efforts are in vain, he fails in his earthly destination, and after his death he is left to eternal damnation. Let us note that even this view, which allows man so little air, cannot be reconciled with the common Christian and Paulinian *Quod non est ex fide, peccatum est.*

Catholicism flirts with the freedom of the will, but it cannot take it seriously. For as soon as man's sovereignty is recognized in the field of ignoble misfortune, part of life appears magically illuminated and metaphysically significant. But according to the Christian view only one thing has metaphysical importance—the way through Christ. Everything else must be without value or meaning. Any other value, no matter how small it is, menaces the uniqueness of the Christ experience. Man's only experience must be Christ. According to the Jewish view, man has many other things to experience, and on the occasion of every experience he can sense the conflict between ignoble and noble misfortune; and where that conflict is felt, it can also be eliminated. This means there is the possibility of a divine revelation. By sharing in this conflict, ignoble misfortune, too, receives a metaphysical meaning, and he who takes up the fight against ignoble misfortune cannot be said to fail in his earthly destination. But he cannot encounter Christ there, for the historically conditioned Christ is offered only under certain circumstances and after certain education or instruction. But such a man's travails may still lead him to God. For God can be found everywhere and is offered without any conditions attached.

The Christian attitude considers the work of redemption *accomplished* by Christ's sacrificial death. What can man add to this?

Here the church distinguishes between an objective and subjective order of salvation. The objective order of salvation has been newly established through the atoning death of the divine man. Thus man has been enabled to return to the state of the first man, the state of sanctifying grace. This implies that, although Christ has died for all men, the benefit is obtained only by those "*quibus meritum passionis eius communicatur*" (to whom the merit of his Passion has been conveyed). Specht elaborates in this manner: "Redemption is not realized in a purely juridical way, as if, by paying one's debt to Christ, one's pristine state has been reestablished without further agency or condition. It is rather done in a moral way, through a spiritual communion with Christ the Redeemer." Here we have another vista on individual grace, the collaboration of individual man. Does the "spiritual communion with the Redeemer" provide grace with personal variations? Here many neo-Christians (particularly Jewish writers) seem to come close to dogmatic and orthodox Christianity. They believe, which means that in some vague form they think they believe, and they connect their belief somehow with Christ; they adjust here and there a statement taken from the New Testament for their own purposes, and they degrade the Old Testament and the Talmud (which is entirely unknown to them). Out of such ingredients a Christian is fashioned, the higher stage of human civilization has been reached, and an offensive Judaism has been overcome all the way. How pleasant to be able to become a Christian in such an easy way, and "out of conviction." But in all truth, Christianity demands much more than these gentlemen think. It is not satisfied with a vague faith which establishes some indefinable "connection with Christ." The Catholic dogmatist (Specht) continues: "Communion with Christ is achieved by the Holy Spirit, but not exclusively in one's soul and invisibly, but regularly also visibly in the Church, which is the institution of salvation as established by Christ, and through the sacraments, which are the means of salvation prescribed by Him." On the other hand, according to Protestantism the only subjective condition for salvation is faith; but that faith must state that my sins have been forgiven by Christ through his sacrificial death, which took place at a certain time in history, *sub Pontio Pilato*. Only that man is a Christian who is able to believe this and to build his entire relation to God on this one factor. There is no other way.

Thus the Protestant as well as the Catholic finds a certain route mapped out; and this way to grace, having been laid down once and for all, bars all real life. This is the basic objection against Christianity, and not the one attacked by Bartmann; namely, that grace weakens man, deprives him of confidence in his own strength and of being really ethical. This objection—it would equally apply to the Jewish idea of grace—can be answered by pointing out the great moral power needed for the "waiting for grace," and for the rejection of false ways. But Christianity expects grace from such a clearly defined direction—not from the entire horizon, out of the vast breadth of all experiences—it leads to frustration, hypocrisy, lethargy, and asceticism. In Judaism individual strength is needed not only in avoiding mistakes but also in the entire province of ignoble misfortune.

According to the Christian plan, these are the stages of justification (the granting of grace):

1) Through the elimination of inner obstacles (vices), a negative disposition for grace is created. It is doubtful whether a positive disposition is possible, for it is always maintained, and rightly so, that grace is always "undeserved," and that it can thus not necessarily follow from preceding states.

2) Through the "first grace" (*gratia actualis*) faith invades one's heart. According to Protestantism, this is the end of the procedure. For even after having accepted Jesus, man remains damnable. Faith declares him to be justified, but he is not really so. Therefore the Protestant recognizes only one mortal sin, the "sin against the Holy Ghost," which means the absence of faith. All other sins are negligible and may even coexist with justification. That it is impossible to be saved without good deeds has been rejected (*impossible esse sine bonis operibus salvari*). Simlarly Luther: "*Ita vides quam dives sit homo Christianus . . . Nulla enim peccata eum possunt damnare nisi sola incredulitas*" ("Here you see how well the Christian man has been provided . . . For no sin can deprive him of salvation, except unbelief"). It would be amusing to collect such apparently amoral passages written by Christian authors, and thus to teach those authors a lesson who, by quoting some misunderstood passages from the Tal-

mud, declare Judaism to be unethical. Even after justification, man remains "morally dead." His collaboration is impossible. He believes, and this suffices. What he does, is as damnable as it is negligible. It is irrelevant. Thus Protestantism, admirably consistent, has shown us where the faulty foundation of Christianity leads. If it is solely Christ's sacrificial death that has metaphysical significance, then the only way for man to communicate with the metaphysical is through belief in that event. All other happenings in the world, including man's deeds before and after justification, are worthless, metaphysically and ethically speaking. Protestantism believes that it is a logically well founded system of Christianity. In doing so, however, it collides seriously with the ethical facts of the world and the human heart, for these cannot be deprived of their value so easily. Compared to Protestantism, Catholicism is a more elastic instrument of grace. It attempts to justify the facts and adjust to truth, but without giving up the faulty foundation of the fast marching route towards grace. This disturbs the tiny parts of the instrument. Logic is replaced by a graceful complication, which makes the study of scholasticism so interesting. After the insertion of innumerable intermediary stages, nuances, and distinctions we stand exactly where the Protestant had been in the first place—in front of the white screen of an existence without value. Yet it remains interesting to follow the Catholic on the path to salvation. For faith alone does not satisfy him. Faith gains form *(fides formata)* through the emerging qualities of love and penitence. This is the third stage. Of course, neither love nor penitence leads necessarily to grace.

3) Sanctifying grace makes its appearance, a process in which man is not entirely passive. But in spite of fine distinctions we do not see what man's share is, since we are faced here with an illusory concession to freedom. After all, the same grace of justification is given to a newborn baby at the moment of baptism. Here we decidedly have a particularly weak point in Catholic dogma, which, in addition, contradicts other parts of its teachings (preparatory acts, freedom, love). One might feel inclined to forget such inconsistencies, but Bartmann states quite clearly: "According to what the Scriptures and the Fathers teach us, the grace of justification consists in an inner and supernatural power, which the Holy Spirit grants us through baptism." The grace accorded to adults depends on the sacrament of penitence. Outside of the sacraments—definite rites—the believing

Catholic does not know of any grace. Through this teaching, Catholicism eliminates the advantage it has in comparison with Protestantism. In Protestantism salvation depends on faith; and, although it is a historically conditioned and narrow one, it is still an act of the soul. The Catholic requires, in addition to this, an act, in order to encounter God. This is almost an exaggeration of the "fast marching route," and at any event much more formalistic than any Jewish teaching, which Christians like to classify as a "legalistic religion." For this reason modern defenders of Catholicism do not put great stress on the sacraments. They speak rather of the cooperation of freedom (in contrast to Protestantism), of the this-worldly reality, of the fullness of life, of the divine penetration of the world, of the sanctification of the physical sphere, although all this does not even exist in Christianity.* At best, it is as a salute to life. Modern defenders of Catholicism blame Judaism for its outward forms, but they disregard the Christian-Catholic forms as well as the contro-

---

* The newest slogan against Judaism, or rather against the Jew as a biological type, is that in the Jew and his *Welaanschauung* there is a "tendency to de-materialization." But this tendency, which I do not deny, is but the effect of European civilization upon the Jew, a conscious or unconscious assimilation, and also a direct counter-movement—the *ressentiment* of the ghetto. The preceding chapters of this book have demonstrated abundantly that in classical Judaism there is no "de-materialization" but rather the opposite—the this-worldly miracle. On the contrary: "de-materialization" and the "negation of this world" is the classical line of Christianity. This is not believed nowadays. People are not familiar with the Fathers of the Church. Here are some choice samples. From Tertullian "ad uxorem": "Why should we be happy to be sourrounded by children? We would rather see the ones we do have to precede us, in view of the menacing troubles, and we ourselves would like to be taken away from this corrupt world, to be received by God, as it was also the apostle's wish." The same author concerning plays: "Thou wilt not applaud those silly jumping, thrusting, and leaping exercises. The art of wrestling, too, is of the devil. Its very movements remind us of those of the serpent. Whatever is there of manliness, straightforwardness, harmony, or delicacy must be regarded as honey on poisoned pastry. Let the devil offer such sweets to his guests." The same author, in *Apologeticum*: "The Christian, without injuring his eyes, does not look at women. Regarding lust he is spiritually blind." The same author writes in "To the Martyrs," "If you remember that the world is but a dungeon, you will realize that you have left a dungeon rather than entered it. And even if you have lost some worldly joys, it is good business to lose something of small value in order to obtain something greater" etc.

versies concerning them, which can be found in any book about
Catholic dogmatics: whether water is the "substance of baptism" or
any other liquid, whether the water must be sanctified or whether
all the water in the world has already been sanctified by the hover-
ing of the divine spirit over it (Genesis 1:2), whether the proper way
of baptizing is *immersio*, *aspersio*, or *infusio*, whether it has to be
done three times or only once, etc. At any rate it is interesting to get
acquainted with that Christian casuistry, since we have been told
again and again that Christianity stands for "spiritual humanity,"
"freedom from the law," whereas the Talmud is said to have bogged
down in superstitious and ridiculous details of the rites, lacking any
common human interest. All of a sudden we realize that the exact
reverse of that commonplace is true.

4) Once justification has been achieved, freedom plays a very
minor and illusory role in Catholic thinking. Through good works,
to which at last a place is being assigned, freedom can lead to a further "increase of grace." The inconsistency and irrelevance of this
is immediately apparent, as it is generally characteristic for Christianity and its rejection of this world that it has no place for the
human freedom of the will. In spite of all attempts by Catholic
spokesmen to admit freedom side by side with grace, the distribution
has never accorded freedom an autonomous working area. It can
only add its two cents' worth to what grace has to proclaim, and
grace drowns freedom's humble voice out so completely that it could
just as well not have been heard at all. According to the Jewish view,
freedom is autonomous, albeit in a small and unimportant sphere.
Several authors (Saadia, Maimonides) recognize it unconditionally.
Where it is acknowledged at all, it is the highest authority.

In Catholicism we meet the problem of the coexistence of grace
and freedom. God offers all men grace and salvation, supernatural
assistance. How is it then that there are evil men who do not make
use of such assistance? Does this mean that man has the freedom to
accept or to reject the grace offered him? Such a freedom would
injure the concept of divine omnipotence. How can God determine
or know in advance the course of the world if it is up to man to
decide against salvation? If, on the other hand, we respect divine
omnipotence, we must come to the conclusion that God grants some
men irresistible grace, so that these will be saved, whereas others, deprived of all freedom, cannot be saved but are, through God's uni-

versal love (?), predestined to a never-ending hell. Why? Because this is the way He has created them?

In view of this dilemma, scholasticism as usual starts to split and to refine the problem but, as we shall soon see, without success. A distinction was introduced between "sufficient" and "efficient" grace (*gratia sufficiens* and *efficax*). Whereas sufficient grace is available to all men, efficient grace is accessible to only a few. This, however, means only a delay of the difficulty, not its solution. For immediately the question arises whether the decisive "efficient" grace is a new divine grace, which overwhelms man beyond his own will, or whether it is man's free affirmation of "sufficient" grace, as was maintained by the school of the Molinists. Thus the Thomists considered them heretics and accused them of Pelagianism, which is the same heresy against which Augustine had fought, and which appears again and again, stressing the omnipotence of human freedom, just because in Christianity there is no room for such freedom. In order to solve the dogmatic struggle, the famous session of the *congregatio de auxiliis* was called, which was continued, from 1598 to 1607, under the popes Clement VIII and Leo XI. Although two hundred sessions were held, no result was achieved. At the end both schools were told not to declare each other heretics. Today's dogmatists teach simply that grace and freedom work together, the details of that collaboration being left to "free theological discussions." Bartmann states that we cannot solve the problem of the passage from "sufficient" to "efficient" grace.

What is at the basis of that difficulty, of that unsatisfactory decision? It is the Christian unification and uniformation of the experience of grace. For the grace of belief, coming from the Christ experience and spelled out in detail beforehand, is in fact incompatible with the freedom of the human will. It shows *ab initio* a distorted image of the world, in which only one reality—the belief in Christ— stands out in full light, and everything else is erased as being irrelevant. It is therefore very unimportant for me to try out my own strength and to do my duty, even if it is based on free will. When the time of faith comes, I shall be able to do my duty in the state of blessedness. Before that, all such efforts are superfluous and meaningless, perhaps even *splendida vitia* (splendid vices), which is what Augustine called the virtues of the pagans. According to Jewish opinion, the grace freely sent forth by God is quite different. I do not know beforehand in which form, at which work, on the occasion of which pleasure or sadness it will overwhelm me. Every way that I go is potentially a way towards grace, and that potentiality is decisive, for it makes the entire world important and metaphysically relevant. But Christ cannot even "potentially" be encountered in experiences which have no direct bearing on the belief in Christ. Here we must draw clear distinctions; for these things are often, and in various intentions, presented in a confused and blurred way. For if Christ is only a spiritual and divine principle, it is easy to believe in him. But then Christ has been identified with God, and why two different words for one concept? Thus Ricarda Huch writes (*Luthers Glaube*, p. 77): "To believe in Christ means to believe in what is divine in man, to believe that man is endowed with spirit." In view of that empty formula we cannot distinguish between Jews and Christians. The truth is, however, that to believe in Christ means something entirely different and has been interpreted thus by all those who seriously call themselves Christians. It means to believe that, at a definite moment in the history of the world, eternal divinity descended into temporality in order to atone for man, and that thus at a definite moment in *time* something happened that made an ultimate decision concerning the *eternal* salvation of mankind. It is this very invasion of eternity in a concrete and one-time point of time which, according to the honest Christian Kierkegaard, represents the paradox of Christian faith (more on this later). It is clear that, if from the innumerable moments in time one moment received such an extraordinarily preferential treatment and was tied up so irreplaceably with eternity, all other moments of time lose all their value as compared with that exalted one. The belief in the specific character of that moment is the only essential thing man should be concerned with, it is the key to all proper being and willing. It is of vital interest to know where to find that faith. Is that faith in a specific historical fact even potentially present in all experiences? It exists where I place it; but I do not experience it in such a way that it arises by itself out of the naturally indifferent stuff of other historical situations. And just that would be needed for Christ to enter existence and ignoble misfortune. For Christ's grace defines its result clearly: Golgotha, Gethsemane, etc., and their supernatural significance. Therefore that grace can never encompass all of existence, which, taken by itself, is not interested in that result. Divine grace, on the other hand, in not necessarily restricted to the form of belief, and still less so to the belief "in this or that," but it reveals itself as a graceful overcoming of a conflict which cannot be solved with human powers. Now that conflict—"the incompatibility of the correlated"—appears wherever there is life, wherever ignoble misfortune hurls itself at noble misfortune, and where man's finite task collides with infinity. This all-present possibility of the conflict clothes ignoble misfortune with metaphysical significance, and thus a place is assigned to freedom, side by side with grace, a freedom which functions within ignoble misfortune. It is just this place which Christianity cannot offer to freedom. For then part of the world, ignoble misfortune, would obtain a metaphysical importance independent from Christ. Here then we have arrived at the basic difference between Judaism and Christianity. It is true that ignoble misfortune is always somehow connected with God, but not with the crucifixion of Christ in such and such a year. Because of this connection with God—through the possibility of a conflict, which can be resolved—ignoble misfortune and man's free deed can become metaphysically important, and that next to God or with God, which in this case is one and the same thing. But such an everyday connection does not apply to the historical Christ. Therefore faith in Christ had to be more exclusive and more jealous than God, Who is available to all and does not have to exclude anything. Thus does the belief in Christ push out ignoble misfortune and, together with it, scholastic casuistry notwithstanding, the freedom of the will, the fullness of life, the facts of existence and the world. Here is, for instance, an excerpt from the autobiography of Hudson Taylor, quoted from William James' *Varieties of Religious Experience* (paperback edition, 1958, p. 197, n. 12), a book, incidentally, which does not refer at all to the Jewish religious experience, and simply identifies religion with Christianity:

> Whilst I was reading the evangelical treatise, I was soon struck by an expression: "the finished work of Christ." Why, I asked of myself, does the author use these terms? Why does he not say: "the atoning work"? Then these words "It is finished" presented themselves to my mind. What is it that is finished? I asked, and in an instant my mind replied: A perfect expiation for sin; entire satisfaction has been given; the debt has been paid by the Substitute. Christ has died for our sins; not for ours only, but for those of all men. If, then,

the entire work is finished, all the debt paid, what remains for me to do? In another instant the light was shed through my mind by the Holy Ghost, and the joyous conviction was given me that nothing more was to be done, save to fall on my knees, to accept this Savior and his love, to praise God forever.

A caricature of this quite consistent point of view, which concerns itself only with the belief in Christ, and nullifies everything else, is found in Zangwill's novel *Children of the Ghetto*. The Catholic governess says to her Jewish mistress: "I am glad that you are doing so many good deeds. I have no need for this, for my soul has been saved already."

There is not so great a difference between that strange view and one of Luther's after-dinner speeches: "It would not even be good for us to do whatever God commands, for this would deprive Him of His divinity, He would become a liar and would not remain truthful. It would also make Saint Paul like one of the Romans, for he said: 'God has included everything into sin, so that He may have mercy on all men.'" Compare also Luther's letter to Melanchthon quoted previously:

If grace is truly that, it should cancel a true sin, and not an illusory one. God does not save illusory sinners. Be a sinner and sin much, but more still, have faith in Christ and be happy in him, for he defeats sin, death, and the world. We must sin as long as we live on earth. This life is no place for justice; but, as Peter has said, we wait for a new heaven and a new earth, where justice will have a place. It is enough that, in the abundant glory of God, we have recognized the lamb which taketh away the sins of the world. No sin can tear us away from that, even if we should fornicate or murder a thousand times a day.

I shall try once more to place the Jewish and the Christian forms of life side-by-side. In doing so, I shall add a few new observations. We shall find new formulations, but not everything mentioned before will be repeated.

The essential and creative element of Judaism is to be found in the clash of the two worlds of noble and ignoble misfortune. Here lies the conflict, and here is the possibility of a solution through divine grace. Is Christianity totally unaware of that conflict? This is quite possible in view of the fact that the entire complex of ignoble misfortune has no place in Christianity. Could it be that the absence of that conflict is responsible for the desperate indifference towards morality which we found in the quotation from Luther cited above? But this is not quite so. In this manner we are likely to exaggerate the difference between Judaism and Christianity, which are, after all, based on the same view of the world. For we must not make the mistake of assuming that the two spheres of noble and ignoble misfortune enjoy equal rights, that they run parallel and are of the same dimension. The fact of the matter is that noble misfortune is above ignoble misfortune, the former encompasses the latter from all sides, just as a vast circle surrounds a much smaller one. In certain cases, ignoble misfortune may rightly be considered a special application of noble misfortune. For what is noble misfortune? Man, small as he is, when confronted with the absolute and infinite God, is in danger of sinking into nothingness. What is indeed the conflict between noble and ignoble misfortune? Viewing man's finite and small task in the light of the eternal God may cause this moral task to seem nothing in view of the humility due to God, and the significance of that deed cannot be maintained. This conflict is solved by the this-worldly miracle. Through God's grace, finiteness retains its importance, which, logically, it lost in the face of the Absolute, or perhaps even by simply looking at the Milky Way. This "miracle"—I have just pointed out its Jewish meaning—is also important to the Christian. It is an intermediary in the conflict between man and God; whereas, so far its role had been to intervene in the conflict between man's action and his infinite humility. But in each of the two cases, the meaning of the this-worldly miracle is different. In Judaism the the ethical sphere of this world regains its significance, relative things do not simply evaporate when confronted with absolute ones. The world retains its outlines no matter how dazzling the light that emanates from the heavens. In Christianity the *I* stands naked before God, without any works, without a this-worldly sphere, since it has lost its importance long ago through Christ. In such a confrontation the *I* cannot be interested in self-preservation, since no independent tasks exist, but only in a complete self-annihilation. The Christian this-worldly miracle implies the annihilation of this world. We can state the two views in short formulas. Jewish: My ethical deeds have not become meaningless to God. Christian: I can bear it to be nothing before God.

What role does ethics, the human-moral deed, play in this entire process? It is the yeast, the ferment, the stimulator. Without the inner obligation to do what is right—an obligation to which we are led because of our sovereignty, our freedom of the will—there would not be that terrible clash with the world of humility. From the religious point of view, therefore, the moral deed has but a limited value. It is not an end in itself, the proper fulfilment of obligations, but rather a germ, a stimulator of a conflict which only God can solve. It is true that this role is of minor value and far down on the list. The moral deed cannot go further down. Since it loses all interest to the Christian, it leads not only to the dissolution of the real world but also to that of the theological system, which cannot any longer allow grace and freedom to exist side by side. This lack of interest in the moral deed is, however, the necessary consequence of restricting grace to one single fact—salvation through Christ. This is the focal point. Isaiah the prophet, however, had said: "God Himself will come and redeem you"—God Himself, without an intermediary, rejecting historical incarnation as the source of the evil. "Then shall the eyes of the blind be opened, and the ears of the deaf unstopped."

Incorrect Distinctions between Judaism and Christianity

Christianity has established a generally valid, abstract formula for grace, instead of recognizing the multifariousness of life. This "grace of generalization" separates Christianity from Judaism.

Once we have thus discovered the real criterion, we are faced with the enticing possibility of rejecting the many alleged differences between Christianity and Judaism that are found so frequently in the literature of all peoples. But I am not writing here an "apologia" for Judaism. The presentation of its positive values ought to make all defensive actions superfluous. Therefore I am limiting myself to a few observations about "incorrect distinctions."

It is not true that Judaism is particularistic and narrowly national or that Christianity is universalistic. I have mentioned this (and also subsequent matters) previously in this book, and I do not wish to be guilty of needless repetitions. I shall, however, quote a reply to a letter of inquiry in the Prague Zionist weekly, *Selbstwehr*.

Love of one's fellow man

You write—we are sure in the name of many others—that you are not comfortable about Leviticus 19:18. You believe that "Love thy neighbor as thyself" can only refer to a member of one's own people, not to everybody, and that apparently only Christ transferred the meaning of that verse to mankind in general. In order not to overlook any matter in this respect, we approached the well known expert on our literature, Rabbi Professor Stark, and here is his reply:

A great teacher in Israel, Rabbi Akiba, declared the law of the Torah, "Love thy neighbor as thyself," to be its core and essence. "This is the basic teaching of the Torah," he wrote (*Bereshit Rabba*, ch. 24). The same remark was made by a younger colleague of his, Ben Azzai, in commenting on Genesis 5:1, which teaches a common ancestor for all mankind and the fact that man was created in the image of God. By quoting these two comments side by side, the Midrash wished apparently to state that they complement and explain one another. For if someone should believe that the word "neighbor" referred to one who shares my faith or nation, the allusion to the single descent of all mankind should teach him that his assumption was based on an error. The fact that such a fear was well founded can be seen from the interpretation of many Christian theologians and Bible scholars. Thus we read in B. Stade's book on the history of the people of Israel (vol. 1, p. 510, n. 3), "It is a sign of arrogance if a Rabbinical assembly tries to convince the Christian public through commandments like Leviticus 19:18 and 24:22 that the Jews are obligated to act morally towards all men, and it is also a sign of arrogance if they thus make of Judaism a religion of human love. These Rabbis are misleading their audience by a wrong interpretation of the German translation of the Bible. They undoubtedly act according to such principles and try to instruct their congregations accordingly, but then they are under the influence of Christian ethics, and contradict Talmudic Judaism." Now I shall not return the compliment of "arrogance" to Stade, for this would be neither Jewish nor Talmudic. We well remember that Stade has, on several occasions, defended Judaism against the shameful accusation of the blood libel, and ingratitude is neither Jewish nor Talmudic. But gratitude must not prevent us from exploring and stating the truth.

Therefore I would like to ask Mr. Stade where the source of the teaching of the "Christian love of one's neighbor" can be found. This is obviously in the Gospels of Matthew (22:35ff.) and Mark (12:28ff.). Now let us see what is being taught there: "Then one of the Pharisees, a lawyer, asked Jesus a question, tempting him and saying: Master, which is the great commandment in the law? Jesus replied: Thou shalt love the Lord thy God with all thy heart, with all thy soul and with all thy mind. This is the first and great commandment. And the second is like unto it. Thou shalt love thy neighbor as thyself. On these two commandments hang all the law and the prophets." In Mark this is related as follows: "And one of the scribes came, and having heard them reasoning together, and perceiving that he had answered them well, asked him, which is the first commandment of all? Jesus replied: The first of all the commandments is Hear, O Israel: The Lord our God is one Lord; and thou shalt love the Lord thy God with all thy heart, and with all thy soul, and with all thy mind, and with all thy strength; this is the first commandment. And the second is like, namely this: Thou shalt love thy neighbor as thyself. There is none other commandment greater than these."

Now my question is this: According to these reports in the Gospels, did Jesus teach here anything new, or did he even intend to do so? Did he not simply answer the question of the Pharisees and the scribes as to which is the greatest and most important commandment in the Torah, by stating that "Love thy neighbor as thyself" (Leviticus 19:18) was indeed the greatest? And since Jesus did not speak German but Hebrew and had read not the German but the Hebrew Bible, he certainly quoted from the original. He must thus have given the word "neighbor" the same meaning it has in the Hebrew Bible. If then the Torah limits the law of "loving one's neighbor" to those who are of the same nationality, the same must be true in the Gospels, since they not only quote from the Torah but mention that this is what they are doing. According to those reports, therefore, the founder of Christianity did only what Rabbi Akiba did according to the Midrash: he declared the commandment of "loving one's neighbor as oneself" to be the most important and essential teaching of the Torah.

In the original the statements by Rabbi Akiba and Ben Azzai read as follows: "Akiba had declared the commandment 'Love thy neighbor as thyself' as the basic statement of the entire Torah. But Ben Azzai said that the phrase, 'This is the book of the generations of man' contains an even greater statement. "Man" refers to all men as a unit and in equality, as it says further on, they were created "in the image of God." (Sifra Kedoshim, Chapter 4, and Jer. Nedarim 10:3).

M. Lazarus (The Ethics of Judaism) also quotes this Midrash: "The revelation was given in the wilderness, i.e. an area which does not belong to anybody. For if it had been given in the Holy Land, the Israelites might say that the other nations had no share in it. Therefore it was given in the wilderness, and it is the property of the whole world. Anybody may come and accept it."

In the Talmud (Gittin 61A) we read as follows: "There must be no distinction between Jews and Pagans with regard to the treatment of the poor, the sick, and the dead" (see Loewe-Montefiore, A Rabbinic Anthology, p. 653). In commenting on this passage Maimonides (Mishne Torah, Hilchoth Melachim) quotes the Biblical verses, "The Lord is good to all; and His tender mercies are over all His works" (Psalms 145:9) and "Its ways are ways of pleasantness, and all its paths are peace" (Proverbs 3:17).

When, in Hebrew, a noun is followed by a number, that noun appears in the singular, provided the number is higher than ten. Regarding this, we find a clever and pleasant interpretation in Vayikra Rabba: "Jacob went down to Egypt with seventy souls. The word is 'soul,' to indicate that all men should be one soul, just as God is One." This is incidentally a good example of the way the Talmud and Rabbinic writings in general deal with grammar—not for the sake of grammar but from their deep feeling for the world.

Disregarding all this, the well instructed and the half instructed, particularly theosophists and writers, insist that the "God of the ancient Jews" was conceited and chauvinistic, and that Jewish religion is arrogant enough to consider its own people "chosen."

Nobody seems to be impressed by Hugo Bergmann's proof (Worte Mosis) that chosenness here implies more duties, and not more privileges. Here is a quotation from his beautiful book, which is unfortunately not known well enough:

A covenant calls for two parties, who obligate themselves to live up to its agreements. But in all stories about Moses which have come down to us the obligation rests unilaterally with Israel (see Hugo Gressmann: *Mose und seine Zeit*). For the obligation which God undertakes in the form of the "covenant" is in fact one placed upon the Jewish people. Through the contract, Israel obligates itself to fulfill God's word. What is God's obligation? To choose Israel, to make of them "a kingdom of priests and a holy nation." But this is again identical with what Israel's obligation meant. The chosenness consists in self-sanctification, in being filled with God. It is true that in times of decadence Israel, too, believed that the covenant obligated God to protect, defend and exalt his people. But the "contract" does not state that at all.

In such "times of decadence," prophets appeared and fought against the falsified concept of chosenness. As Amos said, "Are ye not like the children of the Ethiopians to Me, O children of Israel? Have I not brought out Israel from the land of Egypt, the Philistines from Kaphtor, and Aram from Kir?" (9:7).

Nothing is as hard to uproot as religious prejudices, zealously nurtured by the Christian churches in order to popularize their own advantages as against Judaism. That gigantic propaganda, continued through the centuries, has been successful, even among today's Jews, who do not know much of their own tradition. I have written this book not only in order to relieve my mind and to clarify my ideas but in order to call on others to revise thoroughly their concepts about Judaism and Christianity.

Although Judaism is not chauvinistic, it is not indifferent towards nationality. Thanks to the possibility of the this-worldly miracle, all earthly differences are important to the Jew, nothing must be clouded or passed by. To pour out a jelly layer of "Catholicism" over all nations, in the belief that this will solve the problem of nationalities, is a superficial levelling which goes against the Jewish spirit, which does not wish to minimize the facts. Therefore God's word, through his prophets, addresses all men: "Listen to Me, ye islands, and hearken unto Me, peoples far away . . . And He said: Seeing that thou art My servant, is it too little for thee to set up Jacob's tribes and to bring back the remnant of Israel? Therefore I make of thee a light unto the gentiles, that My salvation may reach to the end of the world" (Isaiah 49:1, 6). But the Jews receive for themselves the yoke of commandments and laws. Although this, too, is a distinction, a wise and pious man said to me once half jokingly;

"The Jews have more commandments than others. Since they are a stubborn people, they had to be strictly disciplined." He who has become acquainted with the terrible lack of discipline, for instance among Jewish politicians, will bless this statement a hundred times. In this respect, too, our Torah proves itself to be a book of the deepest realism, and Moses as a legislator whose look into the future, beyond millennia, can only be explained as a divine inspiration. Only he who stands high above life can understand, predict, and guide life in this way. If the Jews were chosen to carry the heavy yoke of commandments and obligations, it was done with the facts in mind. Without that, mankind would have lost the Jews and their religious tension a long time ago.

The reproof of chosenness is connected with that of the "God of wrath," which I have dealt with earlier in this book. At this point I wish to add that the Hebrew name for God, the vowels of which are unknown to us, consists of four consonants—Y H W H—which are the softest and most tender of the language. It must be a strange "thundering God," whose name sounds so gentle and of whom we are told (I Kings 19:1ff.) that he revealed himself to the prophet neither in a storm, nor in an earthquake, nor in a fire, but "after the fire there was a still, small voice. When Elijah heard this, he hid his face in his cloak and left the cave. Then a voice asked him, 'What wantest thou here, Elijah?' "

Judaism is not the religion of an exclusive and strict justice and of the law, as compared with a Christian religion of the heart and of love. It is not a question of freedom versus grace; nor is it, as compared with the Christian "discovery of the soul," a hodge-podge of rituals.* All this has been mentioned before. All these fictitious distinctions disappear after the one difference has been properly understood. Let us again quote from the Talmud (Makkoth 23): "613 commandments were given to Moses. David formulated them all in eleven (Psalm 15), Isaiah in six (33:15), Micah in three (6:8). Isaiah again in two: Observe righteousness and do justice (56:1), and finally Amos in one: Seek me and live (5:4)" (Montefiore-Loewe, op. cit., p. 199).

It would be difficult to find a more exalted expression of religiosity

* Concerning the other "false distinctions," there is much good to be found in Eschelbacher's little book, *Das Judentum im Urteile der Modernen Protestantischen Theologie*.

than that divine call to the entire world: Seek Me and live.

There is nothing more to be said. For here we face again the only and basic difference between the Jewish and the Christian feeling concerning the world. Live and Seek Me, seek Me while you are alive, in the full breadth of life. Now compare this to the Christian view: No one can come to the Father except through the Son. The prescribed marching route.

Judaism does not show a way. But right now there are obligations to be fulfilled, not because their reward is salvation but simply because this is a human obligation. At the same time, the most distant things have to be recognized and feared; and man must hope that, from unexpected directions and without a previous announcement, grace will suddenly overwhelm him—the love of eternity, which one's own powers could only fear. We are wandering about among forms of life. We do not know from behind which form all of a sudden real life will face us. For this very reason it is impossible to underestimate any one form or even to consider it mere form.

Individual Grace—from a Diary

A book which describes the abstract grace of Jesus and so clearly places the individual experience of grace into the center can be expected to provide a more detailed description of that experience. Here the reader may confront the author with the questions, "How about you? Have you experienced that grace which you mention so frequently? Have you encountered God, and how?"

Suppose the author's conscience does not allow him to regard himself as the founder of a religion, or that he has never experienced grace but only waited for it, or that he did have it but did not wish to convey to others how his soul was in harmony with that sphere of godliness. In such a case he would be greatly embarrassed. In the absence of an individual example his term, a "personal grace," would have been lowered to a mere cliche, and would be at least as abstract as the vigorously rejected grace of abstraction or generalization. Fortunately and quite by accident, I came across notes concerning such experiences, written by a person known to me. As far as I am able to judge, those experiences were not on the highest level, and yet they will do to illustrate our case. We must be satisfied with what is on hand. I am glad that in presenting his inner states the writer tries to be detached. Never does he attempt to mix the scientific mood of the one who merely remembers with the past stage of *ecstasis*. He does not adulterate nor does he wish to falsify anything, but he draws a clear line of separation between the ungraspable transfiguration of the past and the present intention to recall that past as well as possible. Strangely enough some of those who tried similar achievements used an excited and abrupt style so as to hide the fact that at the moment of their writing they were reflecting and not any longer experiencing. Or did they in that manner wish to add credibility to their experiences? Yet even the "excited" method has the advantage of replacing the religious *ecstasis* with the poetic one, and there is a common basis for both. But at this point of the book, where we are interested in clear insights, we must be grateful to our friend for expressing himself simply, almost medically, and for calling things by their names.

Here then are some excerpts from those strange notes:

"Several times during my life I have had sensations which raised me high above the level of ordinary sentiments. I can remember almost all of them, although normally I am not greatly concerned with my past and prefer to leave such interests to my old age. But those events stand out so sharply from the rest that they force themselves from time to time back into my memory.

"Two stages must be distinguished here. I experience the lower one relatively often, but it is only a reflection or an analogy of the higher one. When I was lucky, I experienced such states two or more times in a year, whereas the higher one was granted me only four or five times in twenty-five years.

"The lower level is always connected with works of art, and this happens almost regularly in some cases. Thus I could never recite Hector's farewell words to Andromache without crying, even when this was part of my school assignment. Then there is a second passage in Schubert's second trio for piano. Then there are the first scenes in *The Bartered Bride*, certain sections in the symphonies of Mahler and Berlioz, Goethe's lyrical poems, the Song of Songs, the beginning of Ecclesiastes, etc. This sentiment must not be identified with esthetic pleasure. For I may have esthetic pleasure on a very high level, which leads to enthusiasm, and yet the feeling mentioned above is absent. Nor is it simply a state of emotion.

"On the higher stage, which is much rarer, we have the real inner experience. This stage does not need the help of a work of art, it appears in real life and seems to require the fresh air. It shares with the lower stage merely the accompanying physical circumstances and some details in feeling. Let us first describe these physical circumstances.

"These are a warming up of the head which leads sometimes to headaches, cramps, then tears. The tears may stop, then the cramps again until the tears reappear. The whole phenomenon proceeds thus in waves and, under favorable circumstances, can last as long as a quarter of an hour, although I have of course never really timed it.

"In this entire somatic process, I am tempted to see the antipode of a sexual orgasm, a lascivious eruption in the spiritual sphere, in the direction of infinity, perhaps an ejaculation of the brain. It breaks forth in the midst of hot tears. A feeling of an inexpressibly profound purification accompanies the act, and although it is a painful one, the discomfort is outweighed by that feeling of purification. Perhaps the sacred ablutions and baths prescribed in many rites are meant as a symbol and as a recollection of that rare experience of a tangible and spiritual purification.

"This experience apparently does not depend on the place in which it occurs. Seclusion is not a requirement. Once it assailed me in the midst of the tumult of a metropolitan railroad station, and another time at a place of even less reality. On the other hand, it also happened in a quiet park and by night near a forsaken river.

"This experience is prepared for by great tension and excitement, the details of which I do not want to present here. Once the state has been reached, it is characterized by an extraordinary lightness. At such times I cannot understand why I am not always in that state. I then have the feeling that my entire past was an error, an incomprehensible mistake, and that only unforgivable stupidity and blindness had prevented me from feeling previously so infinitely free and happy. Above all I am sure that from now on I will not allow myself to be pushed out of this natural state. Although my reasoning knows how rare this experience is, at the moment of its appearance it does not seem to be extraordinary or strange but rather the very rule. But while the experience lasts, such reflections are impossible. They appear only afterwards.

"It is in this 'vanishing act' that the two stages differ. The lower one, initiated by works of art, has hardly any aftereffects. The smallest disturbance of everyday life shakes its rhythm, and it breaks off rather suddenly. If, on the other hand, the experience is that of the rarer form, a direct solution of a crisis in life, it affects me many more days and even weeks. My entire existence seems changed and offers a new meaning. It is an incomparable mood of insight, determination, goodness. The feeling of unending duration seems to be confirmed. Although the acute perturbation, accompanied by tears, has gone, the overall image of the world at the beginning of the eruption has not changed. The succeeding problem does not lie in the mood itself—which continues to remain quite natural—but in what manner the world succeeds in reentering quietly, in removing one pebble after the other, until finally the entire structure disappears, as if blown away.

"The next higher level—which has never been accorded to me—may be typified not by a higher intensity but in a more extended duration of the experience. For this reason the Zohar calls the saints 'Sons of faithfulness.'

"Whereas so far I have only dealt with exterior aspects of the feeling, I must now turn to its content. But this is very difficult, and I shall have to remain at the periphery. There is joy involved, but this is not the essence of the feeling. There is strength, expectation, and devotion, but all of this is not central. It is a feeling which seems to imply that nothing is impossible—in a good sense—that evil and sin have been defeated, and that one would never again commit an evil deed or even be tempted to do so. I remember that once when I was in such a mood for weeks I looked at a certain book on my nighttable. It deals with the examination of one's conscience, and I could not understand why I had read that book so studiously and why I had been tortured by it. Once the experience had passed, I understood it again. While the experience lasts, one's soul is different. One believes one's self able to achieve everything properly. One overlooks all difficulties, while standing all the time in the midst of life. Directly touched by that experience, I once could not read the morning paper, which otherwise interests me greatly. At such times distant events, at which we are mere spectators, are too pale. Being part of real life, one stands in its center and needs no reports. One senses clearly that such reports are only distracting.

"At the other extreme would be scepticism, concern with details, transparence. The world would look like a small creek, its bed almost visible. One is sitting on the dry land, trying to get some water, but cannot even reach one drop. Everything can be figured out in advance, is determined by known motives, balanced by gains and losses, animal egoism. There is no riddle. One is in a black mood. I fell into that mood of despair once when a young man told me a story. During the war, while on duty, he had corresponded with a girl whom he did not know personally. She sent him gifts, and they exchanged letters which were full of spirit and agreement. Their relations became more and more intimate. When on leave in Berlin, he met her for the first time and found that she was ugly. After having gone out with her several times, he told her that he wanted merely to be a friend to her, but he could not harbor any other feeling. She had expected more, since the letters appeared to have hinted at a marriage. She ended up in a lunatic asylum, a case of hereditary disposition. What horrified me here was the fact that the story was so clear, simple, all too simple, and self-explanatory. The world became entirely transparent. I could calculate in advance how long one can go on with the affair, which meant how long it was profitable. Everything could be understood. I saw the threads, the entire boring and sober machinery. In such a mood I could not warm up to anything, I could not find anything beautiful or important of itself.

"The exact opposite of that devilish state of transparence is my rare experience, which is so hard to describe. In the former case there is no mystery, and in the latter everything becomes important because of the mystery. This is the way the Zohar puts it: 'Whatever is above is also below, and whatever is below is also above.' According to the Zohar there are things in the upper worlds which correspond to days and hours. Here lies the very depth of the experience—it carries with itself the guarantee of personal immortality. The opposite would be the fear of death, which means the conviction that one does not live a full life. To die is not bad. But to die without ever having done the right thing is what terrifies and hurts. This gives death its terribly serious majesty. He who lives in the 'experience' which I have described is invulnerable, he has already acquired his immortality. For here is the secret: immortality lies in this life, not in the world beyond. It exists before death, not after death. To be immortal means not to have neglected what is right, to have saved part of one's soul. This is what the Bible may have meant by saying that a patriarch died 'satisfied with his life' (Genesis 35:29)."

The rest of my friend's notes deal with Cabbalistic studies. But although, as far as the Talmud is concerned, I may at least consider myself a student, I cannot call myself even that in regard to the Zohar.

Faith and Ritual

These then are the three things in which I believe: the secret, the power of truth, and enthusiasm.

All these three powers, although not equally distant from the higher sphere, reflect it, and it is a sphere which sometimes sends forth rays into our own world. In the upper world everything is solid, absolute, clear. The most subjective phenomenon is enthusiasm; it approaches the absolute from the point of view of man, psychologically. The secret is close to the absolute. In so far as the absolute is turned toward us, it is secret.

Between the two, on the boundary line between the object and the subject, lies truth. Although it is reached by man's subjective experiences, its support and its magic power lie beyond, in the secret. Thus truth is open as well as hidden. It is the revelation of what is hidden.

What are the forms of truth and of the belief in it? For instance, there is this statement: The truth within me cannot get lost. It knows its way already, even if I do not act accordingly. Or: A truthful feeling, expressed truthfully, cannot remain without an effect. A lie cannot be as effective as truth. The same factor redeems art: only the artists's genuine passion, what he creates out of abundance, is of value, and then the fullness of his heart can be felt. This explains why even if a work of art deals with the saddest things in life, one regains his joy in living, although that work may be concerned with the end of that joy. This is so because that work contains truth, and through truth we recognize the absolute and do not despair.

The same holds true of honest love and of an honest deed. Only they have validity. Thanks to their truth the other world, the absolute one, becomes tangible. There is something to cling to, and this is God.

I believe in the secret. People are afraid of death, as if it were so certain that after life everything came to an end, and as if then we would have to find a life which could be explained and defined and run like a machine. But this is not the case. If we try to feel the secrets of a nerve, of a capillary vessel, or of a muscle fiber, the fear of death is lessened.

We recognize the secret also in the fact that things are arranged differently and work differently from what our reasoning imagines a priori. Many comparisons can help us understand how unreal our reasoning is. Suppose we ask ourselves this question: how would we go to work if we had to provide God's creature, Man, with the power of speech? Since we have some uniformity—the sequence of the A B C—we would most probably create some kind of a key board, and the lips would have one key for every sound. But the work of secret is not related at all to our imagination. Sounds are created at various places in the cave of our mouth, at the palate, at the teeth, etc. Apparently accidents are being utilized, and the beautiful order which we have imagined does not exist.

Or again, if we were asked to fashion something that should last long and could do many things, we would perhaps think of armored plate, of precision instruments made of steel, but not of the soft and jelly-like cell which constructs human and animal plant organisms. Everything fluctuates and is in constant motion, and thus durability is created.

Even machines reflect the secret, since they do not correspond to common expectation. Airplanes ought to be flying birds, provided with soft feathers. But the flying machine soars aloft with strictness and energy, filled with murderous power. There is no swan-like wing but a system which beats about crazily, pointed and strong, hard wood, penetrated by earthly weight, difficult to start, and, once in motion, we hear a high and yet low sound, extreme tension, and the impatient exhaust of the engine. If we were to hear that sound from a great distance, we would not expect it to come from the sky, but we would think of a factory, of gravel, and of a dusty road. But lo and behold, it comes from the blue sky. It is flying.

Here someone might ask this question: Where is the connection between these lines and Judaism? Do they not simply apply to a "free religion"? Does not official Judaism, too, have a fast marching route? In Christianity we have Jesus, and in Judaism the Sinaitic revelation, the written and oral traditions with their abundance of customs, festivals, and prayers.

But the position of Christ within Christianity cannot be compared with that of the rituals within Judaism. Christ is considered the Alpha and Omega of salvation, whereas the Jewish rites are only facilitating instruments. Though they must be observed, neglect of a rite does not lead to eternal damnation, as is the case with the failure to believe in Christ. The absolute and irreplaceable importance of Christ to the Christian has no analogy in Judaism.

Furthermore, the Jewish rites form, or are meant to form, a living totality. They do not address themselves to the Jew from the outside as just a commandment, but all of them have to do with the secret of the Jewish national existence. It does not matter whether we consider them the expression of Jewish folk instinct, or whether we believe, as do the orthodox, that God Himself formed them in a way appropriate to the Jewish instinct. This question does not concern us here, and at any rate their rabbinic origin—the source of the folk instinct—has been assured for many of them. What is essential is that through the folk spirit the forms of the Jewish religion communicate in a mysterious way with the individual Jew. It is also essential that they present something creative, in which the individual participates naturally, and not merely through historical knowledge.

The relationship of the religious forms and the life of the Jewish people is a mystery. People have at some time constructed a rational connection, explaining certain religious prescriptions as "hygienic" measures. But this is erroneous. The connection is much deeper. The totality of the laws covers the totality of Jewish national life. Certain religious norms may be compared to the thyroid gland, whose role in the growth of the human body had not been understood for a long time, so that it was considered superfluous, until suddenly new research illustrated its great importance. Thus even in ancient times certain religious prescriptions protected the Jewish people from Hellenization, and even from the Middle Ages onward they have saved them from assimilation. Our "liberal" grandparents were very smart. They found the prayer "Next year in Jerusalem" superfluous, but the enthusiasm of the next generation placed that statement in the center, although many "progressive" rabbis had already eliminated it.

Here is another example: although the requirement of ten men for the recital of certain prayers may be based on a certain mystical intention, its practical consequence was the prevention of the dispersal of the Jews and subsequent assimilation. It facilitated the formation of congregations. The same effect was attained by the strange "dietary laws." We must almost always distinguish between the manifest intention of the law and the latent one. History has always shown that the religious laws of Judaism are more clever than the most clever interpreters. If in some cases orthodoxy denies the connection between the Jewish religion and the idea of a Jewish people, this shows a lack of instinct. It shows that the forms that have been handed down do not suffice any longer, that they start losing their inner meaning, no matter how similar they are to the ancient forms when looked at from the outside. Some people advocate "renewal." But neither their theories nor their lives have given us a satisfactory answer.

I too believe in a renewal of Judaism. But only he who has a strong faith can achieve it. He must have a sense for the secret and for truthfulness.

Behind the strange-looking prescriptions, an apparently unintentional secret is hidden. And that still and humble life of the Jewish folk spirit must be sensed deeply and, if possible, imitated. A gigantic example is the handing down of the text of the Hebrew Bible. This was done under the strangest laws and procedures. The scholars of a certain school—called the Massorah—counted the letters of each individual Biblical book. Thus, for instance, they established that the letter Aleph occurred more than forty thousand times; and they found out which word and letter was exactly in the middle of each book etc. The laws concerning a text are so minute and tiresome that a scribe may rightly congratulate himself if he has succeeded in copying one column without mistakes. We know of cases where an expert scribe had to throw out a column ten or twenty times. For it is strictly forbidden to use a manuscript which has not been copied correctly, according to all relevant religious prescriptions. Shall we call this an exaggerated and bothersome concern? No, here lies hidden a very deep mystery. Scholars are surprised to read in the history of Biblical tradition that there is hardly any disagreement in any Hebrew manuscripts, although at the time of their writing the Jews were already living in the exile. O glorious faithfulness of the dispersed people, driven to all shores, left with hardly any communication with one another, and still preserving the mysterious joint rhythm, as if an invisible conductor were leading them beyond the seas and the mountains. In one such history we read,

> At the time of the earliest manuscripts the text of the Hebrew Bible had already been subjected to criticism by the Jews and been given

a final form, the one which has been preserved in all manuscripts. This speaks for the integrity of the text. . . . The facts testify to the consequences of this exact procedure. A comprehensive comparison could find only a few variations besides errors in writing.

But what do we know concerning the state of the Greek text used by the Christians?

> In the fifth century not one of the editions of the Septuagint was preserved in the original purity of its text, since it had become customary to change the text of the manuscripts without plan or critical delicacy. The efforts of Origen (in the *Hexapla*, the Bible in six languages) produced the opposite of what had been his intention. . . . The manuscripts disagree in innumerable details, and we have not yet been able to classify them in groups [Kaulen].

According to Tischendorf there are 30,000 variations in the various manuscripts of the New Testament that were handed down.

It is clear that a reliable tradition was important to the reliability of the accounts. The solidity of the faith again led to the survival of the Jewish people through the floods of the centuries and the enemies. Without the faithful scholars, who, following an obscure instinct, spent their lives in counting the more than forty thousand Alephs in the Bible, we would not have survived as a Jewish people.

This is how the secret works. It cannot be understood by one who calls the regulations and the abstractions of Jewish life "unreal" or "de-materializing." It was not a flight from reality, but this was the problem: either Jewry would dissolve through the people's accepting a simple life, or Judaism would be preserved, and then rules would have to be applied. Viewed from this point of view, it should be surprising that so much vitality and realism has remained alive among Jews. It is true that the means of preservation applied by the secret of the Jewish national instinct are restrictive and look sometimes like a dangerous *ressentiment*, but the secret itself, which dwells in the midst of those means, is impossible to estimate. It is part of the secret that at the very moment when the means of preservation seem to lose their strength, a new vista opens up—Israel.

Is this an accident? Is it fate? It is the secret which generates fate and the fortunate hour in the distant stars.

10

THE CHRISTIAN

GRACE OF GENERALIZATION:

PAUL AND JESUS

Clemens Ritter and Theodor Haecker

IT IS CUSTOMARY TO HOLD PAUL RESPONSIBLE FOR THE IDEA THAT there is only the one and the same way of grace for all men.

This is true as long as we stick to historical facts. But it is incorrect if behind the lights and shades of history we see the solitary and unseemly lamp of the soul in motion. It is true that Paul quite literally created the construction. Jesus himself mentioned hardly anything about it, but even this proves nothing, since we see Jesus only through the eyes of Paul. The Gospels which have come down to us were written after Paul. Paul himself believed in the Savior Christ. But this was his personal grace, his individual way, and thus religiously correct. But it is religiously incorrect to generalize this way and to require all men to follow it. Now the strange fact is that it was part of his personal state of grace to generalize as he did. He was wrong concerning those to whom he preached, but he was right in his preaching. Thus we come to the conclusion that the grace of generalization was to Paul his own most individual grace. Christianity emerged out of Judaism not only through a Jew but through that man's spiritual movement, which was, Jewishly speaking, religious and proper. The movement was Jewish, and only its petrification was Christian. Although that petrification had been intended, the intent was a movement in the Jewish sense.

As far as I know, nobody has ever tried to write a religious and dogmatic criticism of the figure of Paul from the point of view of believing Judaism. Nobody has ever drawn the line between what is Jewish in this great man and his belief in Christ which was to become his fate. Paul's belief seems so rigid and fanatical that it could be part of the history of Jewish thinking.

Recently Christians have challenged us twice to take a stand concerning Paul, the first Jew who believed in Christ. In Franz Blei's quarterly *Summa*, Clemens Ritter charged the leaders of today's Jewish Renaissance with neglecting the religious problem; namely, the question whether Jesus was the Messiah and God's son. Blei maintained in the article that Jews do not do anything to clarify their position towards the believing Christian. In his epilogue to Kierkegaard's *The Concept of the Chosen*, Theodor Haecker writes, "Since the Jews were chosen, they cannot be spared from coming to terms with Christianity, and this must be done seriously, in spirit and in truth, not in the manner of scholars, artists, philosophers, writers, liberals, . . . Zionists, esthetes, or whatever other subterfuges have been created in the last decades in order to avoid the religious Either –Or: is Christ the Messiah or not?"

The question is justified, and it is important to pose the problem in that manner, although the conceited style smells somehow of the inquisition and the stake. I do not avoid the religious question at all. On the contrary, it is for the sake of the question that this entire book has been written. The preceding chapters contain an answer which some may resent, but at least it does not justify the accusation of being ambiguous.

I do not argue with those who have a personal faith in Christ. Every honest belief is a divine grace granted individually, and rules, laws, and reason should respect it. Since my entire conviction concerns the miracle as a fulfilment and the climax of life, I would do wrong in exercising criticism where all general things become meaningless. No matter how paradoxical it may sound, individual Christian grace—the solution of an individual life problem through belief in Christ—is well compatible with the Jewish religious point of view. What I object to is the attempt to cure all men in one and the same manner, to save all people in one way. Although the starting point and the goal of that way may vary subjectively, it has been laid down from the beginning and objectively, so that it must contain the belief in Jesus as the Christ, the Son of God. Christianity is that attempt at a unification of grace. I have made it clear what I think of Christianity. The concluding chapters will throw greater light on my ideas.

Here I will add just a few words to explain why believing Judaism has to this day by-passed Paul, the author of the generalizing belief in Christ. First of all this by-passing is based on the entirely proper dogma that the grace of generalization has no place in Judaism. But since, as we shall see, Paul has also many Jewish elements, and elements which are imporant to Jewish religious feeling, the question arises again as to why we neglect what is the property of our people and what might still play a role within Judaism; for that intensive part of Paul's religiosity—the feeling of sin and the need for grace—remains important to us in spite of Paul's errors. It must take its proper place within our religious totality; and, properly viewed, it will lead to a strengthening of the religious force in the Jewish soul. How then can we explain this absolute indifference towards such a great figure? We cannot excuse it, yet we can explain it historically. The purely human reason is that Judaism has suffered so much because of Paul. It is difficult to mention his name without bitterness, in consideration for the terrible shame and the horrible misery brought upon us by the church established by Paul. For it was the church which deliberately poisoned the relations between Jews and non-Jews in the Diaspora, relations which at the start had been good ones. Instances can be culled from any book about the history of the Jews in the Middle Ages. What abominable council decisions, papal decrees, hatred and incitement, social oppression, the yellow badge of shame, confiscation of sacred literature, exploitation, inquisition, the fanaticism of the monastic orders, the lie of ritual murder, discrimination, and mass murder. And all this did not come spontaneously from the people—something which might perhaps be tolerated—but was organized by the rulers of the church whose entire wisdom comes from Paul. Generations have sighed under his name. "Whether this be divinely ordained or not, I leave to the insight of spiritual teachers," was stated by a simple city scribe of Breslau, reporting on pogroms instigated by Capistrano's sermons. Alas, it was as ungodly as the life of the innocent originator of all those horrors was godly. Only our poor human weakness cannot view all of this at one time. We must therefore apologize to Clemens Ritter and Theodor Haecker for the poor human weakness which reveals itself in the fact that those Jews, tortured horribly by Paul's successors, have not yet had the time to view objectively the phenomenon of the Jew, Paul, and to gain religious powers from that view. But if Ritter and Haecker should think that we have had plenty of time, I wish to point out that, in consideration of a report like the following, all the time in the world would not suffice to bring about the peace of mind needed for objective observation. Here then is an account of an incident, which is pertinent because it is useful to recall certain facts of life to the missionary spirits, to clarify an opposition to Christianity for certain conceited people who are just now threatening that "it won't go on like this for long. We shall not allow you to persist in your heretic lives." The account concerns a pogrom in Schaffhausen in 1401, following the rumor of a ritual murder.

"When, in 1401, a boy was found murdered in Diessenhofen, the rumor spread that the Jews were responsible for the crime, and another terrible persecution of the Jews started in our country. In Diessenhofen, Schaffhausen, and Winterthur the unhappy people were burned alive, nineteen of them in the last mentioned city alone. Since the city council of Zürich protected those who were in danger, they were only arrested temporarily. Here is a report on the statements made by witnesses during the trial at Schaffhausen:

"Since the Jews of Schaffhausen were burned, and some say that they confessed many things in the house in which they were burned, the servants who were present at the burning were examined. All of them swore by the saints that they told the truth.

"Albrech Mersburg said that he was present when the Jews were led away and burned. Three of them were tortured—Lembli, Manli and Hirz. They had to be taken to the fire in a wagon. Their legs had been cut open, and boiling pitch had been poured in the wounds. These were sewn up and cut open again. The soles of their feet were singed so that their bones were visible, and one of the tortured victims said, "I do not know what I confessed while being tortured." He also said that he did not know anything about it and that he was innocent. The same witnesses also testified that sharp objects were driven under the finger nails of the Jews, and the other Jews cried out and said that they would die innocent, and they told those of Schaffhausen that they were being treated as murderers and evildoers.

"Peter Ellend said: The three were tortured so badly that they had to be driven away in wagons, that they did not want to talk, and that other Jews called them 'You murderers, you evildoers!' The women asked the people to intercede for them with God, since they died innocently. They also said many other things, which he could not repeat.

"Diethelm Rinderknecht said: They tortured the Jews by their hands, by the back of their legs, and by their soles. They had to be driven away in wagons, and when they were taken out they said aloud that they were innocent.

"Hans Etter: The three were tortured, they had to be driven away in wagons; they did not want to say anything, and the women claimed to be innocent; they were singing.

"Hensli Sitz said that some of them had been tortured so badly that they had to be driven away in wagons, and all he heard being said was that they claimed to be innocent."

Paul's Life and Teachings

How Jewish was that life! We find nothing there of Scheler's "relaxation," nothing of the pomp and boredom of the Grail, no pre-Raphaelite idyll. Paul's was a life with the tension of an agitator and it had less in common with the lives of the hermits in the *Thebaid* than with the indefatigability of Lassalle (without his ambition and conceit), with that of Herzl, and with the miraculous energy of some of today's Russian leaders. Saul of Tarsus comes from the great family of Jewish ideologues who nurture their ideas with their very hearts in order to give life to those ideas.

We must of course remember that Saul's religious idea was much higher than any political activity with which it might be compared. And yet there is a parallel in the method—the personal agitation of a great organizer, concerned about every single member of each group, wooing every single man, happy with winning them over, and sad about those who fall off. Read the last part of the Letter to the Romans. What concern and care for the most minute details if they may serve the spreading of the idea, what love and cleverness, what energy and memory! And then—we are reminded of other great Jewish innovators—he had no fear of sinking below his own level. He did not limit himself to the top level of society, neither in regard to intelligence nor anything else. If the intelligentsia did not appear, he preached to those who come, without the slightest disappointment or lack of joy. He showed the same delight with propaganda and seriousness as if the most influential and clever people were on hand. An agitator of a lower level is always characterized by the fact that he adjusts his speech and action to those who are important. If they do not appear, he loses his interest, rattles off his speech, which is all he can do, and thus betrays his own insecurity and unbelief. But Herzl opened the first Zionist Congress as solemnly as if the participation had come up to his expectations. (The great authorities and the official leaders of Jewry had absented themselves.) Jesus spoke his parables to fishermen and publicans. The great propagandist was equally indifferent to the low level of his own activities. Herzl and his first friends personally addressed the envelopes to the invitation for the first Zionist Congress, and Paul sent his personal greetings and thanks to every individual Christian in the Roman community.

I commend unto you Phoebe our sister, which is a servant of the church which is at Cenchrea; that ye receive her in the Lord, as becometh saints, and that ye assist her in whatsoever business she hath need of you; for she hath been a succourer of many, and of myself also. Greet Priscilla and Aquila my helpers in Christ Jesus: who have for my life laid down their own necks; unto whom not only I give thanks, but also all the churches of the Gentiles. Likewise greet the church that is in their house. Salute my wellbeloved Epaenetus, who is the firstfruits of Achaia unto Christ. Greet Mary, who bestowed much labor on us. Salute Andronicus and Junia, my kinsmen, and my fellow prisoners, who are of note among the apostles, who also were in Christ before me. Greet Amplias my beloved in the Lord. Salute Urbane, our helper in Christ, and Stachys my beloved. Salute Apelles approved in Christ. Salute them which are of Aristobulus' household. Salute Herodion my kinsman. Greet them that are of the household of Narcissus, which are in the Lord. Salute Tryphena and Tryphosa, who labor in the Lord. Salute the beloved Persis, which labored much in the Lord. Salute Rufus chosen in the Lord, and his mother and mine. Salute Asyncritus, Phlegon, Hermas, Patrobas, Hermes, and the brethren which are with them. Salute Philologus and Julia, Nereus and his sister, and Olympas and all the saints which are with them. Salute one another with an holy kiss. The churches of Christ salute you.

Incidentally, in view of such warmth of life, we cannot understand how anyone could maintain that Paul was merely a mythological personality and never lived at all.

There was adventure in his missionary travels, which took him from Syria along the coast of Phoenicia and Asia Minor, through Macedonia and Greece, and back to Cyprus and Egypt. In Ephesus he defied an assembly that shouted at him for two hours, "Great is Artemis the Ephesian." In the second Letter to the Corinthians (11:-24ff.) he writes,

> Of the Jews five times received I forty stripes save one. Thrice was I beaten with rods, once was I stoned, thrice I suffered shipwreck, a night and a day I have been in the deep. In journeyings often, in perils of waters, in perils of robbers, in perils by mine own country-men, in perils by the heathen, in perils in the city, in perils in the wilderness, in perils in the sea, in perils among false brethren; in weariness and painfulness, in watchings often, in hunger and thirst, in fastings often, in cold and nakedness. Beside those things that are without, that which cometh upon me daily, the care of all the churches.

Judaism has produced that type more than once, starting with Moses, "the most troubled man on earth"; Rabbi Akiba, that indefatigable zealot and revolutionary; Rabbi Judah the Prince, the great patriarch and editor of the Mishna, who applied to himself the verse from Ecclesiastes, "Sweet is the sleep of the laborer, whether he eat little or much; but the wealth of the rich man does not allow him to sleep." He added: "We, who are concerned with the needs of men, may not even sleep because of this." To the same category of those provided with superhuman energies—without shedding human blood—belong also, *mutatis mutandis*, Jesus, Rabbi Gutmacher, Rabbi Mohilever, Marx, and Herzl. In other nations such an excess of tremendous life energies generated quite different types: the brutal, reckless "Renaissance Man," the "blond beast," Napoleon, Sforza, the Conquistadores, Tamerlane, the heroes of d'Annunzio's novels. Jews apparently do not have such an outlet to aggressiveness. They generate instead the type of the active martyr, the martyr to his work, to whom martyrdom is not an end in itself or the climax of his life but so to say a secondary concern, rather an accident, and yet unavoidable, because his life, which is bursting at the seams, a life in which he dies daily, is from the start directed towards that goal. But he does not know it, nor is he particularly interested in it. For all that interests him is his work. But no matter how immeasurably rich Judaism is in such heroes of humanity it cannot afford to give up a figure like Paul in the series of its great sons. We would be narrow-minded and petty if we were to exclude him in view of the consequences his actions led to without his own knowledge. No, what a touching figure in the midst of our best! In all his troubles and in all his enthusiasm he went on collecting funds for his original community, "the saints in Jerusalem." Without embarrassment he faced the derisive Athenians who "were only interested in talking and hearing of new things" and to whom he appeared ridiculous with his fervor, his teaching of the resurrection of the dead. In Corinth he worked for a Jewish tentmaker; for, possibly a Talmudic saying in mind, he insisted on supporting himself through manual labor, and he refused to be supported by the communities which he had founded. Thus we read in his Epistle to the Thessalonians: ". . . we behaved not ourselves disorderly among you, neither did we eat any man's bread for nought, but wrought with labor and travail night and day, that we might not be chargeable to any of you" (II Thessalonians 3:7f.). When addressing the communities he stressed that point again and again from different points of view. He was familiar with all means of persuasion, using at one time threats, at other times childish words of flattering, always youthful and filled with love, and yet afraid of becoming a martyr prematurely and without need. For this reason he defended himself bravely when facing the Roman officials and insisted on his civil rights at the proper moment, in order not to be flogged. Like a good lawyer he appealed to the Roman Emperor, and he was greatly skilled in utilizing the arguments between the Pharisees and the Sadducees for the purposes of his own trial. Even when in prison he preached and converted joyfully, even when taken out of there in order to address the most unlikely public, the degenerate "King" Agrippa, who made silly jokes, his harlot sister Berenice, and the plump Roman governor Festus, whose "non-Jewish head" cannot digest the Jewish philosophy of immortality. He interrupted Paul's beautiful speech, "Thou art crazy, Paul, many books have confused thy head." And Paul replied, "I am not crazy, revered Festus, but I speak words of truth and reason." And there sits the last Jewish king, blasé, detached, and yet he understands well what was going on, for after all he was a Jew! O what a scene! In all of this

Paul did not rely on anybody, a rugged individualist, not only on bad terms with the Jews but also with the Judeo-Christians, with Peter and the other apostles; following up his differing ideas to the last consequence, so that at the end he could not communicate with anybody but his own disciples and the proselytes of his particular brand. Strangely enough, at the end of his life, in Rome, he found himself again in the narrow circle of the Jews, and "the judges did not look at him the way those at Caesarea had done. Here he was just one of the prisoners from rebellious Judea, a member of the hated people of the Jews" (Zittel). Finally, what irony! he perished during a persecution of the Jews, perhaps while Rome was burning under Nero, and no distinction was made between "Paulinian Christians and anti-Paulinian Jews of the Law." For all of them were Jews, nothing but Jews! At least in death he thus seems united with the fate of his unhappy people! The New Testament is silent concerning the feelings of his last days. Yet one of his last words that came down to us is moved by the Jewish spirit. "It was necessary for me to appeal to the Emperor, but not to complain of my own people." I was over thirty years old when I became for the first time acquainted with that life by reading the history of the apostles. It seemed familiar to me. Paul's life did not arise towards me from the book, but rather vice versa. We might say that in our own days we have seen Jewish analogies to that life.

Here is that man's teaching, as it emerged from his basic feelings.

Strongly impressed in his soul is the dichotomy of inclination and duty, between the instinct and that which has been recognized as good. This is his primary life experience, and he always comes back to it. Thus Romans 7:14ff:

> For we know that the law is spiritual: but I am carnal, sold under sin. For that which I do I allow not. For what I would, I do not; but what I hate, that do I. If then I do that which I would not, I consent unto the law that it is good. Now then it is no more I that do it, but sin that dwelleth in me. For I know that in me (that is, in my flesh) dwelleth no good thing; for to will is present with me; but how to perform that which is good I find not. For the good that I would I do not: but the evil which I would not, that I do. Now if I do that I would not, it is no more I that do it, but sin that dwelleth in me. I find then a law, when I would do good, evil is present with me. For I delight in the law of God after the inward man: But

I see another law in my members, warring against the law of my mind, and bringing me into captivity to the law of sin which is in my members. O wretched man that I am! Who shall deliver me from the body of this death?

The law cannot do that. For the law only tells me what to do, but it does not give me the means to do it fully, which means with devotion and joy. It only shows that I cannot fulfill it properly. Law leads to the "knowledge of sin," or (Romans 7:7f.), ". . . I had not known sin but by the law: for I had not known lust, except the law had said: Thou shalt not covet. But sin, taking occasion by the commandment, wrought in me all manner of concupiscence. For without the law sin was dead." This means, of course, that only consciousness of sin provides the proper life, and the torturing feeling of the presence, but this is expressed with so much despair that the paradox of honesty can be understood fully only by him who has himself suffered under a similar burden of imperfection and longing. I do not understand how in his *History of the Jews* Graetz can render that thought as follows: "Without the law men would have remained ignorant of lust." (Paul states clearly that men would not have become *conscious* of it!) And further: "Only through the law 'Thou shalt not covet' was coveting aroused." And again: "Paul thought that moral laws were obstacles on the road to salvation." He says this nowhere, nor can it be deduced from the passages quoted. On the contrary, consciousness of sin is the first step towards salvation. For this reason the law gives the Jews a certain advantage, and thus (see Romans 1:16 and 5:20) they were the first to receive the Gospel, and only afterwards the Greek. "The law has intervened so that transgression may be complete. Where sin is complete, grace has become abundant"; that is, where natural drives collide with a duty strongly felt. Grace can be fully received where drives and duty coincide.

Paul did not see at all in the law, and certainly not in moral law, a handicap to salvation. He said only that it was not enough, and this is the basic Jewish view, as presented above. I do not know whether by "laws" and "works of the law" he meant only rituals or whether he meant also moral laws and good deeds. It is sure he also demanded good deeds:

For ye know what commandments we gave you by the Lord Jesus. For this is the will of God, even your sanctification, that you should abstain from fornication. That every one of you should know how

to possess his vessel in sanctification and honor, not in the lust of
concupiscence, even as the Gentiles which know not God, that no
one go beyond and defraud his brother in any matter . . . [II Thessalonians 4:2ff.]

He thus seems to insist on the doctrine which is the very core of
Judaism: that, if necessary, one must do what is right even without
joy and against one's own inclination, although unfortunately this is
not the highest level of morality. But it must be done in any case.
Thus does Paul speak up against the works of the flesh (Galatians
5:19ff.; Romans 1:22ff.; I Corinthians 6:9ff.): "Know ye not that
the unrighteous shall not inherit the Kingdom of God? Be not de-
ceived: neither fornicators, nor idolaters, nor adulterers, nor effemi-
nate, nor abusers of themselves with mankind, nor thieves, nor covet-
ous, nor drunkards, nor revilers, nor extortioners, shall inherit the
Kingdom of God." This could not have been expressed more clearly
and is in the same line with the laws and prohibitions of Moses. There
is nothing here of Luther's rejection of "good deeds," of Ricarda
Huch's indulgence of sins, of Scheler's relaxation. In the first Epistle
to Timothy there is no end to Thou Shalt. Paul opens up an entire
moral code. In the first Epistle to the Corinthians (Chapter 11) we
are even instructed concerning rites. A man is supposed to pray with
his head uncovered, the woman's head should be covered; a detailed
reason is given. That women should be quiet in the "assemblies" is
demanded with reference to the law (Chapter 14), accompanied by
a ceremonial prescription concerning the sacred repast. Men cannot
live without customs, but Amos (5:21ff.) and Isaiah (1:11ff.) had
already pointed out that ceremonies are not the most important thing.
To repeat, up to this point there seems to be no difference between
Paul's teaching and what I have defined in this book as Judaism. That
Paul considered circumcision and other rites to be irrelevant has to
do with the basic conflict of his life, about which I shall have to say
more later on. He certainly does not say anywhere that dutiful acts
are irrelevant or sinful or of the devil, but only impossible, which
means not entirely possible without grace.

The central point of his existence has to do with the question of
how he obtained that grace.

The entire life of that disciple and son of a Pharisee centers around
two main axes—rage and tenderness. Yes, Paul was indeed ruthless,
and full of passion. He had a definite need for letting off steam. Only

so can we understand his tremendous activity and the inexhaustible mobility of his existence. How powerful was the energy of wrath and activity that he harbored in himself can be seen not only in the hateful outbursts before his conversion but also from occasional later incidents. If the terrible and merciless words which he hurled at the magician Elymas, the threatening words addressed to the Jews, the first Christians and vacillating communities, or the "heated struggle" during which he separated himself unyieldingly from John Mark— if all of these are documents of the time in which he had already been purified by the Jesus experience and thus "in grace," then we can pretty well figure out what must have gone on in that boiling heart before the soothing influence of the heavens. And yet it is strange that his passion was always coupled with an equally great yearning for love, that its actual goals were love and tenderness. For all that the most secret and the strongest power of his soul wanted was to be a giver, to make others happy, to see comforted faces around him, grateful eyes that, saved from unspeakable suffering, look up to him in divine love. This is all he wants—the noblest and manliest quality of giving love and of receiving redeeming gratitude, this is what his breast feels with a burning wish. The normal sexual path seems to be barred to him. Once he speaks mysteriously of the "thorn in flesh," of a sickness. A "Satanic angel came to slap my face so that I should not be conceited. Therefore I called thrice on the Lord to leave me. And he said: My grace is enough unto thee. For strength perfects itself through weakness." Concerning erotic things, which strangely enough he identified with "troubles to the flesh," he writes, in the First Epistle to the Corinthians, curiously weighing things, ambiguously and, contrary to his nature, without fire and decisiveness. Nor does he claim here immediate certainty, revelation of the Lord, but he relies on his opinion and admits at the same time that he is a disinterested outsider; he wishes that all were like him, and yet he makes concessions to that different world. I hardly need to add that I do not consider this psycho-physical constitution of the man to be decisive, nor do such statements have a Freudian medical conclusiveness. Only a superficial materialism would see in Paul's office sublimated sexuality, and explain that the erotic way out was barred to him. No, his office was the primary factor, a choice of grace dependent solely on the spirit and on God. But Freud is right to that extent that once a decision has been made on another level, sexual-pathological motives can add to it psychic energies, so that the stream of the soul increases in speed, if it is to use one way out to break through, if it is unable to send forth some of its waters another way. With this in mind, we might point out that Paul, when speaking of his relation to his disciples, does often use images from the sexual sphere, and that his life element, his love, pours out over his disciples and his communities with an intensity which may have been strengthened through obstacles encountered elsewhere. When recommending a converted slave to Philemon, he observed: "Look at me—I, Paul, an old man, and now also a prisoner of Jesus Christ, I am imploring you for the sake of my child, whom I have brought forth in my chains, Onesimus, who once was of little value to thee, but who is now highly valuable to thee and me." At another occasion he referred to "my children for whom I have labored again." Or: "I have begotten you in Jesus Christ through the Gospel." "We have appeared among you as tenderly as a mother who cares for her children. Thus have we been attracted to you, not only to offer you the Gospel of God but even our life; for we love you."

Into what situation has this soul been pressed, which only wanted to love and to give itself away? "Strictly trained in the law of the fathers, at the feet of Gamaliel," his passionate disposition, his will not to remain in the abstract but to turn his feelings seriously into deeds, causes him to persecute the first Christians in Jerusalem. "He destroyed the community, invaded the homes, dragged men and women away, and had them thrown into jail." Being jealous for the law, he is commanded to act thus by the duty which he follows with the very passion of his soul. Rage, fire, eternal rebellion—this is what he needs. But tenderness, love, and being loved? He would like to be surrounded by happy and comforted faces, and he looks into weeping and disturbed eyes which hate him as the one who disturbs their peace. His misfortune is that he has that power, and that he must utilize it dutifully. His blood compels him to bring salvation, while his duty tells him to bring suffering. A symbol of that terrible collision, he is present at the martyrdom of Stephen. Those who stone the martyr place their garments at his feet, which indicates that he led the entire action, although he cannot bring himself to lending a hand. This shows the tear in his heart. He tries to do his duty, but he can never do so fully, in spite of the force he applies to his feelings of love, for what his reason calls law is in such a sharp contrast with his natural disposition. He is a witness to his own demoralization. For if duty is only accompanied by passion and energy, whereas love works against it, the soul degenerates and loses its impetus, it can only imitate duty in a mechanical way, deprived of life and sensation. But Paul wants to live in his duty, he does not want to shirk his sacred task nor to tire. Out of such tortures we can understand his later insight which tells him that the law is not sufficient for salvation, and that one can never do it fully. Then he is sent to Damascus with the order to arrest the "Messianists" in the synagogue and to chain men and women in order to take them to Jerusalem. He was torn out of his surroundings and out of his office, which had perhaps become rigid already. He was lonesome when together with his own group, lonesome after so many excitements, about which he had time to meditate while on his journey, time to consider all details and possibilities. Terrible days lay ahead, and now he might have to act for the first time on his own responsibility. When thinking of the inevitable duty and of the horrid scenes of the future, he may well have accused himself in these words: "Alas, why do I not suffer instead of causing others to suffer? Why am I not among the persecuted instead of being among the persecutors?" Until his heart stopped, and his tortured senses refused to serve further and, out of anxiety and frustration, the vision breaks forth: "Saul, Saul, why doest thou persecute me? He said: Who art thou, lord? And he replied: I am Jesus, whom thou persecutest." Paul fell to the ground and was led to Damascus, where for three days he was blind, refusing to eat and to drink. Then he betook himself to the leader of the persecuted, but not in order to destroy but to join the community of those who were threatened by dangers and arrest. The crisis was solved. Supported by the vision—he was to recall it again and again to the end of his life—he started on a new life.

After having made common cause with the powerless Judeo-Christians, who were oppressed everywhere, all the forces of his soul can go into action, for all of them have the same goal, and do not oppose the demands of duty any longer. For the new duty says: Be as jealous for Jesus as you had been for the law. Now, fortunately, he is not provided any longer with instruments of power—swords, trials, jails—but only with means of love and the spirit. He may take up the cause of the weak. He may bring comfort, tenderness, and refreshment to all, and all his energies are spent in spreading such gifts of love. He was entitled to see grace in that new harmonious order. For grace is the coincidence of inclination and duty. He admits that he was lucky in being allowed to be on the side of the oppressed: "Therefore do I feel well in weaknesses, mistreatments, in despair, persecutions, and distress, for the sake of Christ. For when I am weak, I am strong." Now a newly recognized duty bids him do what he would have done anyhow out of his own: love, to bring love, to arouse love, and to suffer for love's sake. It is not only this wish of love but other wishes of the heart too which find their due place in the new order. He can put his energy to use in the organization of new communities, and his always raging soul against the conservative Jews. This was harmless enough, since the new political situation did not allow murder or jailings. He may rage even against bad communities, like the Corinthians, but all this can be done in love ("Shall I come to you with the stick or with love and the spirit of mildness?") The tiniest parts of his soul have been changed so that each of them can be active at its new place without interfering with others, as had been the case before. Unity has been achieved. This explains the great vitality in all his statements, the energy in standing up to humiliation and suffering, the immortal hymn to love, dictated by his immeasurable happiness:

> Love is long-suffering, love is good, love is not jealous, it does not violate customs, it does not look for advantages, it cannot be incited, it does not take revenge, it is not happy with injustice but with truth. It covers up everything, it believes everything, hopes for everything, tolerates everything. Love never succumbs . . .

When did that great man actually take the step that was to separate him forever from the sphere of Judaism? It was not the fact that he brought the good tidings to the pagans. For that mission to the heathen, that universalism, was an inheritance from ancient Jewish times. The prophets had said it again and again: "I make of thee a light to the nations," "listen to me, ye nations, hearken, ye islands." Nor is it important that, as I shall discuss later, Paul's rejection of this world gave Jewish universalism a particular and false variation. The inspired apostle's path through the pagan world is deeply Jewish. Not only that, the energy of his propaganda is of the noblest Jewish kind, but more so the self-denying emphasis with which he objects to any Jewish privileges. He states in his sermon that Jews and pagans are alike. Since, at that time, Judaism was some kind of moral aristocracy and, in the sphere of the spirit, God's court, it is fitting to the real democrat to stretch out his hand to the ones below. At that time the will to be together with others was a real resignation and a descent; today, when Judaism is despised and close to dissolution, this would be undue eagerness. Those who want to minimize Paul's figure often maintain that he went to the pagans because the Jews did not want to accept his teaching. This I cannot believe. Even if all Jews had embraced the Gospel, Paul would have gone to the heathen because of his anti-aristocratic and universalist motives.

The separation must have been caused by something much deeper. So far I have failed to explain why it was just the Jesus experience (the vision) which was empowered to change Paul's heart so much, and to provide him with a new duty, which means the belief in a duty which then ran parallel to his drives. That central circumstance can of course not be explained at all, since it is *the* miracle, something which cannot be handled rationally. Only some side phenomena are accessible to a slight touch. Thus it seems to me that the image of Jesus who suffered out of love had all the prerequisites for creating in Paul the longing for suffering and for teaching him the mistake of making others suffer. Whether he had only heard about Jesus or had actually seen him (II Corinthians 5:17), his image appeared to him as something sweet—the fate of being persecuted, to give comfort with all one's strength, to be active and yet to remain innocent. His model gave him the belief in the possibility of such a fate, just as we may have been sustained in many a night of despair by remembering a selfless, pure, and upright friend. That in the midst of the chaos created by human cowardice and craftiness such a thing is possible—truthfulness, strength, and the will to do good by disregarding material advantages—this is sweeter than anything else, it triumphs over our despair which sometimes fools us into believing that everything is but lies and emptiness. But in Paul's case the "nightly consolation" was of a longer duration—it lasted a lifetime. That it had the power to turn his entire inner constellation upside down was the divine grace, without which his struggle would have been in vain.

Now a unity arose in his soul. He did not believe in redemption by his faith in the pattern of Jesus, but immediately through Jesus' deed, through his sacrificial death. Not that that death gave Paul the courage to sacrifice himself, too, and showed him the way; but Jesus had died immediately for him, and not only for him—this was his further conclusion—but for all of mankind. It was this faith—man can be saved by Jesus' sacrificial death—which he called "grace." Those who had that faith lived in grace, and only through that faith could everybody attain grace. My own Jewish way of thinking tells me that there are as many ways to grace as there are human beings endowed with grace; thus for Rabbi Elihu Gutmacher it was the rise and the inner appropriation of Zionism, for Dante it was "Beatrice" and the clinging to her. But Paul knew only one way for all men—the faith in justification through Jesus' suffering. Thus the free grace of an infinite God is narrowed into a limited belief in an historically determined event. That event, having become an experience to Paul, had from then on also to become an experience for all mankind. Consequently, Jesus had to become "the son of God," a term which, coming from Jesus, meant only familiarity with and closeness to God, as evident from many Hebrew prayers current to this day; furthermore, eschatological ideas arose; and, since the anticipated end of the world and the Last Judgment did not materialize, everything was interpreted spiritually. These stages in the development of Christianity have been described frequently. But I have nowhere found the first step—Paul's idea to deprive his personal experience of grace of its individual character, and to force it upon all mankind. This started the false foundation of Christianity, and here is the key for uncounted confusions. We must be honest enough to admit that it was not all the fault of successive generations, but that Paul himself is responsible for the first step on the way down, although he was not conscious of it. For his faith was his own experience, and we can well understand that, compared with that experience, the entire visible world vanished, that "through the cross of our Lord Jesus Christ he was crucified to the world, and the world was crucified to him." It is this experience which cannot be imitated, for it occurred on his own path, not on that of other people, who, chosen for another grace, wait in vain if they expect grace from this one direction exclusively. All that other people could learn from him—and falsely so—was his disinterest in other this-worldly experiences. That disinterest had been meaningful to Paul, since he had been enriched by the decisive and inspiring factor of his existence, whereas with his successors this disinterest—lacking the great experience—led to disinterest in everything, to the rejection of this world. Traces can already be found with Paul. He is already the enemy of the flesh, and this in a very general way, without the more delicate and tragic problems of Judaism; and, although several statements of his abound with life, in others he is a pure ascetic, and his *"argumentatio ex negative"*—namely, that he must fight circumcision since otherwise he would not be persecuted (Galatians 5:11)—sounds modern, a case of inverted egocentrism. This is his weakness, and later on it was to grow into gigantic proportions. Here starts the deceptive supremacy of the "noble misfortune." For we have to pay a penalty if we change grace from an immediate relationship between God and man, which allows material things to remain in their proper places, into a relationship to a godly man, a relationship which is only halfway metaphysical. Divine grace as an entirely metaphysical and incomprehensible fact does not disturb the earthly proportions of light but illumines everything uniformly. But a grace which comes through the deed of a divine man comes down on earth like a meteor, spreading light and darkness, disturbing all magnetic needles, stopping all growth. We may believe in divine grace and still go on doing our work on earth humbly. But if the son of God has himself intervened in that work, I have become superfluous and my work unnecessary. The spirit has expropriated the flesh. Whatever else happens is unimportant and irrelevant.

A final word concerning his propaganda. He violated the idea of Judaism not by going to the heathen but in the way he went there. He went in complete disinterest in anything earthly, with no consideration for the political situation and the national preservation of Jewry, which alone guarantees the preservation of essential spiritual powers. In every nation there exists such an irreplaceable spiritual quality, and by eradicating a nation the world becomes as impoverished as when an individual experiences the decline of a natural feeling. The man who saw the entire world crucified tried to eliminate the natural factor radically and to overlook the natural differences and advantages of nations. From Paul's point of view it would have been possible to establish in all pagan countries communities willing to accept Jewish-Christian doctrines. Thus the Jewish teachings could have been integrated with national dispositions to form new entities; and Judaism, even after accepting "the grace of Christ," could have retained its national and racial qualities. All nations that differed in the flesh but were related through Christ could have been united in one "league of nations." Instead, Paul directed himself towards a hodgepodge and attacked the Jewish teachers who at that time, urged by a proper instinct, emphasized more than ever the preservation of certain forms, which in the face of the threatening political downfall were to safeguard the spiritual life of Judaism for millennia. Paulinian wishy-washy thinking can be refuted by the events of the year 70—the destruction of the Jewish State—which Paul was not destined to see. Paul did not think of dissolving Judaism; if he had been asked, he might well have opted for the maintenance of the Jewish nation, provided that its Jews believed in Christ. But since he was generally disinterested in affairs of this world, he was not concerned with providing the necessary means for all eventualities. As seen from Romans 11:25ff., the eternal survival of Israel and Zion was taken for granted by him. Even as an apostle to the heathen, and with all his hatred for the unconverted Jews, he had a warm feeling for them. Yet he did not see the danger. At his time the Jewish community still flourished, and complete dispersal was not foreseen. But if the entire nation had followed him without the outward forms as prescribed by the sages of those times, complete assimilation would not have been avoidable after the political downfall of the state. Therefore the Mishnaic teachers who lived during the period of the early Christians were entirely right to oppose—at a time of complete political disorder—those who, in their alienation from the world, wanted to destroy the last bulwark of national cohesion, the Jewish law (Halachah). From that time stems the statement: "In all the world God has only dwelling place—the four cubits of His Halacha." Those four cubits were not to be tampered with. Therefore Paul and his memory were rejected by his contemporaries. Today we may call this a tragedy, although he saw in it salvation—that his personal grace was at cross purposes with the state of his people, which required different support.

Strictly speaking, Paul did not make the mistake that we have called the basic error of Christianity. He did not say that on earth there is only noble misfortune, compared to which avoidable misfortune, placed in human freedom, lost all importance. For himself he accepted the fullness of the experience, lived a full life, and received grace, in whatever form it was offered to him. But as far as others were concerned, they were told by him which road to grace to take. But since not everybody started out as a persecutor of sects, not everyone can be changed at this juncture. Nor does such a change always lead to a propaganda activity, which, in Paul's case, took its place next to noble misfortune. But his teaching points out to all his successors noble misfortune exclusively, and in addition gives faulty information concerning the road to be followed. Even in his own case, the idea that Jesus' death had redeemed him from all sins made him underestimate his own place before God. For Paul's grace was not really derived from the fact that Jesus had died at the cross; rather, his grace came directly from God, its essence being that that death on the cross so overwhelmed Paul—or better, that Paul received so much power to harbor that death faithfully within his soul—that his heart could gain a new duty in harmony with his secret desire. In any case, the idea of vicarage meant to Paul a real experience which allowed him to take the meaninglessness of everything else in stride. His successors had to make do with that meaninglessness. This was an unforeseen confirmation of Paul's statement: "One hath died for all, therefore all of them have died."

Jesus of Nazareth

Every Jew, whether he is a believer or a non-believer, is placed by the believing Christian before the following dilemma:

Since Jesus called himself the son of God, two possibilities arise: If we assume Jesus to have spoken the truth, Clemens Ritter was right in stating as follows: "From the Christian point of view this is the ambiguous position of the Jew: the son of God has appeared among them. The son of God has been put to death by them. The two sides of this paradox explain their greatness and their downfall." In that case the entire history of the Jews is a gross error and a crime. It means that all prophets had the appearance of the son of God in mind as the unique moment in the history of mankind, after many preparations the Jewish people were eventually "chosen," God's incarnated majesty appeared among them and in their own country, speaking, of all languages in the world, Hebrew and Aramaic—and yet it was the Jews who failed to recognize God, who rejected and betrayed Him. What can the Jew of today do but hurriedly leave that accursed community? If Jesus spoke the truth, Jews must become Christians. Nothing else is possible. If Jesus lied in claiming to be the son of God, he was either a lunatic or a traitor. We cannot see in him an honest, important, and respectable man, in view of the fact that he had maintained himself to be the son of God. If this is true, the Jew must become a Christian; if not, the Jew must reject him instead of admiring "primitive Christianity."

To a consistent Christian it must therefore be abominable to hear it said by a Zionist that Jesus is important to us Jews not as an object but as a subject of religiosity. Such a Christian must ask himself: "How can a liar, who falsely ascribes to himself the attribute of divinity, be considered the subject of religiosity? Is this not merely a nice excuse, a flight from decision?"

Whatever I have said so far concerning the apostle Paul questions the questioning of the believing Christian. To us Jews the seemingly inevitable dilemma of the believing Christians is unimportant. We have a third way of coming again and again back to the pure and individual divine grace, instead of having recourse to the belief in Christ.

Here then is that third way: We see in Paul's faith in Christ his individual way to grace, which we cannot criticize any further. But we must reject objective claims which go beyond that.

The understanding and the explanation assumed here are not a psychological understanding or explanation. This must be emphasized, because nowadays explanations are often suspected of being psychologisms. But only those psychologisms must be rejected which reduce psychic facts to a lower level, which "explain" relations to a higher world by referring to needs, nerves, unconscious desires, and material motives. Thus higher processes, directed towards infinity, are traced back to the lower and finite work of the soul. A man's extraordinary enthusiasm for an idea is "explained" by pointing to his surroundings, his education, and his sexuality. It is ridiculous and shameful first to omit what cannot be explained—the idea—then to explain that which can easily be explained in many different ways, namely, what idea has taken possession of man, and under what circumstances. Thus psychologism claims to have explained the entire phenomenon, including that part which had at first been excluded. Psychologism is at work whenever a factor is traced back to something known, without consideration for individual features. The reader should be aware of the fact that my analysis of Paul did not deal with his secret. That analysis did not go back to what is known, to lower sensations which can somehow be explained, but to the unknown, to that which can be explained least—pure and individual divine grace.

Paul believed that Jesus was the son of God, sent out to eradicate sins and to redeem mankind. Did Jesus himself believe that? Did he believe himself to be the Christ?

We certainly see Jesus only through Paul's temperament. Paul's epistles antedate the Gospels, and certainly the Greek translation which has come down to us. But Jesus spoke Aramaic. Nobody can deny that the Gospel of Saint John is greatly influenced by Alexandrian philosophy and is thus a multi-colored, unreliable work. But even the synoptic Gospels have gone through the school of Paul. This means that even what has been reported by the closest witnesses had to pass through the censorship of Paulinian construction.

But then "the dilemma of the consistent Christian" disappears. We do not have to answer the question whether Jesus told the truth when he called himself the son of God. Perhaps it was not he who made that statement but only Paul. To him that claim was a God-given grace; as such it is not debatable, since it makes no sense to try to understand someone's most individual affairs. And even the spreading of the tidings is part of that grace. We cannot pass judgment on the value of Paul's grace for others. So far as it has to be rejected, it has been discussed in previous passages.

In a certain sense this means that I am evading a discussion of Jesus. This is so because I do not wish to criticize a man who is the object of religious veneration for many people, and the source of true grace for some. Those who really believe and share in the grace of Christ will not be offended by the following lines, for the Jesus who appears in them is not theirs.

I am of the opinion that the historical Jesus did not call himself the son of God in the exclusive sense which the church preaches—that God has just once become man. "The son of God" is not typical to the New Testament. In the Old Testament that phrase is used frequently in order to describe an intimate and proper relation to God. This is the case in the Book of Hosea, in Psalms 2 and 82, and in II Samuel chapter 7. Furthermore it is strange that the term "son of God" in its exact and Christian sense is only found in John with any frequency, whereas those passages in the synoptic Gospels which mention it may well be later interpolations, and some earlier sources seem to be opposed to John. Thus, in the Acts of the Apostles, Jesus is simply called "the righteous one" (22:14), in the First Epistle to Timothy "the man," in the synoptic Gospels often "the prophet," and in Luke (18:19) Jesus clearly distinguishes himself from God. This is just one of the contradictions within the sources.

Therefore we cannot really know whether Jesus called himself the son of God in the sense adopted by the church. But Jesus may have called himself the Messiah. This is not non-Jewish, even if the mission fails. Thus Rabbi Akiba saw in the war hero Bar Kochba the Messiah, and the unfortunate outcome of Hadrian's war did not harm the reputation of the great teacher. In those days redemption was required and expected, since the Roman rule made life unbearable. Everywhere it was believed that the times had been fulfilled, and the Kingdom of God had arrived. Jesus was one of those who believed themselves strong enough to bring about that kingdom. We cannot understand how he could believe that so firmly, but then we cannot understand any individual grace. How firm his belief in himself and in his Messianic mission was, how deeply convinced he was of being the son of God in that sense can be well deduced from the consistency and the harmonious security of his short life. It is this peace of mind which impresses the quiet reader of the Gospels; there is a personal coloration of the accounts in a way not found in any other biography. What an idyll on the shore of the Sea of Galilee, where the most important things happened in infinite softness. Although his entire life had to end in a catastrophe, we do not have the obscurity and the abruptness of Paul, no breaking point, no forcefulness. Nothing else was so clear, so self-understood, so tender—in spite of all firmness—as that life which was directed towards the greatest thing, and at no time later has mildness been found so well integrated with tragedy, and sweetness with immensity. What lightness in the strict idea of leadership, which comes to him so naturally. As Paul leaves Jerusalem for splinter groups, so does Jesus long for Jerusalem, for the common cause of his people and the center of mankind. There is never a dichotomy between his mission and his will, between inclination and duty. The tempter in the wilderness, Gethsemane—this passes so easily that it may not even be called a serious battle. The moment the conflict arises, it has already been eliminated. One might be tempted to say that here grace has reached its highest intensity. In spite of great suffering, happiness hovers above the figure that guided earthly and heavenly things into one direction. And yet earthly things were not absent. The parables show a man who is well acquainted with human beings, their drives and their professions. But he does not know everyday life, the annoyance of banality. For everyday life is here integrated with the highest things—animals, trees, the landscape, the fig and the thistle, rain, sand, the peasant, mustard seed, yeast, the pearl fisher, the money lender, the prodigal son and the wealthy administrator, oil and wheat, purple and byssus—all elements of daily life have a share in his knowledge of divine things. His speeches teach us what the "this-worldly miracle" is. He is not an angry ascete, he accepts the ointment from the hands of the pious woman, and he wishes his disciples to be merry in the presence of the bridegroom.

Regarding the parables it should be added that those of the Talmud not only have the same vividness as the ones spoken by Jesus but they share a deep national analogy of style. In the Talmud, which has been so often slandered, and which is widely unknown, we find the same material in the parables: the king, the loyal and the disloyal servant, the manager, the fox and the fish, the economy with interest and the repayment of debts, sowing and harvesting, trade and manual labor. The same raw material, the same vivid style, which grasps things with its strange ideas. To Jesus' parables of the camel and the needle's eye, of the splinter and the beam in man's eye, parables which are so unforgettable because of their remarkable strangeness—to these parables we should compare that Talmudic passage where an easy death, the soft exhalation of the soul, "death by the kiss of God," appears "as if one pulled a hair out of milk," whereas painful death is one in which the soul leaves the body "as if one pulled a thorn out of a hide of wool." There are even literal likenesses by the dozens. But just because their ideas were apparently independent from each other, the parallel originality and the common impulse are even stronger.

Starting out from the style, our attention goes to what Jesus has in common with the great men of our people. What distinguishes him from them has already been mentioned: the serene certainty which shines above all the terrible seriousness and the horrors of his life like the breath of youth. We cannot penetrate that personal atmosphere of the man, which he owes to his individual grace. To try to penetrate it would be an act of impiety—not only in this case, which happens to be that of Jesus, but in all cases. The power of divine grace cannot be grasped rationally, and it is quite possible that such a power can work miracles, visible miracles in the strictest sense of the word, which means reversals in the course of nature and causality. But this must not blind our eyes regarding what is of a national and common character, side by side with personal particularities. Only a rabid anti-Semite fails to see in Jesus what is typically Jewish. He appears as the Messiah, for he wants to save Jewry. Now some Christian theologians maintain that the Jewish ideal of the Messiah was a political one, dealing with a victorious Jewish king, who wishes to reestablish the independence of the Jews and to chase the Romans out. This ideal does indeed exist. But side by side with it there is the reflection that in view of the terrifying Roman supremacy all resistance was useless. A reading of certain passages in Josephus' books will confirm that view. Jesus was one of those who thought that the Jews could be saved only through the spirit. Several centuries later that same thought inspired Rabbi Yochanan ben Zakkai, when, after the fall of Jerusalem, he asked of the conquerors only one thing—to be allowed to teach the Torah in a house of study at Yabneh. That house of study was to outlive the Roman throne by centuries. It is still alive, and we Jews live by its power. Jesus chose a similar way— salvation through inner purity, through repentance and intensification, through "fences" around the law. The Sermon on the Mount says it again and again: The Law commands this or that, but I am giving you an even stricter order. He inclined to interpret the law in a more stringent way. He did not abolish the law but made its observance more difficult, corresponding to the critical situation of Judaism since it could only be saved by pulling itself together. He wanted to be strict and refine moral sentiments. This has happened frequently in our spiritual history. Thus Rabbi Akiba considered a greeting usury, if the debtor had not previously been that friendly towards the creditor. The same teacher admonished his congregants to visit the sick as an act of loving one's fellow man, since failure to do so was considered tantamount to shedding blood, and shedding blood means "a diminution of the divine image." Is this not exactly what we read in the Sermon on the Mount? "Ye have heard that it was said by them of old time: Thou shalt not kill; and whosoever shall kill shall be in danger of the judgment. But I say unto you That whosoever is angry with his brother without a cause shall be in danger of the judgment." Jesus taught that nothing shall be taken away from the law. He adds; he does not abolish. Unlike Paul, he is not indifferent to customs. This is so because his personal grace differs from that of Paul. He lives in an even light, whereas Paul knows only one event illumined by lightning, and everything else in fog and obscurity, worthy to be forgotten. When Jesus scolded the Pharisees for "tithing mint and rue and all manner of herbs and passing over judgment and the love of God" (Luke 11:32), he added: "these ought ye to have done, and not to leave the other undone." Thus tithing was to him an important custom and law. No trace here of the negation of this world, of the dissolution of the Jewish community. On the contrary—the thought that, by strict observance of the law and by turning inward, the menacing doom can be avoided is a genuinely Jewish one; it recurs frequently and was particularly appropriate in those days, when the downfall of the State was imminent. Rabbi Meir stated: "Great is repentance; for the sake of one man who repents the whole world is forgiven." In the Talmud we are told of a man who for forty years partook only of the juice of figs in order to forestall the fall of Jerusalem. In that connection Rabbi Yochanan ben Zakkai said to the Roman Emperor Vespasian: "If there had only been two like him, the city would have been saved." Even the idea of vicarious participation has its Jewish analogies, as in Isaiah's famous chapter 53. Indeed those who were close to the generation of Jesus considered him to be a part of Jewish spiritual history. Thus we are told that Rabbi Akiba reported to Rabbi Eliezer about a Scriptural interpretation given to him by a disciple of Jesus of Nazareth, and that he liked that explanation (of Micah 1:7). Although we are told in that connection not to associate wih Judeo-Christians, the very prohibition presupposes a close communication in spiritual matters at that time.

Jesus apparently never emphasized the Paulinian idea that only through his own sacrificial death could men be saved. We find such ideas for the first time in the Gospel of Saint John. Of course Jesus' thought that everything was coming to an end may have tempted many to neglect their daily work and "ignoble misfortune." But he was not yet as unpolitical as Paul. The Jewish Temple, it is true, was to be destroyed, but also to be rebuilt. Similar prophecies had previously been made by Isaiah, Ezekiel, and others. In spite of later interpolations into the synoptic Gospels, no one-sided restriction to "noble misfortune" could be achieved. There was no disinterest in this world nor in the natural differences among nations or within one's own nation. A strange and moving proof comes from a Talmudic passage, which did not pass the censor. There we are told that Jesus was indeed one of the three worst persecutors of the Jewish people. One commentator places his ghost next to the ones of Balaam and Titus in the netherworld. He asks them what to do in order to gain greatness in the world. Whereas Balaam and Titus advise him to hate the Jews and to annihilate them, Jesus counsels to love them and to be kind to them, to which the Talmud adds: "Come and see the difference between a traitor in Israel and the prophets of the world!" In Matthew it is stated unequivocally that Jesus believed himself to be sent only "to the lost sheep of the House of Israel." "It will not do to take bread away from children and to throw it to the dogs." To his apostles Jesus said: "Do not travel the roads of the heathen and do not enter the cities of the Samaritans, but go ye rather to the lost sheep of the House of Israel." This in spite of the fact that in the last resort his teaching is addressed to all men. But because of the this-worldly miracle its practical application is bound up with earthly differences, which can never become irrelevant, not even when looked at from the most exalted viewpoint. "Be ye clever as the serpents, and without deceit as the doves"—Jesus commands his disciples. This statement alludes to the fact that being human contains a task that can hardly ever be solved—to live simultaneously for the sake of the noble and the ignoble misfortune.

Christian dogma is kind enough to recognize what is Jewish in Jesus, since it is part of the miracle of the hypostatic union that God was incarnated in Jesus. It then becomes difficult for the church to make peace with the national-Jewish claims of its founder. Thus we read in the collective work *Religion, Christentum, Kirche*: "Jesus himself was only sent to the lost sheep of the House of Israel, as he emphasized several times. He does not want to preach to the heathen. Even when he turns his healing power to one of them, he only yields to force. As long as he lives, his disciples, too, were to avoid the dwellings of the pagans and the Samaritans." What then does the pious author—who, incidentally, added the words "as long as he lives" out of his own—have to say about those passages which contradict Jesus' "catholicity"? Only this statement: "The divinely ordained short duration of his earthly ministry was one of the main reasons—perhaps the only one—for this limitation." This doubtful "perhaps" is then accompanied by the alleged concession that Jesus, contrary to his radical stance in other respects, is said to have made to the spirit of the time. The author adds further: "What Jesus announces is meant for all mortals, his God is the Father of all human beings, the love of one's fellow man which he approaches is meant to embrace the entire world." Now this kind of a "catholicity" and universalism is genuinely Jewish and, as shown previously, by no means particularly Christian. It is not universalism which separates Christianity from Judaism but the fact that the former, while being universalistic, disregards national differences and anticipates a uniform mankind, whereas to Judaism national differences are recognized, and the coming unity of mankind is prepared with the instruments of the present. Jesus is therefore in good Jewish company in his delicate feeling for the national particularity of the Jews and for what had to be done at once. The Revelation of Saint John the Divine is also a clearly national-Jewish book with its "144,000 sealed ones from all the tribes of Israel fighting the animal with the seven heads" (Rome). Paul took the first step in denying this world, and the Fathers of the Church followed suit.

There are, it is true, several passages of a Paulinian character attributed to Jesus. These are perhaps later interpolations. All I want is to point out that essential features of the Jesus figure do not harmonize with the Paulinian construction but they are Jewish in the sense of the old anti-Paulinian mood. It is then a mere matter of taste that those things which do not fit the theory and have enforced for themselves a tradition which contradicts an ad hoc theory, seem to me much more alive and true than details which are used to support a system. It is the irrational elements in the story of Jesus which do not allow me to accept the theory that Jesus was merely a mythological figure, composed of Asian and Greek elements.

11

THE

CHRISTIAN–PAGAN AMALGAMATION

The Christianity of the Future

THE READER WILL HAVE OBSERVED THAT MY CRITICAL WAY OF OPPOS-
ing Christianity did not go in the direction of history, starting with
its "founder." On the contrary, it was the youngest layers of Christianity, those of the Middle Ages, which were mainly exposed to my
rejection (in the Ninth Part of this book); then, proceeding to the
origins, I have pointed out that not everything Paul said must be rejected as being Christian, nor does everything Jesus said have to be
rejected as being Paulinian. By thus reversing the historical process—
trying to ascend from the river to the purer source—I have achieved,
in more than one sense, what some theologians call "cleansing Christianity of Jewish dross."

But the final word has not yet been said. I caught the Christian
stream at its middle section, where, having run through the clever
discussions of scholasticism, it passes by the cities of the sixteenth
century with their religious concerns and their decisive attempt—
though following the wrong direction—of reestablishing the first
Christian wave in its purity. But there is another Christianity, that
of today. There is the delta of the river, where the broad, vast water—
without falls—lazily carries along the soil of its banks and of its bed,
hardly distinguishable from the land around with its few trees; for,
although it takes pieces of earth with it and broadens thus step by
step, we might also say that the dry land sucks up the liquid and
mixes with it as in the process of boiling.

Doing away with allegories: Christianity, having entered the world opposing paganism, discovered—and not by accident, but following lawful reactions—within itself stronger and stronger affinities to paganism, and ended up by forming with the latter a mixture of ideas and feelings, a mixture which is now being used everywhere in Europe and America, in private and in public. This Christian-pagan amalgamation—the final link in Christian development—dominates today's world in such exclusiveness as no *Weltanschauung* has ever formed. Perhaps it is this exclusiveness and omnipotence of its rule which makes it invisible and unnoticeable, so rarely observed, and hardly ever challenging an analysis. For only friction directs our attention to forces.

Yet counter-forces are at work, not only within Judaism but also within Christianity itself. For here is something miraculous: A false construction, like that of the Christian "grace of generalization," can, if nurtured with the greatest energy, complicate the path to individual grace for centuries, but it cannot bar it forever. With every newborn soul, the idea of truth is born anew. Even after having been corrupted a hundred thousand times by means of doctrines, the next time it grows into a counter-force, although it may be a feeble one. Thus we have many such counter-forces in Christianity at the very instances where living religiosity is at work. Examples are individualism within Protestantism, and neo-Thomism within Catholicism. Particular mention should be made of Thomas Aquinas, for it is he who made the remarkable statement, "*gratia natura non tollit, sed perficit*," meaning, "grace does not eliminate nature but perfects it." This statement leads to many wholesome possibilities.

Here might be the right place for me to point out the many values of Christianity in order to appease those who feel offended by the above presentation of mine and the concluding criticism contained in the present chapter. And yet this might obscure matters, since I would rather write a one-sided book than one which gives everybody something to hang on to.

I never called Christianity a lost cause. Around its basic construction—and this I believe indeed to be "lost"—so much human kindness has blossomed forth in the last centuries, so much has grown out of the life blood of Christianized nations—some of it in connection with basic Jewish thoughts—that the entire complex cannot fade away. And yet the Christian-pagan epoch of mixture, which we have now reached, is not far away from death. But three components fight hopelessness: common humanity; national vitality, which will not go back again to pagan self-deification, and which will therefore strive towards a new future; and the Jewish religious heritage offered to all nations, which has never been entirely possessed, but neither has it ever been completely rejected, as indeed it cannot be. Now, by virtue of its faulty foundation, Christianity stands outside that development. But Christian tradition has created such a tremendous treasure of feelings that do not depend on the foundation—think of the intimate recounting of the legends of the saints and of the manner in which the figure of Christ has been modified and given life—that these elements, combined with the three "components," could well constitute a new religious life, without severing the historical connection at any place. Nothing of what has moved past times passionately can be judged irrelevant or meaningless by subsequent development, and a passionate error—even that of the "faulty foundation," fought for with fateful passion—has always had more reality than a cold insight.

But instead of losing myself in fantasies concerning the Christianity of the future, which is of no concern to me, I would rather come back to the figure of Kierkegaard, illuminated by all the rays of irony, enthusiasm, and courage, a man whose Christian and Nordic soul has created all by itself that mood of the "this-worldly miracle" in which Judaism lives. Here lies the true guarantee for a future Christian life, which must come as close to the basic Jewish thought as it is now removed from it and close to paganism.

Kierkegaard's Faith

"In time eternal salvation is decided by the relationship to something historical"—thus does Kierkegaard formulate his faith, Christian faith. He does not identify himself in the least with those nonsensical attempts to water down Christ's death on the cross into a mere abstraction, an ongoing historical process, a symbol which repeats itself daily and in every man, and similar banalities that annihilate the particularity of Christianity. Rather, Kierkegaard clings to the fact that, at a certain moment in history, which can be determined exactly, God has become man in order to redeem men, and that the eternal salvation of every individual depends on belief in that unique event. "It is difficult to become a Christian because you can become a Christian only by means of the paradox of basing your eternal salvation on your relationship to a historical event. It would be a mere excuse and a play with words to turn Christianity into an eternal history and the God who exists in time into an eternal becoming." Thus we see that Kierkegaard, the extreme subjectivist, embraces a form of grace which is valid for all men, and objective. He sees the confirmation of true faith in the absurdity of having to accept a temporal condition for eternal salvation, an objective factor for the most individual feeling of being saved. If this objective uncertainty does not exist, faith has nothing to conquer; it loses itself in cold knowledge or, lacking this, in an "approximation of knowledge" or "mediation." Thus we read in his "concluding unscientific postscript to the philosophical fragments":

Let us take Socrates. Today everybody fools around with proofs, some offering more, others less. But Socrates retains the problem—if there is immortality. Does that then mean that, compared to a modern thinker with his three proofs, Socrates was a doubter? Not at all! On that "if" he bets his whole life, he dares to die, and, with the passion of infinity, arranged his entire life so that it might be acceptable—provided there is immortality. Is there a better proof for the immortality of the soul? But those who possess three proofs do not arrange their lives accordingly. If there is immortality, their lives must be an abomination to it; is there a better way to refute their three proofs? The "little" uncertainty helped Socrates, because his passion for infinity was of great help; but the three proofs are of no help to those others, because they are and remain Philistines, and their three proofs prove just that! Thus a girl who hopes faintly to be loved by her beloved may possess all the sweetness of loving because she placed everything into that feeble hope; on the other hand, a married woman who has experienced more than once the strongest expression of love has had "proofs" and still what counts is lacking. Socrates' uncertainty was thus the deepest expression for the fact that eternal truth stands in some relation to existence, and that existing man must remain a paradox as long as he exists. And yet Socrates' lack of knowledge contains perhaps more truth than the objective truth of the entire system which flirts with the demands of the time and lives on the opinions of university professors.

Here is the paradox: an existing man, becoming and imperfect, factually possesses a relation to something objective, absolute, infinite. Kierkegaard states: "Modern speculation has done everything in its power in order to let the individual transcend himself objectively. But this cannot be done. Existence puts on the brakes." Reviling the Hegelians, he says that the only way through which man can transcend himself is by committing suicide. Thus Kierkegaard remains strictly within existence, an existing and subjective person who is continually becoming. That in him something perfected—truth—can be found, is the paradox, and it can only be hardened through objective proofs, and it can only be believed by means of the paradox and through passion. "Only in a moment can the single individual find himself existingly in a unity of infinity and finitude, which transcends existence. That moment is that of passion." The paradox is therefore the relation of finite I with God, a relation which I have called "the confrontation with infinity," but it is to be taken as an act of cognition, not as a mere "fear of God." That infinity must be sensed as something positive, as truth, as a principle that, in spite of its infinity, is in touch with a finite being, meaningless in the face of infinity. That "touch" can never be proven, but it can be believed in passionately as the paradox, by wagering one's entire existence on it. It is this risk which characterizes faith. Such a life "thanks to the absurd" is life in the this-worldly miracle. "Objectively there is only uncertainty, but it is this uncertainty which lends impetus to one's infinite passion, and truth lies in the courage to choose with the passion of infinity what is objectively uncertain." To say that so far we can agree with Kierkegaard would be arrogance, because that statement implies the idea that we might have reached that point even without him, and that we allow him at best to accompany us. On the other hand, it would be equally immodest to call him a teacher and a guide where we would have gained some insight independently of him, so that agreeing with him is not only a rediscovery but fulfilment. A geographical map, too, agrees with a certain region, and yet nobody would fight the notion—which would mean to agree with it to a certain point—that both are of the same kind. This is what I meant when I mentioned above the fruitfulness of the "Christianity of the future" and the guarantee for it. Such a guarantee is inherent in Kierkegaard's religious fruitfulness. For instance, he is not satisfied with setting up the concept of a "confrontation with infinity," but, in his *Non-Scientific Postscript*, clearly faces the fact of a general religiosity ("Religiosity A"), and bravely approaches the existential and living aspect of man—the fact, thus, that we are dealing with an individual of flesh and blood. Here is truly a "vademecum to a blessed life," and although I may not agree with it fully, having the impression that the Christian "Religiosity B" somehow influenced its sister A, I must admit that I have not found such a moving presentation of religious duty in any Jewish books of ethics. This is what I wanted to point out, and this is the result and the end of my observations, once we omit all allegories and courtesies in order to cling to plain truth: Christianity, as a body of teaching, cannot teach Judaism anything but can learn from it; but in the field of Religiosity A, where there is still much to be learned, the Jew can indeed learn much from a Christian who lives seriously in his Christianity.

Now I have arrived at the distinction between Religiosity A and Religiosity B, established by Kierkegaard, which enables us to accept the one without the other. We can see at this point that Kierkegaard constructed a building with two stories, and he is clearly aware of it. But before reaching this juncture, we are bothered by the following conclusion: Since faith is only possible as a paradox, and since the dependence of man's eternal salvation on a historical event is the most paradoxical thing imaginable, do we not just have to accept the belief in Christ?

But a closer look will show that Kierkegaard's Religiosity A will do for that paradox, and the specific Christian religiosity is not needed, although the more pretentious may not agree with this. For the paradox has no limits, and if a man wants to try out his strength by believing only what is absolutely unreasonable, imagination has a field day. This may lead to fanciful things, to lunacy, perhaps also to playing comedies. Therefore I may have to apply to Kierkegaard the ancient phrase "*qui nimium probat, nihil probat.*" For once the shield of the paradox of faith is allowed to cover up all fancies, there is no end to it.

But this should not lead to our rejection of the entire argument concerning the paradox. Among the stages of the paradox there is an excellent one, called by Kierkegaard "the climax of the paradox," and although it is supposedly the second stage, we can well imagine more of them. I rather believe that the "excellent" and most serious stage is the first one, at the point where the paradox begins to escape the claws of reason and, forced by logic, deviates from the common truths worked out by rationality, yet deviates only as much as absolutely necessary. In such a self-restriction the paradox would prove that this is not a case of wandering about in some nonsense but of sacrificing common sense for the sake of a higher value, for being able to live with dignity. This minimum of the paradox is identical with a maximum. Therefore we remain with Religiosity A, renouncing further aspirations, which would threaten to turn the entire paradox into a plaything.

Here is one way of formulating the paradox of Religiosity A: Whatever you see and experience is finitude and conditioned. And yet you must, if at all possible, believe that everything has an infinite and absolute meaning, and it is in your own personal experience ("grace") that you will find that infinite and absolute meaning. This corresponds also to Kierkegaard's definition of Religiosity A, if we take into consideration that in the *Non-Scientific Postscript* he does not mention any more the this-worldly miracle, which he had described so clearly in *Fear and Trembling*. The religious task is not any longer to live before God but to feel annihilated and extinguished by him. This is the way Kierkegaard contrasts Religiosity A and B:

> What is gratifying in the sphere of Religiosity A is the immanence and the annihilation through which the individual does away with himself in order to find God, for the individual himself would be an obstacle. This can only be noticed in the negative side, in self-destruction which finds its proper relation to God within itself and suffers therein. For God can only be found after everything that it is in the way has been cleared away, every finitude and, above all, the individual himself in his own finitude and his disputatiousness in the face of God. In Religiosity B, gratification lies outside—the individual, in order to find God, must relate to something outside. It is paradoxical that this seemingly esthetical relation to something outside is nevertheless supposed to be the absolute relationship to God, whereas in immanence God is neither "something" nor is He outside the individual. The paradox says that "God is in time as an individual man," and the individual relates to something outside. This cannot be imagined, and here is the paradox.

To Kierkegaard therefore, infinite truth not only cannot be proven but is self-contradictory. It contradicts not only experience but its very own sphere.

Subjectivity is truth. The paradox arose because eternal and essential truth entered into a relationship with existence. Now let us go one step further and assume that eternal and essential truth is itself the paradox. How did that paradox arise? Because eternal and essential truth is placed side by side with existence. In that manner truth becomes a paradox. Eternal truth has arisen in time. Here is the paradox.

This is clearly the "second story" mentioned above. It starts with the words "let us go one step further." It is not only superfluous but it threatens the first floor.

Kierkegaard's emphasis on subjectivity is marvellous. He thus stresses the most individual grace. God encounters man where man has only himself, no example, no guardian, no assistant, no agent. With this view Kierkegaard steps outside official Christianity, which is the belief that a historical event can establish for all mankind a metaphysical revolution and new metaphysical conditions. Yet, through the absurd, Kierkegaard secretly enters Christianity again. He seems to say: "I can be saved only *ad personam*, through my subjective experience. This subjectivity, this accident, takes hold of eternal truth. This is the paradox. But it is this paradox that I believe in." Since here we are still in the sphere of Religiosity A, Judaism is still in agreement. But where is that eternal truth to be found? "Ever since my childhood I have heard it stated that it lies in a unique and finite event, which is nevertheless valid for all of mankind. Can there be anything more paradoxical? My subjectivity not only grasps eternal truth in a paradoxical manner and attains eternal salvation in this belief, but eternal truth is in itself paradoxical."

Kierkegaard admits—and welcomes the fact—that the paradox of the second power leads necessarily to the negation of this world. There is of course a difference between "relating oneself in time to the Eternal" (Religiosity A), where time, through the this-worldly miracle, can have a very important meaning, and "relating oneself in time to the Eternal in time," where the this-worldly miracle has been condensed into one moment and been absorbed once and for all. "For if eternity is present at a certain moment in time, existence has been forsaken by the hidden immanence of eternity." Having reached this point, Kierkegaard can no longer cling to the this-worldly miracle in the purity in which he had conceived it when writing his

Fear and Trembling. It is true that it is still better to live in the face of God than to fade away. But it is not any more a joyful regaining of worldliness but only a semblance of life, without its elan. According to Kierkegaard, all relative and finite goals have lost their interest when one is required to be constantly concerned with infinity and the absolute, and to live a religious life. One could as well enter a monastery. But one does not do it—according to Protestantism, subscribed to by Kierkegaard—for this too would be a finite expression for something infinite, it would be an outward application of an inner relation to God—vanity. The religious man lives in this world as a stranger, although he refuses to stress this situation. "He is incognito, but his incognito means looking like others." Existence lives on as a humorous mask of religiosity. For the religious man is always aware of the contrast between his powerful position in the world and his absolute powerlessness before God. "To have many men's fate in one's hand, to recreate the world and then to understand that everything is a jest before God—this is serious indeed." This is the form to which Kierkegaard's this-worldly miracle has shrunk. This world only means a humorous contrast to the religious, a camouflage to prevent inwardness from being visible from the outside. According to Judaism, however, this world is the immediate expression of religiosity, no expression *per contrarium*, no veil or diversion for inwardness to hide in but the resurrection in the miracle, no meaning for the world because of the soul. Kierkegaard concludes therefore that all men are religious, they only hide it.

Am I taking Kierkegaard's "infinite resignation" seriously enough? Some passages are repulsive to me, like the following formulation: "If the religious man does not want to give up a certain thing, he does not have the proper relation to eternal salvation." Or again: "Existence is composed of infinity and finitude, existing man is infinite and finite. If, then, eternal salvation is his highest good, the moments of finitude have once and for all, through action, been lowered to something which must be given up in view of eternal salvation." Perhaps it is my own eudaemonism which refuses to accept such a Christian rigidity, the identification of "eternal salvation" and "resignation." My book has previously pointed out that the this-worldly miracle ought not to be misinterpreted as eudaemonism. I have always been in the danger of becoming a prey to eudaemonism. For this reason I am afraid lest my concept of the this-worldly miracle contain a grain of eudaemonism, which would prevent me from accepting Kierkegaard's austere concept of resignation.

But a thorough self-examination taught me that it is not eudaemonism that makes the difference; rather Kierkegaard, coming from his construction of Christ, allowed the this-worldly miracle, which he himself had established in *Fear and Trembling*, to change to "resignation," which originally had only been meant as a passing stage. My own concept of "infinite resignation," obviously differing from Kierkegaard's, does not mean that "moments of finitude" have to be given up once and for all, but that we cannot do them justice in the normal course of life, unless a miracle harmonizes the conflict, which could not be solved otherwise. The resignation which precedes the this-worldly miracle therefore does not mean a renunciation of life but of a normal regulation of life. Kierkegaard says: Live, and know also that to God finitude is without value. This book teaches: Live, and cling to the value of finiteness, and know that this value, unless opened within you by God through a miracle, is unattainable on the normal level of life.

Of Paganism in the Past and Always

The following presentation of pagan religiosity has two purposes. First of all it is meant as a check of the this-worldly miracle, and it is supposed to prove that this miracle is as far removed from Kierkegaard's negation as from eudaemonism and unmetaphysical things. Furthermore, the development of the pagan idea of God will above all show up those instances that further evolved in Christianity.

Having these two purposes in mind, the following pages cannot possibly describe the full wealth of what ancient times had to offer. I will not look at the world and the history of old but rather at the world of our own days, a world which is pagan, and has really never ceased being so.

Paganism takes the material world as something unavoidable and, in the widest sense, natural, so that the supernatural world, too, appears to it only as a direct continuation and straight development of the visible one. Thus the drives and forces of this world are approved of and sanctified. Where these forces are at war with each other, the primitive spirit is content with a pacification by natural means. The right of the stronger one becomes true right. Only when a harmful drive threatens to annihilate all other forces entirely, the interest of general sanity—that of the individual or of the group—requires that the strong and evil elements be repressed by even stronger ones, and thus forcibly broken. The goal is not a profoundly different order of the visible world, and the rights of unlimited power—those of the individual or the group—are not touched. This pagan attitude is not only taken by Kallikles (in Plato's dialogue *Gorgias*), who, anticipating Nietzsche in astounding details, explains morals and the law as a slaves' revolt and *ressentiment* against the upper classes, but Socrates, too, has that opinion. He uses the technique of a chess player, who, faced with an inexperienced opponent, defeats him first in three moves, before starting a serious game. "My dear Kallikles, you say that by nature the stronger man is the better one, and that a law which restricts him is unnatural. Now who is stronger, the masses or the individual? The masses are, and it is they who make the laws. Therefore the law is not against nature, not even that law which restricts the stronger man." To Socrates the scoffer, what is decisive is not that morals are moral but that they are stronger than immorality.

In this view—and in innumerable others of ancient times—a completely different, invisible and absolute world, a "new heaven," is neither established nor desired. Only Plato's teaching of the ideas occupies the boundary. Therefore Socrates was rightly accused of not believing in the gods of the city and of introducing new ones.

Most gods of pagan folk belief are nothing but intensified human beings. A simple ladder leads from the world of man to that of heroes and gods, and the highest rung is only quantitatively, not qualitatively, different from the lower ones. This can clearly be seen on Achilles' shield (*Iliad* 19), where the gods are depicted as being simply taller than ordinary men. Such primitive concepts of power and strength come close to the terrifying faces, weapons, and larger-than-life teeth of certain Negro fetishes, except that the Greeks used symbols which were esthetically nobler. Their gods are human beings who eat better than we do, the liquid in their veins is not just blood, they are stronger than even the heroes, they are born but do not die (which is not the same as immortality). It is typical for the pagan concept of God to intensify human dimensions and passions, and to form the upper world after the model of the lower one. The passing from nature to divinity is so unnoticeably slow that God himself seems to become part of nature. This may explain the strict and so pathetically worded Biblical prohibition of making images representing God. This means not merely a formal separation from the pagans but a very essential one. The same protest, from a different direction, can be found in the parodies of Jacques Offenbach, where the underlying idea is this: Since gods and demigods are only human beings, let us have a closer look at them! This is a typically Jewish criticism of the prolongation of visible ethics into invisible ones. This became quite clear to me when, in 1915, I gave lectures on ancient literature at a school for Jewish refugees from Eastern Europe in Prague. I must admit that it was only on that occasion that I began to understand the historical fight of Judaism with Hellenism (Maccabees) and the permanent difference between the two worlds of civilization. Getting in touch with those refugees did not revolutionize my feeling of what is Jewish, but supplemented and strengthened it in such a way that it rose from mere theory to the level of knowledge based on practical experience. My students (girls from age 15 to 19) sensed vividly what is beautiful and exalted in Homer's description of human beings. They particularly sympathized with the weaker ones, the defeated Trojans. But when it came to gods, I almost failed in calming the revolt of those simple souls, who found them either abominable or outright "funny." My humanistic training was surprised at this barbarically respectless opposition, the real meaning of which dawned on me only slowly.

Paganism in all its forms is the attempt to construct the supernatural world upon the visible one by way of induction. That attempt is doomed to fail. If earthly, finite life does not yield any meaning, unearthly life, lying in the same direction, must show the same meaninglessness, only in a larger measure. This explains the hopelessness in Homer's visions of Hades, the lack of freedom of the gods, behind whom there stands always the obscure and all-defeating moira, which pushes Hector's death scale to the bottom, in spite of Zeus' wishing the opposite, a scene which is a horrifying symbol of determinism. From this vantage point, we can appreciate the boldness with which the Jews connected an entirely ungraspable meaning of the world with their God, and from there they derived the world in a deductive way.

The world appeared to the Greek as confused and miserable

(deiloi brotoi). Consequently the superhuman world had no meaning either. To the Greek this was an independent fact, and, reflecting on our own world, revealed its own lack of sympathy and
interest. Homer's gods, therefore, are driven on by raging passions
as long as they are involved in their own—very human—affairs, but
in relation to human beings they are bloodless, cold, and even sar-
castic and evil. Thus does Apollo explain his lack of interest in human
affairs:

> Thou who shakest the earth wouldst call me a fool
> If I were to fight thee for the sake of mortal men.
>
> *(Iliad 21)*

When looking over his own way of life and that of the old man,
Achilles can say only this to Priamos concerning the gods:

> Thus did the gods weave the fate of poor mortal man,
> Afraid of living in grief, they've rid themselves of sorrow.
>
> *(Iliad 24)*

When the gods do interfere with human fate, they do so only in
the human sense, out of finite and limited motives. As a rule they
enjoy the spectacle of human and divine regrettable deeds, being
mere innocent bystanders:

> Among the other gods broke forth the heavy
> Feud of the fight. . . . Kronion,
> Sitting on Olympos, heard it, his heart rejoiced
> In glee, when he saw the gods entering the fight.
>
> *(Iliad 20)*

This divine fancy in wars is really only a reflection of the Greek
attitude towards the world. Betrayed by human and superhuman
powers, the Greek was left with only two sentiments: a terrible fear
of the core of things, and an intensified clinging to the multi-colored,
evanescent shell. This explains the fear of death, which bursts the
shell and reveals the terrible core, which one would have liked to
hide:

> Out of his limbs the soul flew to the depths of Hades,
> Mourning its fate, severed from strength and youth.

This is basically how the famous and serene spirit of the Greek looks, and we find many variations of this immanent hopelessness in Greek lyrics of all times.

Homer's greatness and eternal youthfulness lie in the great nobility with which he spread the safe ground for his calm narratives in spite of the difficult situation in which the human heart finds itself. It was just the passion and the consistency of his narrative which was meant to tell the knowledgeable reader something of the raging waves beneath him. One wrong word might cause the whole structure to collapse, and he walks along like a somnambulist, concentrating on the visible world, mankind's sole possession, the "multi-colored shell." This explains his clarity, his well-known epic and unpsychological method, which is based on ethical phenomena, not on esthetical ones. It is a flight to the surface of the world. In continually repeated epithets, he evokes reality as with a magic spell, telling it to be firm and rigid, so that the black juice of its vessels should not emerge. Those epithets are not of a "decorative" nature, as assumed by philologists, but a most serious part and parcel of a poetical ethos, the halting points and crutches of a world of anxiety.

The purest expression of pre-Platonic Greece was Homer's man. Completely chained to the visible world, he feels doubly chained when fleeing to the gods. Since he cannot solve the struggle within him by referring to an invisible "ought," he is bound to minimize that struggle. In Stoicism that harmonization becomes the ultimate wisdom of antiquity and its legacy to the subsequent centuries. But Homer offers a more original solution, and this explains his value and charm. His solution is not in the realm of philosophy but in that of poetry, although I am convinced that those two spheres are not so hermetically separated as sober reason may assume. Subterranean passages lead from one domain to the other, subterranean rivers, united, flow through their foundations. Only this explains why all through antiquity Homer was considered a teacher of philosophy. Such a strong sentiment is not justified by the scarce ethical maxims and statements extracted here and there from his works. But the entirety of the works of art, their uniform style, which is identical with their uniform ethos, did its share in educating the best men in a thousand different and speechless ways. This ethos was directed towards a lessening of the inevitable contrasts in life, which hurt each other in cruel manners. But Homer's solution is not that of stoicism, which wanted to cover everything up with indifference and apathy, thereby strangling joy as well as suffering. No—Homer's men attack each other mercilessly and endowed with full feeling, and the pages of his books are filled with ever-renewed streams of blood and tears. But the form of the presentation, by which we mean the entire poetical complex, not only technical and formal matters, is like a second, superhuman world, which dissolves all earthly forcefulness into harmony. This dualism of form and happening may stand for the missing dualism of God and creature. The form, which means poetical fashioning, is Homer's true divinity and transcendence. Thus we have the symmetry of the vivid metre, the harmony in the violent dialogues (often quite unrealistically: only one speech and one reply); the well-measured characterization of the personages, so that Paris is not entirely a coward, and Helena not quite without honor; the slow evolving of the events, the dwelling with episodes, the detailed description of seemingly everyday acts, the latter not being an artificial "transfiguration" of every day life but rather the expression of the Greek idea that there is nothing hidden behind the visible world, which is our ultimate, highest, and inestimable value. Whatever is visible, from the royal palace to the "divine sows' herd," is therefore provided with the greatest dignity in the smallest details. Even when men fight, they call each other divine, no matter how deeply they despise one another. They do not forget that they are border cases, dignified positions of life at the edge of nothingness. For in this world the absence of metaphysics is a reversed pantheism. Nevertheless it was quite clear to ancient man that this process of harmonization neglected something essential. Like a bad conscience it expressed itself in fear—fear of the gods, whose tyrannical power without moral controls had been set up, fear of any exaggeration in man, of the *hybris*, which at any moment threatened to bring to an explosion the careful balance of earthly states. The gods hate human *hybris*, and they characteristically persecute all exaggeration, not only in evil but also in strength, in innocent joy of living, in happiness—in short, exaggeration in good things. David, on the other hand, danced before the Ark of the Covenant. Intoxicated with God, he was not concerned with harmony, good taste, and manners. The Greek had to be harmonious. Antiquity with its clearly defined plastic forms, its symmetry, its great line turning back towards itself, its Stoic and Epicurean contentedness, which forbade all excess in joy and suffering—that antiquity is a crystallized mistrust of God. Their arms held tight to their bodies, these men go through life, careful not to touch too many things, and not to touch anything with violence. Dionysian passion must be sent away into obscure earthly cults, into orgiastic mysteries and to ancient mythologies. Apollonian life in the light of the day is left with little more than an artificial system of self-sufficiency, of stopping before the end, of a well-balanced mediocrity, of *nil admirari*, as expressed so elegantly at the end of Horace. Catullus, not so clever, and raging into the climax of his feelings, rejects that symmetry, which was only a sleeping draught used to deaden the yearning for God. Therefore he starts immediately to clamor for just gods. His shout drowns all that the unhappy and odious Romans had produced.

Homer is the Alpha and the Omega of ancient Greece. Homer, the artist and the religious man, untiring in recreating visibility in details which move us to tears. While with other poems details are mostly boring, here they are a religious factor. For, since Homer has only the visible world, he would lose everything, if he lost that. Perhaps he was considered blind in order to indicate that the many things he has seen had not been viewed in natural light but as something essentially unviewable, the physical world replacing the metaphysical.

Pagan Science

Paganism is not an historical type. We are in the midst of paganism right now, with additional Christian ingredients.

The following trends in modern thinking are mainly emanations of a prevailing paganism: evolution, biological-scientific *Weltanschauung*, monism, the Marxist theory of socialism, historicism. All these branches of science take it for granted that everything was bound to lead to where we stand now. In order to support this unprovable assumption, all extraordinary, free, spontaneous, miraculous phenomena of the past are comprised in one law, and derived out of the "natural" bases, which, however, are merely coincidental in most cases. This means a disregard for the ethical will and divine miracle, so that they are abolished for the future, too. Thus science has emasculated itself. Based on one element of paganism, the continuation of this world, it has reached the second pole of paganism, a position alien to life, and will forever be a spectator instead of interfering.

Now it is true that art as well as science must have a certain distance from life, they must be bystanders, and not intervene in life. Outside of paganism that makes good sense. But within paganism the situation differs, because here that passive attitude is the only and ultimate meaning.

Paganism just views what has become historically, it states and describes the facts but does not even have a critical view of them. Pagans look at them with dull eyes, assuming that what has developed is automatically proper. This abject kow-tow before the data and facts, the pagan overrating of nature and what has evolved organically is seen also in the materialistic concept of history as well as in the concept of the "positive order of law," for this too is the unconditional recognition of history. It is also the source of the Prussian State idea of Treitschke, the ideal of the physiocrats, of liberalism, and of the Manchester school. It is not surprising that so many divergent phenomena are based on the same origin. Paganism is at work whenever a natural drive of mankind, a natural force, or the entirety of natural necessities is presented as something inevitable, as something ultimate and unchangeable, or as something to be respected under all circumstances. In other words, paganism denies the fact that freedom and the experience of grace may counteract causality. This negative sign is shared by all variations of paganism. They always lack the redeeming leap into non-causality and freedom. Nevertheless there is room for many variations, depending on what drive one worships—the lust for power of the State, or that of a few aristocrats. In every case, however, "pagan science" makes the mistake of projecting into the object of science itself the legitimate attitude of science towards that object. Standing outside while looking at life leads to a view of life as something equally passive, something which does not have the strength to place itself under a new law but must eternally continue by the norms of the past.

A very instructive example is the biological branch of sociology. Darwin had stated rather carefully that "man may be subject to a violent fight for survival," since, according to him, the selection of the fittest is the very result of that fight. Immediately sociologists proved that man must be subject to the misery which surrounds him, and only those who cannot resist become its victims. ("Jewish sentimentality," incidentally, would be of the opposite view.) This animal doctrine of "racial hygiene" is supported by the theory of the absolutely unchangeable aptitudes, and other opinions of unconscious paganism. It is easy to calculate what effect such "science" must have on politics.

Here is a statement by Nietzsche: "To gain a bird's eye view which makes one understand that everything works the way it is supposed to work, that all 'imperfection' and the suffering resulting from it are highly desirable"—this is the sum total of his own life and of paganism. At no time has man lowered himself more than in this "bird's eye view."

The Christian–Pagan Amalgamation

Homer's Zeus just looks at the fights and enjoys doing so. This typical attitude of antiquity—in order not to have to see the chaos in the center of the world one views the beautiful surface of the things— ought to be compared to a remark made by Schopenhauer: "The optimist tells me to open my eyes and to look at the beautiful world of sunshine, mountains, valleys, rivers, plants, animals, etc. But is the world really a kaleidoscope? There is a big difference between seeing and being."

Here we note with surprise how close the Christian attitude is to pagan evaluation. Schopenhauer gave us only the ultimate consequence which results from the Christian view—"there is a great difference between seeing and being." A pagan and Homer could have made the same observation, the only difference being that Homer would come to the conclusion that he should content himself sagely and calmly with seeing things, whereas the Christian suspects even a beautiful appearance as deceit.

This tendency of "looking at things" is one of the most important meeting places of paganism and Christianity. Here is another formulation: To paganism, material things are everything; to Christianity, nothing. But both views lead to the same result: Material things must be left to themselves.

It is an outcome of the disregard for this life that Christianity (in some of its extreme positions) does not grant man an independent task outside of attaining the state of grace. It does not recognize the existence of "ignoble misfortune," which must be fought by the human will and its freedom before God. Indifference towards this life leads to indifference towards morals. Here is the place of Scheler's relaxation and of the indulgence of sins as mentioned by Luther and Ricarda Huch. It is also the place of a vast and expanded form of amalgamation. If we follow the Christian doctrine to its end, we do not see a supreme ethical supervision; man's inclinations have free play, and only grace can sanctify them. Before the appearance of grace, man's drives are allowed to do what they wish; and, although this may fill the genuine Christian with pain and repentance, he cannot do anything about it. For striving for what is ethically good is "of the devil" and wants to decrease Christ's merit. It is in this treatment of the drives that the Christian meets the pagan within himself; for the pagan, too, gives the drives free rein, because they are proper, innocent, and incorrupt. The difference in motives goes together with a similarity of the consequences—a conscious capitulation of man in view of the course of nature.

In all this we must remember that these two tendencies of amalgamation—indifference towards politics and ethics, and relaxation in view of the I—represent the more delicate and honest way in the collaboration of Christianity and paganism. But there exists also a third amalgamation, whose structure is much less delicate. Here paganism and Christianity do not work with or against each other nor are they competitors, but they have divided the spheres peacefully between themselves. Here Christianity claims for its self-denying doctrine the nobler, but unfortunately ineffective heaven, leaving to paganism, as represented by the State, the earth and reality. The ideals of Christianity are so exalted as to be unrealistic, and therefore the pagan lack of ideals must be acknowledged in the domains of life. The wolf and the lamb have concluded peace, and man is caught in the middle. Achad Haam was right: "Since Christian nations were unable to base their mutual relations on the moral basis of their religion, national egoism remained the absolute ruler in international relations, and 'patriotism' . . . rose to the rank of absolute moral basis."

To show that I have not invented that form of amalgamation, I quote from Chamberlain's book *Deutsches Wesen*: "Luther teaches that a Christian ought not to defend himself, not even when he is in the right. But this does not prevent him from standing up, at another passage, for man's right to protect himself and his loved ones, and from reviling those who fail to do so."

Did Chamberlain reject the way out of the tragedy, did he find it terrible that there is an amalgamation between a world-denying Christianity and real paganism? But this is not amalgamation any longer, but a coarse physical mixture. We have two railroad tracks, one of them carrying a train to heaven, one to this world. Therefore they can never collide. But this is exactly what Chamberlain lauds, continuing: "Few people have had the moral courage to accept so freely two opposing trains of thought. This example, which has been chosen at random, shows us the coexistence of the two worlds of religion and politics. Religion prohibits self-defense, politics demands it. If I do not obey the command of politics, I am a crazy saint, and false religion will defeat the true religion." Or, in another passage: "I am warning the Germans of those who preach to them sobriety, self-control, and love of one's fellow; they are wolves in sheeps' clothing or, at best, real sheep. . . . Only enthusiasm raises the average man above himself and enables him to do noble deeds." The noble "enthusiasm of the average man" is certainly a pious wish, perhaps a mischievous mistake. At the end we read: "No matter how old Germany is now, rising Germany is young. . . . For the same reason almost everything in Germany is incomplete: the State, society, taste. Only two things have been completed: the army, and genius. These two belong together. German genius has willed and created the army of the people." Here is the amalgamation of Luther and militarism, and the combination is not even too artificial. Even Ricarda Huch admits that Luther had to strive for a "strengthening of authority," since according to his view man cannot act ethically "without weakening the force of his heart"—State authority, therefore, in order to save man from ethical "relaxation."

Christianity is partly responsible for the outbreak of the first World War. For Christian-pagan amalgamation, arising from political indifference, indulgence of drives, and State-Church morals, prepared the soil for the bestialization of politics. Nevertheless even today Christianity is thought of as being an element of peace. The religion of love, the image of its noble founder, the palm and the cross—in a hundred allegories we are kept under the impression that, if Christianity had only been left alone, it would have been able to prevent the war. As a matter of fact, if we take Christianity allegorically, the Christianity of the surface, we do have the appearance of gentleness. But allegories and the surface are nonessential, as long as the inner channel of the Christian view of the world points to another direction—to silent toleration or even affirmation of war, at least to a weakened resistance towards suffering and cruelties. Parenthetically, I wish to mention that both Christianity and Judaism have been misused for purposes of war, and this has been done on both sides of the fence. But these are abuses of Christianity and should therefore not be taken too seriously. After all, every idea can be misused, although in some cases the resistance to abuses is greater than in others. Thus Judaism resisted war and more. The direction goes from the Book of Judges to the decisive peace ideal of the prophets and of the Talmud, where a majority decision, based on Isaiah chapter 2, declares that weapons of war are not to be considered an ornament. We may also point out that tournaments and the odious "poetry" of hunt are forbidden to Jews by the Talmud and later legislators. In Judaism we find hardly any inclination towards an amalgamation with paganism.

But in Christianity such a tendency is present not only in cases of abuse, and this is a regrettable consequence of its rejection of this world, an attitude which, as I have shown, is an inevitable derivation from the basic idea of the "grace of generalization." The honest Christian, not the one who hypocritically incites to war, proves the justification of the blind faith in Christ—negation of this world—*laissez-faire*, indifference towards politics—triumph of the pagan beast.

In Theodor Haecker's epilogue to Kierkegaard's "The Concept of the Chosen One" we find the Christian self-contradiction referred to previously. On the one side, all suffering is recognized as necessary; on the other hand, war is assailed passionately.

Christianity, denying this world, is basically indifferent towards all the institutions of this world. Haecker expresses this quite clearly:

> Beyond the fulfilment of his duties the honest Christian is not interested in the existence of a certain form of state. . . . To establish a metaphysical connection between Christianity and monarchy is only a reminder of a purely human church policy, which has lost all meaning by virtue of this war. Those Christians who are also con-

cerned with the State . . . will live to see times in which they recall Cromwell. The church, too, changes its views.

This is the ultimate in self-contradiction and the lack of logic. If, to the Christian, forms of state are irrelevant, why is Haecker so violently opposed to militarism and dictatorship, whose sting he feels and whose shortcomings he objects to? Against my own will I must truthfully admit that the pagan party of those who are in favor of war is allied with a Christian party of those who tolerate the war and at the very same time write pamphlets against it. Deeply rooted in the Christian attitude is the misconception that there is no alternative between its own indifference towards this world and an all-comprising affirmation of it. This implies a complete misunderstanding of Judaism, which represents a third view, not between, but above these two; namely, in the sphere of the miracle. Therefore Haecker believes that, if the Jews cling to their racial distinction, they interpret the covenant with God "selfishly, imperialistically, and in a Prussian and German way." The truth is that in Judaism the respect of the this-worldly differences looks to infinity, to God. Here we encounter again a deep contradiction: the very same people who, because of their religion of grace, should be against "doing" anything, misunderstand universalism and become the worst "doers" in the question of nationalities. In that field, as Haecker points out, a handful of missionaries are enough to spread the word of God to Chinese, Japanese and Negroes, but Europe can disappear, since it has not deserved anything better. For the rest, we expect God to reveal Himself again as He had done to Abraham, Isaac, Jacob, Moses and the prophets. "The knowledge does not grow out of the people's soul, it is there already in the germ." This indifference towards the divinely given data of this world is typically Christian. One manufactures a universal mankind, a spiritual porridge, an abstract and vacuous space. A girl has every right to feel offended if her lover does not notice her new hairdo. Nor would she believe his assurances if, to make up for his default, he were to insist that love did not depend on her hairdo. Such a lover might be considered a fool, since we would tell him that too general a declaration of love stems from a badly hidden indifference. In the same manner do Christians make declarations of love to mankind. No matter how things stand, whether the world is well off or miserably bad, whether we talk of a German tribe or the Japanese, it is one and the same thing, as long as God reveals Himself. But such a love which makes no distinction concerning the beloved object is no love. "To love in any case"—means saying too little, not too much. It is true that God may reveal Himself in a new and unforeseen way. But to conclude that man is allowed to neglect His earthly and distinct forms of revelation—which applies to nations and to individuals at the point where, in the depths of their souls, they encounter God—this means giving in to a coarse paganism, which sweeps all values onto a dungheap, above which God can still reveal Himself.

The history of the Christian-pagan amalgamation is that of the history of Caucasian mankind. Initially Christianity did not agree to that pernicious alliance. At the beginning, its impetus, which had grown out of Judaism, had been strong enough to reject the pagan monsters. In the Middle Ages there was an almost equal balance between Christianity and paganism. Christianity maintained itself through the high civilization of the Middle Ages, an economy within the framework of supply and demand, and Gothic art. The Renaissance in turn stressed paganism. At that time Christianity did not offer any resistance, but a mixture started. The form in which Christianity reacted to pagan penetration was not a fortunate one. The Reformation emphasized Paulinian ideas, apparently most remote from paganism. But exactly where the tension between Christianity and paganism is strongest, the amalgamating trends seem to be most intensive. Where the contrasts have been driven to the extreme, the slightest accident can bring them together. Early Christianity, still under the influence of the Jewish this-worldly miracle, as well as certain forms of Catholicism could still defend themselves somehow against the pagan worship of the drives. But once this world has been removed from Christianity, nature, which can never be subdued, fills the vacuum, and the two become integrated. The world a valley of tears? Capitalism was happy to hear that one. The less value there was in the world, the more useful it was to capitalism as a field for its pagan rule. If mankind had been fortified—*more Judaico*—in its dignity through the this-worldly miracle, it would not have agreed to such a dishonorable embrace. But when Columbus had discovered the first American island, he wrote in his diary: "These kindhearted people must make good slaves," and here is his daily prayer: "May it please the good Lord in His mercy to let me find gold mines." His

Christian and pagan instincts had concluded peace. Here is the decisive factor, the tragic guilt of Christianity—it was not strong enough to resist seriously an intensified paganism, which broke irresistibly forth with the growth of the population and the greater chances for amassing fortunes. The appearance of the *Homo capitalisticus* can be explained by the change of the state of affairs, together with the lack of real resistance from Christianity. Sombart has shifted the problem by overstressing the importance of the passing from irrational man to rational man. But that passing is only the assimilation to a changed situation: a greater number of people, more traffic, a higher turnover, and therefore the "ration-ality" of those who remained bold pirates and warriors only as long as this had been the only way for making a profit. Here too, Christianity said Amen. By being indifferent to this world, Christianity aided those pagan attacks. In 1494 it was a monk who started bookkeeping by double entry. Where Christianity and paganism came closest, in Italy, early capitalism blossomed first.

12

JUDAISM AND INTERNATIONALISM

As all misfortune resulted from pushing out the Jewish in-
gredient in Christianity and from the subsequent Christian-pagan
amalgamation, so can redemption come to the world only when
Christianity frees itself from paganism.

This could be done by emphasizing the Jewish component in
Christianity. Tired of paganism, Christianity will have to go back to
its origin, Judaism.

It can of course not be predicted in what manner Judaism would
exercise its influence on Christianity. A direct way seems neither
desirable nor possible. Nevertheless, if Jewish thinking were really
known in the world, it would have a reforming and invigorating
effect on religiosity, and stimulate a creative development within the
material on hand.

Today Jewish thinking is unknown among the peoples, and the
Jews themselves prevent it from becoming known. Judaism has
adopted a form in which it cannot express itself. This is the universal
significance of the new Jewish State, which will perhaps create an
adequate form of Judaism sufficient to itself and to the world, and
able to influence the latter. At least it would reveal the possibility of
a life which is neither the Christian negation of this world nor its
pagan continuation but an amalgamation of both. For today only the
two extremes are recognized. If the third way appeared in actual life,
the relation of the nations to it would differ from a relation to a mere
theory.

The above allusions are in strict opposition to what the best known
representatives of our time have stated. Two entirely different reno-
vators of Christian thinking—Richard Wagner and Tolstoi—appear
as witnesses in Chamberlain's book on Wagner, in which the latter is
quoted as having declared that "Christian religion has been corrupted

by utilizing Judaism in the forming of its doctrines." In general, vilification of Jewish thinking has become so much an everyday occurrence that further proofs are unnecessary.

Did Wagner or Tolstoi know Jewish thinking before they condemned it? "Jewish thinking" is presented these days as a hodgepodge of mistranslated Biblical passages, deliberate misunderstanding of Talmudical statements that ought to be explained historically, evil qualities of assimilated Jews, and a general unanalyzable discomfort in the presence of things Jewish. It is so much easier to learn from uneducated individual Jews than from consulting Jewish literature or through getting acquainted with those Jewish circles to whom Judaism is the very source of life.

Invisibility and ambiguity are typical for today's Judaism, as far as it strives for assimilation. The symbol for the new Palestine is visibility.

Although it is essential to Judaism to become visible and to influence the nations religiously, their dissolution is not intended. Influencing the nations must not be done in a direct manner but as a liberation from the illusion that only paganism and Christianity exist. The natural religious creativity of every nation must be brought to the fore.

This is exactly the opposite of national dissolution. This was the basic error of the liberal-Jewish concept of the "mission"; in this, as in other respects, it was an imitation of Christianity. Jewish liberalism tried to minimize national differences and to adulterate Judaism. They become like us, and we become like them. In the night all cows are gray. In the happy future, of which liberalism dreamed, all religions and nations were anemic and looked like each other. On the other hand, influencing the nations according to my own concept would leave the nations untouched, and the influence would not necessitate an adulteration of Judaism but a strengthening. This kind of a "mission" would be quite different from the liberal one. In consequence of the concept of the this-worldly miracle, the nations—although finite forms of the infinite spirit—would retain their importance even in the confrontation with infinity, and their particularities would remain valuable to God. This is the very Jewish concept of nationality. When Micah speaks of the world as a domain of peace, with Zion as its center of learning, he still emphasizes the independence of all nations: "For let all the nations walk in the name

of their god, we shall walk in the name of the Lord our God forever."
The different gods referred to here cannot apply to the national gods
of the pagans, for from Zion comes the teaching of the One God;
but the allusion may be to various national features, which shall not
cease even at the end of the days, when the entire world will live
harmoniously together.

In the Jewish concept "internationalism" is an aim, and not something which can be created overnight by decree. Nor does it imply
an eradication of all national differences into an abstract humanity,
but peace among the nations, which will go on developing in their
own ways, and a common tie—that of a human and proper relation to
divine grace. Christianity, on the other hand, is an illicit anticipation
of internationalism, and disregards the national dfferences before
God, which means in the absolute life of the spirit. This may look like
universal love. But I have already shown that such a general love is
based on indifference and on the rejection of this world.

The nations are entirely subordinated to the concept of mankind.
But there are two kinds of subordination. Pearls may disappear altogether when dissolved in an acid; or they may be placed side by
side on a string, maintaining their individuality and increasing their
beauty in the brilliance of being together. Could it really be in the
interest of humanity that national and cultural values, say, the music
of the Italians, the Norwegians, the Czechs, should be eliminated in
favor of a unified, abstract, human music? The truth is that every
great musical creator produced his works out of the depth of his own
nationality, and thus did his share towards a common and human
music. Even where a genius like the Frenchman Berlioz recreated
Italian motives, he did so as a Frenchman—he did not mix Italian and
French features.

Today's objection against the stressing of national sentiments is a
fortunate reaction to the pagan overemphasis of the national concept.
For too long "patriotism had been the last refuge of the scoundrel"
(Samuel Johnson). Like everywhere else, we have two opposing
views—yes and no, pagan and Christian—and all possibilities are supposedly exhausted, so that he who escapes from one extreme ends
up necessarily with the other, and Judaism, the redeeming third
party, and existing on a different level, is overlooked and remains
unknown. In the chapter titled "Judaism beyond the alternative" I
have shown this to be true concerning the concepts of State and

worldliness, and I do not have to repeat this for the complex of nationalism. The Christian idea of nationalism means an elimination towards the abstract, and the pagan one, eternal war, coupled with unconditional affirmation of all national power schemes. The Jewish concept of nationalism can neither be traced back to a denial of this world nor to its affirmation but only to the this-worldly miracle, which means maintaining the finite form in the face of the all-dissolving power of the infinite spirit, and this not for the sake of the form—which would be pagan pride—but as divine grace, as a meaning once destroyed and paradoxically regained, making the spirit visible, a spirit that ought to disappear in the material world but is, miraculously enough, enriched by the material world in essence and dignity. The this-worldly miracle means that under certain circumstances finitude can add to infinity.

Here an objection may be in place: Usually nations do not live in the sphere of the miraculous but on the extremely realistic level of coal mines, ports, frontiers, armament budgets, all of which are (allegedly?) needed for their existence. At this moment it is quite fashionable to wage war against nationalism, to rage against all forms in which it may appear. This may be done from a pacifistic, bolshevistic, or neo-Christian standpoint. Now it does occur that someone stresses loudly that he is not thinking of nationalism in the common martial and imperialistic sense of the word, and that he may recognize the spirit as the highest principle. Not only today but even during the war he may have fought the lunacy of war in pamphlets, lectures, and action, thus getting in trouble from censorship, the police, and military tribunals. Yet he would feel terribly ashamed and he would sneak away in never-ending disgrace if some "revolutionary" were to call him a nationalist. He will never recover from such a mistake. He has been "recognized," which, in our crazy world of journalism, means that whatever he has done to clarify his unusual concept of nationalism is pilloried by a decree of the literary office. Such a man is flogged with statements made by great philanthropists and geniuses—true or fake—the climax being a book by that wise Indian Rabindranath Tagore against nationalism, and then he is thrust into the abyss. It would be in vain to point out that Rabindranath Tagore was only thinking of the European, capitalistic, mechanized nationalism, that he travelled through Europe in the national costume of India and gave a lecture concerning the integration of the Western and the Eastern spirit, which must mean the preservation of both; thus he is not a foe of cultural nationalism. But all this is in vain. The word "nationalism" is enough to degrade someone. Our time has no time for a more delicate distinction.

Anti-nationalists usually maintain that nationalism is dangerous and worthless. Whenever the one objection is proven to be faulty, the second view is raised again. The basic attitude runs somehow like this: "Why do I have to prove how dangerous even a mild form of nationalism is to world peace, since this fanciful idea is worthless anyhow? I admit that nationalism has certain values. But even if those values were gigantic, we should not do anything to promote a trend of thought which is so inimical to universal peace."

We can gain much by separating the two arguments from each other and by attempting to take care of them one after the other. Is nationalism really a threat to universal peace? This is true only if we are to assume that the world is not large enough to hold all nations. If nationalism turns into a chauvinistic national imperialism, the world does indeed seem too small. But we ought to see in nationalism a moral program, without denying its objective and natural presuppositions. But material things are vitally necessary for the solution of spiritual tasks. Nevertheless the nation can only claim a minimum of such material presuppositions. Concerning this, I have previously stated as follows: "Spiritual things cannot thrive in pure air, they require a territorial and material foundation. Yet it can accomplish great things with very little means, and better so than when possessed with the greatest wealth. Now it is this physical minimum of spiritual achievements which every nation has a sacred claim to. But the great European powers are saturated in that respect." "A minimum"—but then the concept of nationalism does not contain any danger regarding world peace. This means that the misfortune of national conflicts, as we are experiencing it now, does not belong in the field of noble misfortune, as if it were an indissoluble tragedy of mankind; most of it can be eliminated, provided that these minimal conditions do not oppose each other hopelessly. Here we see that legal formulas will not do, but that the nations are expected to have a decent attitude towards each other. It is not enough not to hate each other, they must be willing to give up individual claims for the benefit of other nations. Such an attitude cannot be created by law. It is true that an international court can create a code, just as it exists already for individuals. But for duties to become natural love and to unite with deeds of grace—this is as necessary as it is unenforceable; it must be left to God, it is the miracle. We see thus that not all suffering that arises from national division is ignoble and curable. This life too expects humility and hopes for the divine miracle. It would not even be desirable to escape the religious superstructure by some trick, for instance the leap into politics. Such a politics would remain foolish and imaginary. But that insight must not prevent us from taking those measures through which human power can be helped within a well-defined sphere. Such a measure is the ennobling of the concept of nationality. About this I wrote in my book *Kampf um das Judentum,* a book which, together with my essay "Sozialismus im Zionismus," contains the practical application of what is presented in this book:

> We are in dire need of a new nationalism to replace the old one. The European nations are not eager to put that new concept of nationality into practice. They do either too much or too little—they are either imperialistic or, in a cosmopolitan and Christian monotony, they want to eliminate the various instruments in the human orchestra. It is therefore up to the new Jewish nation to demonstrate how a nation can be a nation and at the same time reduce the concept of nationality. For this is the crux of the matter: We must learn to renounce whatever is not absolutely necessary to the spiritual essence of the people.

Now we come to the second argument of the anti-nationalists. They maintain that nationalism is worthless. A nation is identical with mankind, so far as it is accessible to me immediately. It is accessible to me because I am related to it through natural factors, such as a common language and civilization, education, country, etc. The most important of these, however, is race. Ethnology can not yet answer the question whether the idea of race plays an important role concerning non-Jewish nations. But those nations do not need to refer to a common descent, since they have a language and a territory in common, in addition to blood ties and a certain spiritual legacy. Only we must not look for a "pure race"; as long as a group intermarries for many generations, living within definite boundaries, we arrive at a group who feel physically and mentally related to each other. The case of the Jews is different. They are a race apart, for most of them married only within their own group since the time of

Ezra. Whether they are a definite race or a mixed one, even the mixture has led to constancy. The existence of the Jewish race—a fact which can be felt—has only been denied by some "Israelites" eager to assimilate.

The racial ties of Judaism are of course much stronger than those of education, civilization, language, and the state. For this reason the Jews should be called a people, not to mention their religio-cultural and linguistic connections, like Yiddish and Hebrew. (The latter had always been the language of literature and of correspondence among the educated; and now, in Israel, it has been completely resurrected, from medical journals to railroad tickets, stamps, road signs, and songs sung by children.) The racial unity of the Jews warrants also that again and again men appear who properly understand the religious feelings and thoughts handed down by the Jews, and express them in ever new variations. This explains the steadfastness and naturalness of Jewish thinking, although individual analogies of these thoughts may also arise among other peoples. It possibly appears there in a particular development, and perfected to a degree unknown to Jews. The combination with an alien character and creative genius can lead to unexpected heights. Since I am admitting this, I cannot be accused of chauvinism if I state that the perpetuity of their thought can only be guaranteed by the Jewish people.

The people are the natural domain of the spirit, their spiritual leaders depending on their own nation. Only within the nation can the spiritual leader influence those below him in education. In spite of that distance, their spirit is related to his; for secret connections established by the instinct flow between the heights and the depths of the people. Here we detect the divine miracle, a fact to be revered: within the people, the spirit knows of a path on which it can communicate with the lesser spirits, and on which sometimes it receives more from them than it can convey—the refreshing immediate touch with the natural sources of life.

The nation is the basis for natural communication, of which we do not have enough, and there are far too many misunderstandings. Even a sober utilitarianism would therefore prohibit interference with those channels of communication, those circles that have the spirit as their radius. All this is self-evident and does not require further elaboration. But the Jewish attitude towards this world yields an even more important result: we must appreciate the national molecular forces not merely out of cleverness but out of a religious devotion concerning the spiritual forms of this world.

These values are placed in proper relief when placed side by side with the worthlessness of a cosmopolitan equalization. Once I was horrified when reading the following report in a newspaper:

In a Far Eastern Movie

The movie has conquered the entire world, and in the picturesque world of the Far East it is as popular a means of entertainment as it is with us. The pictures are the same as in the Old World, but the public and the surroundings are different and thus lend a movie performance in the Far East a charm of its own. Here is a report about a visit to a movie in Siam: Whatever is supposed to stir the spectator does not make the slightest impression on that audience, but when they see a car racing along, or a horse race, or people beating each other, they yell out loud in delight. When the scoundrel commits a crime, the people hiss, which does not always imply disapproval but also pure pleasure. Their greatest joy is in seeing a fight and beatings, and the more blood flows, the better. War pictures two years old and more—mostly of American vintage—are viewed with indifference. The orchestra does not even try to adjust the music to the action. When the most tragic things appear on the screen, we hear gay dance music. The somber and simple interior of the movies contrasts with the light colors of the garments worn by the viewers, composed of various Eastern races, like Chinese, Siamese, etc. The ancient national and popular entertainment of Waiyang, an open-air theater, has been completely replaced by the movie. The Siamese do not even pay any attention any more to these plays but crowd around the light-colored posters announcing "the great sensational drama The Tigress of Paris, or The Hit of the Year: The Secrets of the Harem." The movie has penetrated the most remote places in the interior of Siam, where half-naked natives crouch in front of the screen, which, in the midst of the wonders of the tropical night and the jungle, shows them the sensations of New York and Paris.

Apparently there is such a thing as education at great speed. I prefer the slow maturing of national civilizations in their own atmosphere.

Here several questions arise. Am I not defending an overanxious isolationism? Do today's nations really represent forms of the spirit which have the right to maintain themselves religiously in the face of infinity? Why do we wish to survive, since all of God's children fade away? (All nations have perished, and out of Roman colonists and autochthons the Middle Ages created new nations.) Why should we object to the rise of new mixtures? Why not create a new race? Does it not mean to abuse the this-worldly miracle if we ascribe a never-ending importance to a passing stage of mankind? Does such a deification of accidental phenomena not lead to quietism?

Such questions and objections do not lead anywhere. It is enough to have shown the relevance of the national element from the most exalted point of view, that of the religious conscience. How to utilize that relevance, and how to square it with other relevances, is a different and very complicated problem. We must of course promote the mutual influence of national cultures, for this leads to understanding and enriches all cultures without endangering them in any way. A small scale mixture of races can be very beneficial. But the result of such experiments should not be the complete destruction of the existing nations. Care should be taken that, side-by-side with the mixture, there remains, in part of the people, the ancient type so that further evolution is made possible.

Judaism comes to the nations. For many centuries it had come to the heathen in the Paulinian deterioration. In the shape of Christianity it has done much to shake up mankind, but the typically Christian rejection of this world, the indifference towards ignoble—political, social—misfortune, weakened more and more the original Jewish impetus, so much so that it could mix with pagan forces, and today is visible everywhere in the hypocritical civilizations of Europe and America. Through divine providence, we Jews were driven out of the Holy Land together with our product, Paulinism, so that in the countries of the pagans we might observe with our own eyes how our gifts affected the instructed nations for better or for worse. The result was not fortunate. In order to become aware of the evil consequences of our teaching, we have been taught a painful lesson, especially ever since the crusades. Now we are returning to our own homeland. I am finishing this book in the important year 1920, when the national homeland of the Jews rises anew. I hope that my people's religious forces will awake. Again glad tidings will come forth; it is the undiminished clear Jewish message of redemption. For we have learned something. The millennia of the exile have shown us the abominations of paganism and the inability of Christianity to overcome them. People cannot say that we are coolly experimenting with the flesh of other nations. We have paid dearly for that lesson by suffering more than others, until this very year. Nor can we foretell when the cruelties will come to an end.

To claim that Jewish martyrs suffer for the sake of all of mankind sounds paradoxical today, just as paradoxical as the assumption that the establishment of a Jewish homeland is a concern for all nations, of common human interest, and that no man of good will ought to withhold his cooperation. And yet this is the case, and the future will prove me right. Zionism provides Jewish religiosity with a body, which it had lost. Now this book has demonstrated that possessing a body is not a lowering of the idea but is rather a distinctive sign of religiosity; it adds something to the idea, when elements that are less clear and still more enriching accompany God's incomparable purity. Therefore the embodying of Jewish thought—Zionism—is what Judaism must demand of itself in the way of religion. Other religions may be able to do without materialization; but it is of the very essence of Judaism that it cannot follow suit. For it cannot exist as a pure idea, which is characterized by the consideration that the finite form does not have to lose its importance when being dissolved into universality. On the contrary, empowered by the this-worldly miracle, Judaism can regain unlimited significance on a higher level. At the beginning of this chapter I pointed out that Christians, too, should welcome the fact that Jewish religiosity adopts a proper shape, and that the streams of spiritual influence emerging from that shape are of an inestimable significance.

Now I wish to address a word to my fellow Jews.

He who has read so far and is now disappointed that a book, which, after all, did not avoid the subject of world politics, ends up in an apparently narrow task, a small corner of the map, a local concern of the Jewish people—such a one has not understood this book or has forgotten everything he has read. For the basic religious feeling of the this-worldly miracle is that the limitation to something concrete, clear, and real can have a divine significance. Generalization—sometimes disguised as "love of all," "revolution," "the greatest horizon," "embracing the cosmos"—produces abstractions and is an outcome of that enormous indifference fertilized in the hearts of some by the genius of plain boredom. The hardest task for mankind is not to fool around with the miracle but to leave it at its proper place, neither to deny it rationalistically nor to abuse it in areas where reason ought to rule. A concrete, rational, and limited thing can have meaning, which it does not lose when looked at from the viewpoint of the infinite miracle, although it may raise that meaning to a higher level. This is basically the Jewish teaching, and no particle of it must be removed, or else the whole tumbles down into the ever-ready categories of Christianity or paganism.

But why does it have to be the State of Israel? Is the Judaism of the Diaspora not equally concrete in its effect, stimulation, and influence on other nations?

The answer to this is that the Diaspora will remain anyhow, since Palestine can at best become the home for one-eighth of Jewry. Whatever is therefore to be expected from the Diaspora will occur anyhow. Those who are ready to compare all martyred Jewish revolutionaries with Jesus forget that he worked in Palestine among Jews, and told his disciples "not to enter a street of the pagans." Therefore did he have great chances for success.

Only a hard-core reactionary can deny that the Diaspora has given much to its Jews and to their host countries. But this is not enough, although some Diaspora Jews, proud of their race, believe the Jews to have such a mission. Others go to the nations because they have no faith in their own peoplehood. I do not agree with either group. I definitely reject our role as instructors to the world, since, no matter how serious we are, it remains a game. True seriousness is only the deed within one's own material, in a homogeneous Jewish organism of a people constructed from the bottom with all layers. But even if we were to sacrifice our very lives in the task of teachers, it would be too easy to approach alien masses from the outside, to play foolishly with their instincts, to be unreal in the obscurity of unknown realities, to create an order that reflects the subject and not the object. But, tragically enough, it is not only too easy but also too hard. For we would not promote our own ideals but burden them with our alien race, which in turn leads to objection, enmities, and counterarguments. The end of our ideals will be that they will be crucified.

But I saw a man with a thinker's forehead, with fiery and yet kindhearted eyes, with callous, tanned, unnaturally big hands next to his delicately built body. He had been a student in Russia, and now he works the soil in Palestine. He is the type of the good new Jews, who, while in Palestine, symbolize the idea of the Jewish religion for the benefit of all.

Recalling him, I am coming to the end.

EPILOGUE:

CONCERNING THE TALMUD

IN THIS BOOK THE READER HAS HEARD THE TALMUD MENTIONED AGAIN
and again. But it was not referred to in the manner in which it is
usually presented—as something quaint, which can be done away
with by a smile—but as a living help in the despair of our days and
of all days.

Whereas the Kabbalah, the Zohar, and Hassidism have by and
large found advocates, the Talmud has not yet been duly appreciated
outside of Jewish orthodoxy, with the possible exception of the books
by R. Travers Herford.

And yet I think that great strides could be made if Jewish thought
as expressed in the Talmud were to become known to non-Jews as
well as to modern Jews, although it is almost impossible to read the
Talmud—in the original or in a translation—without the help of an
instructor. And even a teacher might not be interested in those matters with which this book has dealt. The difficult problem can only
be solved by those who know how to sail freely "on the sea of the
Talmud." Although I myself might be able to read the Talmud in
just that way which is needful to mankind, I am only learning, an
apprentice in the study of the Talmud. In order to know it properly,
a lifetime is required, and I approached the sources only a few years
ago.

A new anthology of the Talmud ought to have the aim of discuss-
ing the period of the Talmudic sages, and to show what form the
lives of the individuals and of the community adopt if they are based
on what I have here described as the Jewish attitude towards the
world. Above all this would involve the criticism applied to misfortune in the world; part of it, the noble one, being humbly accepted,

and the other one rejected energetically and fought in moral freedom; the resulting "incompatibility of the correlated"; and finally
the experience of individual divine grace, love, and the this-worldly
miracle. Such an anthology might give a new and un-pagan direction
to our entire spiritual life. In the curriculum of the high schools I
would place it next to the beauty of Greek poetry. (The Talmud
states that "Greek beauty ought to dwell in Jewish tents.") If such
a Talmudical anthology is to serve its purpose, it must not be made
too easy to study, for it is of the essence of the Talmud that it must
be conquered by the efforts of its disciples. Without that effort, the
important benefit of slow spiritual training and of a complete re-
adjustment in thinking and feeling would get lost. All Talmudical
anthologies known to me suffer from the fact that they make it too
easy for the student. They look like a collection of anecdotes, like
a book of quotations. The book I have in mind should not be a presentation of some choice "pearls," torn out of context, but of longer
passages, which allow the reader to acquaint himself with the style
of the Talmud. It should not be written in a *feuilleton* style, which
makes something out of nothing, whereas of the Talmud we may say
that it makes out of something—nothing; for it is so sparing, and it
expressed itself by omitting self-understood links. The reading of the
Talmud therefore implies a search and a new creation, a solution of
contradictions. How important such a study is can be seen from the
Yiddish idiom, in which "to learn" means to study the Talmud.

Europe does not appreciate the Talmud. But sometimes pamphlets
against it appear on the literary market. Thus Europe harms itself
without harming the Talmud. Here is a typical quotation, printed
in Hungary:

> The Talmud is of interest to everybody. It is indeed more interest-
> ing than any charming novel, and no book is more interesting. No
> pornographic book contains more filth, and no collection of anec-
> dotes is more exhilarating. We have here a prescription for usury,
> fraud, for the Jewish will to subdue the world, the most abominable
> laws concerning women, horrifying mercilessness, and so-called
> miracles. One cannot put the book down before having read the last
> line. One would only harm oneself by not purchasing this book.
> Those who have read it will agree. Since we live among Jews, it is
> in our own interest to know their moral code, by which rabbis are
> trained. Again we recommend it warmly to every brave Christian.

Judging from the price of the book—just a few pennies—it must be a very thorough work!

But even Jews—particularly the liberal ones—do not like the Talmud too much. Here is a quotation: "A gigantic collection of tiny quotations and strange legal cases. The Jewish spirit, roaming wildly, remained hopelessly attached to every ceremony, and on the thin threads of shockingly petty sophistication. All in all a strange alliance of casuistry and mental vagabondage."

For my own part I must humbly admit that I am only learning. I pass no judgment, I just learn. Nor shall I write an essay "The significance of the Talmud for today's civilization," or something like that. I am not ready to do that. My entire book may be considered an attempt to write an introduction to such an essay. I am just learning, I do not know anything yet. I live in the midst of the discussions held in these many volumes, I detect basic ideas or moods, and I have talked of them here and there in this book. I have not arrived at any conclusions. But from time to time I get an idea of that great ironical fact that for many centuries mankind had a great treasure, but it was unknown to them, or worse still: it was half known, laughed at, and reviled. A man who was crucified because he wanted to bring salvation is worshipped, and at the same time people have been crucifying for many centuries that which could bring salvation.

Every study concerning the Talmud points out how much knowledge can be found in that work about astronomy, geography, history, chronology, numismatics, linguistics, medicine, etc. But as far as the essence of the Talmud is concerned, all this is irrelevant. It does not even lead to a more eager study of the original; scholars content themselves with quoting from secondary sources. No book has been quoted more often while being neglected more universally. It has been said that many people still agree with the medieval "scholar" who referred to "Rabbi Talmud."

The Talmud also contains many binding decrees in the field of religion and the law. The overall name for this approach is Halacha. This has nothing to do with the scientific by-products exploited by our scholars. But to the Talmud, Halacha is the main concern or, at least, one of the main concerns. Still in the process of learning, I appreciate at the moment only the other side of the Talmud, the Haggada, which is narration and meditation. Here we are not concerned with stern obligations but with examples. The Talmud itself tells already about an argument between those who followed the Halacha and those who preferred the Haggada. In the Talmud the two are inseparably intertwined. The dry separation of "Halachoth" was accomplished much later, when the immediate religious life had already become obscured.

Here is indeed the noblest mark of the Talmud—life, unending vitality in God and in the spirit. The spirit and virtue live here a charming, natural, and even sensual existence among these men. For many centuries there ruled a mood of the this-worldly miracle, no less so than in the Song of Songs. To be imbued with this is the proper meaning and benefit of studying the Talmud. The desire and the duty are integrated, the highest things are performed in a moving and childlike naivete, martyrdom takes its place next to jests, and the genius of an indestructible national will hovers serenely above the smoking ruins. It is true that we find also heart-rending grief. But in the main there is strength, tension, hope, hope for the miracle gushing forth from the depth of the soul. Therefore the Talmud is not for weaklings. It wants to raise lions' souls, but lions of goodness and spiritual strength. Whatever animal forces there are in man flows here mysteriously towards higher functions. This does not mean that animal instincts are overlooked puritanically, but they reveal themselves openly and without a false shame. On some tombstones in the old Jewish cemetery in Prague ripening grapes are carved, a symbol of the great scholarship of the deceased. What to others might be a symbol for intoxication, stands here for spiritual wealth. The same holds true of the Talmud. We find here an exuberance which makes the reader magnanimous and gay. This is far removed from the narrowmindedness that I once came across while staying overnight in a Munich hotel. Above the Bible on the nighttable there was a small plaque, reading: "Please do not read the Bible for entertainment." The Talmud shows no trace of such unctuousness. On the contrary, all human sounds are there, and the composers use all registers. The Talmud may indeed be compared to an organ, which, although playing sacred music, sends forth living holiness, pulsating, clever and tender, sweet and yet deeply moving. It has no secrets but opens itself to all who come close. It does not expect to be approached in fear but seems to say: "Above all, learn. Whatever your intentions may be—study or something else—learn! For soon you will learn to learn for learning's sake." I cannot understand how one can manage to find coldness and casuistry in a work which is so clearly based on enthusiasm and faith. But where faith is lacking, everything seems bald and cold, as it happens always to some clever critics who project their own cleverness into the poets' works. They get caught in details, and they are neither willing nor able to see the total. But we who are willing have been caught by the fire when we read, at the conclusion of each volume, the mutual relationship between the reader and the book, perhaps without its equal in world literature: "May thou be proud of us, O tractate . . . , and may we be proud of thee. May we think of thee, O tractate . . . , and mayest thou think of us. Do not forget us, O tractate . . . and may we not forget thee, neither in this world nor in the world beyond." We have mentioned previously a statement that contains a similarly overflowing gratitude: "If we had come into this world merely to hear this, it would have been enough." There is another Talmudical legend, which shows the same kind of an intimacy and relationship in the spiritual sphere: A certain rabbi devoted himself particularly to the study of the tractate of Haggiga, which deals with sacrifices. When he died, forsaken by all the world, a brilliantly white womanly figure appeared by his deathbed, keeping watch by night. It was the Tractate Haggiga.

Even the literary form of the Talmud is attractive. Everything has been extremely condensed, it is an extract of thinking, and often only one word represents an entire train of thought, so that the language serves only as a reminder, never as an end in itself. Reports are made as written in shorthand, with abbreviations recognized by private agreement of the parties, with no consideration for beauty, purity of language, or even grammar. Nevertheless the style is forceful and clear. "Evil spirits surround us as rubbish lies around garden beds." On every page the reader is surprised by parables.

The Talmud does not report on things of average quality, but on deviations, the abnormal and the bold. Since, therefore, the Talmud could be easily misinterpreted, it sometimes became a danger for the Jews. The Talmud is not afraid but talks out with passion, regardless of consequences. Thus Rabbi Simon bar Yochai said: "Even the best among the heathen should be killed." But this is not a law of the Jewish religion, rather has it been preserved for the sake of its incisiveness; it was the cry of despair of a man who had been persecuted by Roman tyrants and had to hide in a cave for thirteen years. This is easy to see; however, an evil intention does not wish to see but is looking for an argument. Not everything in the Talmud is Halacha, some things are meant to be paradoxical. Even a Jew well versed in the Talmud has a hard time to extract a binding Halacha out of the discussions by the Rabbis, as preserved in the Talmud, discussions which are an ongoing process, for in them are contained development and life. We must honor and love our ancestors for having kept up their courage in the midst of the surrounding hostile nations, and part of that courage is that they did not pose as saints, whether they were such or not; in other words, they did not give up the natural rhythm of their hearts in order to please others. For those early generations of the exile, the period of the Talmud, had not yet been domesticated. They still lived the living existence of their piety and of their evil desires, they lived through their struggles; and, without looking right or left, they preserved those statements, customs, and events that seemed to them strange, great, striking, outside of all rules, and filled with personality. They were not patriotic army chaplains, and therefore they were not interested in making a good impression on the non-Jewish public. For this reason the majority of the decisions reported in the Talmud are not abstract decrees valid for everybody, but they are accounts of the strange ways in which the great teachers interpreted those laws arbitrarily and even deviated from them. The Talmud is dominated by outstanding or individual cases, not by boring commonplace generalities. Thus we hear that Rabbi Gamaliel took a bath on the night after his wife's death, although he had laid down a law against such practice. When interrogated by his own students, he replied: " I am not like other people, I am sickly." When his slave died, he accepted mourners' visits, although he had taught that a master ought not to mourn for his slave's death. "My slave was different," was his justification, "he was a righteous man." In connection with these exceptions which the master allowed himself, the Talmud quotes some sayings with which great teachers concluded their daily prayer, for "he who does not introduce some change in his daily prayer does not pray properly." Some other teachers are reported to have made favorite statements of theirs after a fast or after having ended the reading of the Book of Job. It all sounds like a loving recollection of the habits of our own forefathers. It does not say "Thou shalt." The sole intention is to give examples of depth, wisdom, and emotion. When we are told how our sages honored their parents, the extraordinary and—to our own taste—exaggerated signs of respect are not meant as laws but they shake us up. The exception is thus preferred to banalities, since these do not have to be reported. Thus we find in one place a charming fairy tale concerning King Solomon and the demon Ashmoddai, and elsewhere stories about ghosts, strange dream interpretations (although not so strange any longer after Freud, which is just one example of the fact that things considered ridiculous today will perhaps be understood by succeeding generations). In another tractate we read about the horrors of the siege of Jerusalem, the famine, the fall and the destruction of the Temple, the legends about Titus, punished by the tortured people in the form of a fly. Everywhere we find the most vivid colors. Rabbi Yochanan sat down in the front of the ritual bath house and said: "When the daughters of Israel come out of the bath they shall look at me so that their children will be as beautiful as I am." Rabbi Simon ben Gamaliel, seeing a beautiful pagan woman on the steps of the Temple, recited: "How great are thy works, O Lord, thou hast made them all in wisdom." The Talmud is not dominated by a mechanical formalism but by a verse from the Psalms, as interpreted by the rabbis: "When it is time to work for the Lord, the Law may be abolished" (119, 126; see Montefiore-Loewe, *A Rabbinic Anthology*, p. 131). Further: "The Law has been given to the people that they may live and not die." Or: "It is better to live on the Sabbath the way one is used to live on weekdays, rather than be dependent on other people." Or we find the following good-humored and anti-formalistic story: A certain rabbi visited his colleague. The host gave his guest a cup of wine, which he emptied in one gulp; he gave him a second cup, and again his guest emptied it in one gulp. The host then turned to his guest with these words: Do we not have a tradition that he who acts in that manner is considered a glutton? No, answered the guest, it does not apply here; for your cup is extremely small, your wine is not strong, and my stomach is extremely big." This story is immediately followed by a law. There are many contradictions in the Talmud, and he who cannot stomach them should not read the Talmud. For there is no life without contradictions, and it is of the essence of the Talmud to be very much alive, and at the same time to make great demands on sanctity, to live in such a demand and to be surrounded by it as by a motherly secret. The piety of the Talmud is not a filing system, and it does not command you beforehand which numbers in the songbook are next. Rabbi Akiba added spice to his religious sermons by inserting three hundred fables about foxes, most of which are unfortunately lost. But here is a beautiful one:

Once the Roman government prohibited the study of the Law. When a Jew found Rabbi Akiba busy teaching he asked him whether he was not afraid of the authorities. He replied with a fable: A fox, walking along the river, saw a school of fishes. He asked them: Why are you running to and fro? They answered: We are fleeing from the nets spread out by men. Thereupon the Fox: Please come out to the dry land, and we will live together as our forefathers used to do. The fishes replied: Are you really known as a smart animal? You are not clever but a fool. If we must live in fear while in our own element, much more so at the place of our death! This applies to us, too, concluded Rabbi Akiba. Now we are sitting studying the Torah, which promises us long life for doing so, what then would happen to us if we were to forsake it?

The lives of the great teachers were as unsystematic as their teachings. Before being converted, the great sage Resh Lakish had been a robber, and we are told of his pranks, which remind us of Samson's. Akiba was a shepherd, and his wife made it possible for him to study by selling her own hair. After many years of schooling he returned to her at the head of a long procession made up of his own students. He took part in Bar Kochba's war of liberation and died as the result of torture inflicted upon him by the Romans. According to a legend, Rabbi Meir was the descendant of Emperor Nero. He was a disciple of an apostate; and once, when his teacher rode on a horse on the Sabbath, his student walked humbly beside the horse. He is the author of many profound thoughts, among them the following: "As there are many opinions concerning eating, so is it with women. Some people refuse to go on drinking after having found a fly in their cup, others throw the fly out and go on drinking, others again suck the juice out of the very fly first." He also said: "When a child is born, his fists are closed, as if to say: The entire world is mine. But when he leaves this world, his hands are stretched out, as if to say: I have not taken anything out of this world."

We do not yet have good legendary biographies which would take together all the rays around the person, with him as the center. Such books would support and perhaps even surpass the anthology which I have suggested. For a mere collection of sayings would not prove that the content of the Talmud or its spirit or its basic mood is identical with what I have described in this book as Jewish religiosity. But such a proof could be brought by studying the lives of the saints and teachers, although every quotation might be disproved by a counter-quotation; for the Talmud is the book of contradictions. But as a living idea continually balances logical contradictions, so does the idea of a life demonstrate how literary contradictions come to naught when faced with the power of a real form of existence, which somewhere, in deep abysses, is connected with the instincts and the mysteries of the Jewish people.

INDEX OF PERSONS